The Sybase SQL Server Survival Guide

JIM PANTTAJA

MARY PANTTAJA

JUDY BOWMAN

WILEY COMPUTER PUBLISHING

John Wiley & Sons, Inc.

New York • Chichester • Brisbane • Toronto • Singapore

Publisher: Katherine Schowalter
Editor: Theresa Hudson
Managing Editor: Robert Aronds
Text Design & Composition: North Market Street Graphics

Designations used by companies to distinguish their products are often claimed as trademarks. In all instances where John Wiley & Sons, Inc. is aware of a claim, the product names appear in initial capital or all capital letters. Readers, however, should contact the appropriate companies for more complete information regarding trademarks and registration.

This text is printed on acid-free paper.

Chapter 1 is based on previously published material found in *Relational Database Journal,* article entitled "Roles of the SQL Server," January/February 1994. Used with permission.

Chapter 2 is based on previously published material found in *SQL Forum Journal,* article entitled "Top Ten Mistakes Using SQL Server—Log Management Mistakes," Volume 2, Number 6, November/February 1994, and article entitled "Top Ten Mistakes using SQL Server—Transaction Design Mistakes," Volume 3, Number 2, March/April 1994. Used with permission. *Sybase Magazine,* article entitled "Locking Behaviors and Why They're Important," Summer 1994, Sybase, Inc. Used with permission. *Relational Database Journal,* article entitled "RDJ Advisor—The SQL Server Response," August/October 1993 and November-January 1994. Used with permission.

Chapter 8 is based on previously published material found in *SQL Forum Journal,* article entitled "Defining and Using Useful Indexes," Volume 1, Number 5, September/October 1991, article entitled "Top Ten Mistakes using SQL Server," Volume 2, Number 2, May/June 1993, and article entitled "Top Ten Mistakes using SQL Server—Mistakes Three and Four," Volume 2, Number 4, July/August 1993. Used with permission.

Chapter 9 is based on previously published material found in *Sybase Server Magazine,* article entitled "Hot SQL Techniques," Fall 1994, Sybase International User Group Inc. Used with permission.

This publication is designed to provide accurate and authoritative information in regard to the subject matter covered. It is sold with the understanding that the publisher is not engaged in rendering legal, accounting, or other professional service. If legal advice or other expert assistance is required, the services of a competent professional person should be sought.

Library of Congress Cataloging-in-Publication Data:
Panttaja, Jim.
    The Sybase SQL server survival guide / Jim Panttaja, Mary
Panttaja, Judy Bowman.
      p.   cm.
    Includes index.
    ISBN 0-471-12745-0 (paper : alk. paper)
    1. Relational databases. 2. Sybase. 3. SQL Server.
I. Panttaja, Mary. II. Bowman, Judith S. III. Title.
QA76.9.D3P3438   1996
005.75'65—dc20   96-10798
                                      CIP

Printed in the United States of America
10 9 8 7 6 5 4 3 2 1

C O N T E N T S

Chapter 7 Replication Server   **157**

Chapter 8 Designing Databases   **173**

Chapter 12 System 11 Tuning Features

F O R E W O R D

Since our first meeting six years ago, at a Sybase User Group session on Secure Server, I have been consistently impressed by Jim and Mary's ability to get to the heart of arcane technical issues and communicate their understanding clearly and accurately. They not only have a wealth of experience teaching and implementing complex client/server technologies, but also an ability to focus on the practical use of technology for business that makes their information useful to anyone trying to build business processing systems in this arena. While the center of this book is the core database technology, it also covers the surrounding issues essential to the successful development of client/server application systems. From discussions of effective approaches to project management, to the mysteries of scalable online transaction processing design there is a rich feast of knowledge here. Experienced developers can graze on tidbits of technique and learn the latest twists of Sybase System 11; those who are unfamiliar with Sybase have a series of well-planned meals to digest the Sybase architecture. In both cases, however, the authors' energy and expertise provide excellent insights into how to use Sybase and how to approach the development of client/server systems. This book embellishes their popularity as presenters and trainers and deserves to reach a wider audience than those who have had the pleasure of attending their training programs.

Jonathan Vaughan
VP Applied Technology Chase Manhattan Bank, N.A.

P R E F A C E

Who You Are

If you picked up this book, you must be interested in working with Sybase SQL Server. You may be new to the software, looking for a clear approach to a complex product, or a veteran, interested in solutions to particular problems. Novice or expert, you'll find lots to think about in the *Sybase SQL Server Survival Guide*—it's a distillation of years of Sybase SQL Server consulting experiences. It will help you avoid common mistakes, teach you some neat tricks, and give you new ideas about how database management systems work.

How you use the *Sybase SQL Server Survival Guide* depends on what you need.

- A SQL Server beginner may want to read the book from cover to cover.
- A database specialist interested in learning more about a particular topic can pick the appropriate chapter and dive in.
- A busy programmer looking for a specific technique (perhaps how to write a trigger that propagates changes made to primary keys) can use the index to find the relevant sections.

As much as possible, topics are treated so that they can stand alone.

What This Is

The *Sybase SQL Server Survival Guide* is intended to make you successful with Sybase SQL Server System 11: Think of it as a database consulting firm in book format. Use the book to save time and avoid some painful learning experiences. It is not a replacement for Sybase manuals, which you will need for syntax details and tool-use specifics, nor is it a one-book guide to SQL Server development. Rather, it helps you work through the many alternates that SQL Server and the SQL language present, giving advice on what works and what doesn't, what is efficient, and what is extensible.

Sybase SQL Server Survival Guide has twelve chapters divided among five general sections.

1. Understanding SQL Server

   Chapter 1 gives an overview of what SQL Server is, what client/server means, and how relational database management systems work. It also includes some historical background, a brief review of SQL Server components, and a list of new features in System 11.

   Chapter 2 concentrates on key technical issues (locking, transaction management, and the query optimizer) where understanding the syntax is not enough: You have to consider the implications of each alternative.

2. Planning

   Chapter 3 looks at the disciplines, skills, and tasks you need at each stage in a project. Since SQL Server is a complex system, using it requires a lot of planning. Users often skimp on this stage, to their later regret. The *Sybase SQL Server Survival Guide* provides database-specific project planning checklists to help you evaluate your resources at each stage of the project and think through your requirements before you start writing any code.

   Chapter 4 gives detailed guidelines for programming standards, both in general and for SQL in particular. The rules are complemented with plenty of examples.

3. Considering application specifics

   Chapter 5 zeros in on the relational model. It shows that you have to think differently when you use the relational model and works through examples comparing procedural processing and relational processing.

   Chapter 6 explores client/server issues in more detail. You'll see information about tiered architecture, connections, error handling, data access, transaction management, concurrency, and security.

   Chapter 7 is a review of Replication Server. It discusses the architecture and gives some examples of how different configurations work.

4. Developing

Chapter 8 walks you through the process of designing a database, from using entity-relationship diagrams and normalization to creating objects, to testing and tuning. There's a comprehensive section on choosing indexes and some suggestions on modifying your database design for better performance.

Chapter 9 is all SQL, all the time. You'll find a review of SQL syntax and an interesting collection of SQL tricks, including how to generate cross tabulation output, create serial numbers, use SQL to generate code, and deal with a hierarchy. The chapter also includes code for cursors, stored procedures, and triggers.

Chapter 10 concerns physical issues—creating and using database devices, setting up mirroring, and using thresholds to monitor space use.

Chapter 11 deals with system administration: managing users, importing data, setting database options, and using DBCC. It also provides some guidelines on backing up your database.

5. Tuning

Chapter 12 focuses on the new tuning features in System 11. These include changes to the buffer manager that let you set up named data caches and bind objects to them, variable sized I/O pools, a new cache placement strategy, and partitioning for heap tables. You'll also see updates on the transaction log, the lock manager, the housekeeper function, and handling configuration options.

These topics represent areas where users often get lost and signal for expert help. The *Sybase SQL Server Survival Guide* can get you through these rough spots by providing context and explaining the tradeoffs various solutions offer.

Who We Are

This book started out as a collection of notes Mary and Jim Panttaja put together for clients, including sections on methodology, SQL coding, tuning, and more. Their company, Panttaja Consulting Group, Inc. (PCG) specializes in the development and deployment of client/server applications for customers. They are experts in the Sybase and Microsoft SQL Server, Powersoft products, and associated technologies, and have been working with SQL Server since 1988. Mary and Jim began their relationship with Sybase teaching classes under contract to Sybase. Mary is the President, and Jim the Vice President of PCG. PCG has its corporate headquarters in Healdsburg, California, and a development and training center in San Francisco.

As the notes became a book, Mary and Jim added material from their database journal articles and user group talks, focusing on the topics that were most helpful to their clients. The result was a loose collection of explanations, approaches, and tricks. At this point, Judy Bowman, another database consultant, joined the book effort, filling out chapters, doing some reorganization, and adding her own tips.

As you read through the *Sybase SQL Server Survival Guide,* you'll probably notice the three authors have different concerns and styles. Mary likes to start with methodology. Jim is interested in the practical aspects of coding. Judy wants to make sure explanations make sense and flow logically. In most cases, one author wrote a section and the other two reviewed and revised it. We've included some true-life stories from the consulting front. They're set off from normal text like the following one:

MAN

A man with a duck walks into a room . . . [whoops, wrong set of stories]

We hope you find here information not available in Sybase manuals—overviews connecting disparate parts, useful examples, explanations that go beyond syntax. Our goal is to pass on information we've learned in our years solving problems for SQL Server customers.

ACKNOWLEDGMENTS

Terri Hudson, our editor at John Wiley & Sons. Bruce Prendergast, our co-author on another project who contributed to some of the chapters. Tom Bondur of *SQL Forum Journal*. Tom used to book Mary and Jim when he coordinated client-site training at Sybase, and more recently has published our articles in *SQL Forum Journal*. Karl Fischer, former editor of *SQL Forum Journal*. Valerie Anderson, Jim and Mary's first contact at Sybase, and now a member of the Panttaja Consulting Group, Inc. board of directors. Stacey Burch, Jim and Mary's first contact at Microsoft when they began teaching classes. Peter Thawley of Sybase.

Jonathan Vaughan of Chase Manhattan Bank. Jonathan encouraged us to put together a set of guidelines for using SQL Server. That's where the book started many years ago.

The entire staff of Panttaja Consulting Group, Inc. They all had to put up with this project. Especially our VP and General Manager, George Loyer, who bore the brunt of putting up with this project, and Russell Barber and Patrick Wright who reviewed many of our articles before they went off to the publications.

The Authors

D E D I C A T I O N

To our mothers, Glo and MaryEvelyn. Glo would have been proud (but probably would have preferred it was in Latin). MaryEvelyn claims not to know what we are talking about, but is always there for us.

Mary and Jim

To my mother, Mary Jo, who doesn't think much of computers or databases, but has always loved books.

Judy

1

What It Is

Overview

This chapter introduces SQL Server and puts it in context. It begins with brief descriptions of the relational model and client/server architecture and goes on to describe SQL Server features. Topics include:

- ◆ Historical perspective
- ◆ Relational model
- ◆ Client/server architecture
- ◆ Sybase SQL Server products
- ◆ New features (System 10 and System 11)

Most of the ideas introduced in this chapter are treated more fully in other sections of the book.

Historical Perspective

The first relational database management system (RDBMS) was proposed about 25 years ago. Commercial products became available in the 1980s and, after a short struggle, won the database market. Although there are now other contenders (such as object-oriented database products), most database application development projects use relational database management systems.

Sybase introduced SQL Server in 1987, advertising it as a "client/server" solution, designed to separate client and server functionality for new levels of performance. Sybase also located the fundamental business rules in SQL Server, rather than in the client side of the application.

Primarily a UNIX vendor, Sybase teamed with Ashton-Tate and Microsoft to make SQL Server available to the PC world. Gradually, Microsoft got more involved with SQL Server development on its platforms and in 1994 the partnership terminated, with each party taking responsibility for an independent product line. The Sybase and Microsoft product lines address similar customer needs, but in different ways.

Before describing Sybase SQL Server, let's review some underlying concepts: *relational* and *client/server*.

Relational Model

Dr. E. F. Codd first wrote about the relational model of data in a paper entitled *A Relational Model of Data for Large Shared Data Banks* published in the Association for Computing Machinery journal *Communications of the ACM* in June 1970. A *relation* is a mathematical set and as such holds elements in no particular order, contains no duplicate elements, and allows no decomposition of the individual elements.

Relations are often described as tables, with rows and columns. Table 1.1 shows an example of the publishers' table from the pubs2 database used in many Sybase examples.

The rows are horizontal; the columns are vertical. However, it is important to remember that the rows and columns you see here have an order, while in the relational model there is none. (The order of rows in a table is affected by the clustered index, if there is one.) It's also critical to keep relational tables conceptually separate from data files.

TABLE 1.1 The Publishers' Table from the pubs2 Database

pub_id	pub_name	city	state
0736	New Age Books	Boston	MA
0877	Binnet & Hardley	Washington	DC
1389	Algodata Infosystems	Berkeley	CA

The relational model is a way of looking at data, paying attention to the data structure, data manipulation, and data integrity. Because of this, the underlying set basis of relational databases affects how you work with them in important ways.

Data Structure

Creating a database and its tables requires identifying atomic elements and determining their relationships, eliminating duplicates, and setting up ways to protect data integrity. You implement a database from the design by translating your requirements into SQL statements (pronounced "ESS-QUE-ELL" by some and "sequel" by others, it is the dominant relational database language). The RDBMS handles the underlying physical storage systems. Relational database theory requires that logical design be independent of physical issues.

Data Manipulation

Manipulating data also has special requirements. Because of their basis in set theory, relational databases are designed to manage *sets* of data, not individual *rows* of data. Using relational databases means replacing procedural thinking with relational methods. The main relational operators are projection, selection, and join.

Projection is listing the *columns* you want to include in the result set.

```
SELECT pub_id, pub_name
FROM publishers
go

 pub_id pub_name
 ------ ----------------------------------------
 0736   New Age Books
 0877   Binnet & Hardley
 1389   Algodata Infosystems
```

Selection (also called restriction) is setting the conditions that determine the *rows* you see in the result set.

```
SELECT pub_id, pub_name
FROM publishers
WHERE pub_id BETWEEN '0700' AND '0900'
go
```

```
pub_id pub_name
------ -----------------------------------------
0736   New Age Books
0877   Binnet & Hardley
```

Joining is working with data in more than one table by comparing related columns.

```
SELECT pub_name, title
FROM publishers, titles
WHERE publishers.pub_id = titles.pub_id
AND title LIKE 'Net%'
go

pub_name             title
---------------------  ---------------------------------------
Algodata Infosystems Net Etiquette
```

While procedural logic finds each row and loops through operations on that row, relational logic steps through the operations and applies them to all qualifying rows. For a very small data set, the procedural and relational solutions might be comparable. But for a medium to large data set, or nested operations, the relational method can be much faster. The logic may also be easier to follow. Chapter 5 gives more information on relational thinking.

Data Integrity

A relational database also must have ways to support data integrity, user authorization, transaction control, and recovery. Some of these capabilities come from SQL commands that you execute, such as:

♦ Creating defaults, rules, and unique indexes
♦ Granting and revoking permissions
♦ Explicitly declaring transactions
♦ Dumping the database

Others are the responsibility of the RDBMS, such as:

♦ Logging
♦ Locking
♦ Managing user connections
♦ Handling transactions
♦ Running recovery processes

These functions take place "under the covers." You need to understand how they work so that you can use them to your advantage, but you don't need to run them.

Client/Server: Tiered Architecture

The classic client/server architecture is a server process (most often a relational database management system), a client process, and the communication between them.

The server process handles data storage and manipulation. The client process handles information presentation. The two processes are deployed on independent scalable platforms appropriate to their functions. The client machine is often a PC, for example, while the server machine may be a mainframe, a mini, or a souped-up PC with a multiuser, multiprocess operating system. The successful client/server setup takes advantage of native hardware and operating system resources and handles communication between the client and server computers efficiently.

The application's client component takes care of all interaction with the user. It

♦ Provides the dialog with the user
♦ Collects and validates the user's input
♦ Extracts data from the database and presents it to the user
♦ Submits data modifications to the server

A client process needs to know how to construct requests, use the protocol, and deal with results. Clients can be windowed applications, reporting tools, batch processing written in 3GLs (third-generation languages, such as C), or whatever you can build using the client API to communicate with the server. In most applications, what the user sees on the client side is a graphical user interface (GUI) that has a consistent look and feel with the host environment.

A server process runs constantly on a network. It knows how to "listen" to one or more networks for messages. These messages are structured in a formal client/server protocol and contain a request for services. The application's server component

♦ Manages the connection with clients
♦ Stores the physical data and maps it to the logical structure
♦ Manages users
♦ Manipulates the data (processes requests and transmits results to the client)
♦ Handles security

Many client/server implementations, including Sybase, provide *programmable servers*. This means that some application logic resides in the server, so that you can modify data structures and business rules without needing major changes to the applications. In Sybase's case, this logical layer consists of stored procedures, triggers, defaults, rules, constraints, and views. A programmable server performs all the normal server functions previously listed; in addition, it maintains business rules and executes transaction logic.

But client/server systems can get more complex. Servers can talk to servers. And, in many environments, client applications can talk peer-to-peer to other client applications. That's where multitiered structures come in. They include capabilities for

♦ Working with heterogeneous databases
♦ Isolating certain functions from the rest of the application
♦ Enabling systems to service many users
♦ Interfacing with object servers
♦ Providing interactions with the outside world

Many client/server systems are data-centric—their main function is storing and manipulating data. However, they can also offer *open services*, such as gathering real-time data, communicating with the outside world (sending e-mail if some event takes place inside the server), and setting up gateways into external or legacy data systems.

Sybase System 11 and Its Components

Sybase SQL Server is a relational database management system built on a client/server architecture with programmable server and open services components. The term "SQL Server" is sometimes used for a family of products. Technically, it is only the database server, the relational database engine. Some of the related tools are bundled with SQL Server, but others are sold and priced separately. The basic product set includes SQL Server, Open Client, and Open Server.

Other products with specialized functions are:

♦ Replication Server
♦ MPP
♦ OmniSQL
♦ Sybase IQ
♦ Powersoft products
♦ SQL Server Manager
♦ SQL Server Monitor

Sybase uses a dialect of SQL called Transact-SQL (T-SQL for short). It contains some extensions to standard SQL, including the ability to create stored procedures and triggers, procedural commands, and administrative tools.

SQL Server

SQL Server is the RDBMS controlling all database activities. It runs as a single process on the server machine, processes all requests from client applications, and ensures data recoverability. It has these responsibilities:

◆ Controlling physical disk storage, including mapping the logical design to the physical layout and maintaining the logical design
◆ Manipulating data, parsing Transact-SQL, optimizing queries, and transmitting results to the client
◆ Managing the internal activities that protect data integrity, such as logging data changes, handling transactions, controlling network connections and multiple users, and locking

Basically, SQL Server is an operating system within an operating system, with added features for database functionality.

Managing the Logical Design-Physical Storage Connection

When you first install SQL Server and later create new databases or add space to existing ones, you (as the system administrator or sa) assign some amount of system disk space as database devices. The disk space can be raw partitions or operating system files or some of each, depending on the limitations of your platform. SQL Server stores system tables, user data, and indexes on these devices.

SQL Server completely controls the database devices. After you specify devices for a given database, there is seldom any reason to pay attention to the physical storage except to note how much space is available or to do advanced tuning.

As a relational database management system designer and developer, you view data in terms of tables, usually with associated index structures. But data is stored on disk in quite a different structure. SQL Server handles mapping the logical database objects to physical disk locations.

SQL Server stores all data in 2K pages (except for Stratus, where pages are 4K) written to the appropriate database devices. When you insert, update, or delete a row, SQL Server determines which page or pages are impacted and makes the changes. You can determine which pages a given object is on—and which object is on a given page—but you don't need to manage this, except in special circumstances.

SQL Server also handles index maintenance. As tables are modified, entries are added to or deleted from the index structures. When a page is almost empty, the last row is moved to an adjacent page and the page is freed. When a page is full, it is split. In both cases, SQL Server takes care of mapping the logical layout to the new physical pages.

When you define database objects, SQL Server keeps track of the object definition in a set of system tables (collectively called the system catalog) where it records what is in the database and how the objects relate to each other. The system catalog records information such as:

♦ Descriptions of all columns, including datatype and size
♦ Permissions associated with all objects
♦ Text of commands creating views, stored procedures, rules, defaults, and triggers
♦ Definitions of all indexes

SQL Server supports a large number of system stored procedures that get specific kinds of information from the system catalog. See Sybase documentation for description of system tables and system stored procedures.

Handling Queries and Data Manipulation Commands

In some ways this is the most obvious requirement of a RDBMS: to parse the SQL language and translate it into executable code. When a client program sends SQL commands, SQL Server checks the syntax of the commands and the existence of all referenced objects. If the SQL text passes these two tests, it is translated into an intermediate form and optimized.

Extracting data from a relational database is a very complicated process. A wrong decision about the sequence of obtaining the data can be disastrous (slow). It is the optimizer's job to analyze the query and decide how to do it. SQL Server optimizer considers the query structure, table structure, available indexes, and statistics showing the distribution of data in order to determine the best query plan. All of these items are critical.

As SQL Server processes a query, it

1. Converts the query into an internal tree structure. This allows queries that look different but have a similar structure to be optimized in the same way. Differences in order of tables in a FROM clause or variations of comparisons in the WHERE clause do not impact the query optimizer.
2. Uses cost-based algorithms to determine the indexes and table access orders requiring the least number of physical and logical inputs/outputs (I/Os). SQL Server uses index statistics to make accurate predictions of the number of I/Os for various candidate

query plans. In addition, SQL Server detects a number of special cases of SQL syntax.

3. Generates a query plan and makes an executable version of the query implementing that plan.

4. Executes the query plan and extracts the data from the database. It uses the temporary database (tempdb) if necessary, for work space (sorting, grouping, temporary tables).

5. Packages the data and sends it across the network. SQL Server and the client keep track of where they are in the transmission of data.

Maintaining Data Integrity

An application submits data modification statements (INSERT, UPDATE, and DELETE) to SQL Server. The application either includes *explicit* transaction management statements (BEGIN TRANSACTION, COMMIT TRANSACTION, and ROLLBACK TRANSACTION) or sends each data modification statement as an *implicit* transaction.

If any statement in a transaction fails, or if the transaction does not get to the COMMIT TRANSACTION statement, SQL Server rolls back the entire transaction. From the perspective of the application, the transaction is atomic: Either the entire transaction completes or no part of the transaction completes. SQL Server implements this transaction behavior.

SQL Server maintains commonly referenced data pages in cache, saving subsequent reads, and making it possible to combine several logical writes into one physical write.

SQL Server logs all data modifications (INSERTs, UPDATEs, and DELETEs) and all transaction activity (BEGIN TRANSACTION, COMMIT TRANSACTION, ROLLBACK TRANSACTION) in a system table called **syslogs.** SQL Server writes log pages to disk whenever a transaction is committed. The data pages may not be written to disk until much later (when there is a checkpoint operation or when the page is aged out of cache).

The log is a physical log—recording the actual data changes made—not a logical log. It's not readable to the human eye and you cannot use it as an application audit trail. (You can use Sybase's optional auditing capability by installing the sybsecurity database or build auditing into your application with triggers, stored procedures, or application logic.)

The transaction log contains the data image in before and after states.

◆ In an INSERT the new row is recorded in the log.
◆ In a DELETE the old row is recorded in the log.
◆ In an UPDATE either the whole old and new rows or just the data changed is saved in the log, depending on the specific UPDATE.

The log has three purposes:

1. Transaction rollback. When a transaction fails or is rolled back by the application, SQL Server uses the log to recover the data to the original state.
2. Recovery when you restart SQL Server. If processing is interrupted, the log ensures that committed modifications are written to the database and that uncommitted modifications are not. This is possible because the transaction log contains the before and after version of all rows modified by the transaction.
3. Incremental recovery using transaction log dumps. If you perform transaction dumps (backups of the transaction log) you can use them for database recovery after media failure by loading earlier database dumps (backups of the full database) and then applying the transaction dump modifications. Your backup schedule should include both full database dumps (often time-consuming operations) and transaction dumps.

SQL Server manages client network connections, keeping track of each client location and current context, and sending data rows and messages to the appropriate client. SQL Server can operate in mixed network environments where different clients are using different network protocols.

To the computer operating system, SQL Server is a single process managing multiple database clients. (Some relational database management systems generate server processes for each user/client.) For each connection, SQL Server uses separate internal control structures to manage requests and to schedule work. This mechanism allows for very fast context switches from one connection to the next and supports parallel processing. Locks keep transactions from interfering with each other.

SQL Server allows many users to simultaneously access the same database. Typically each user requires 50 to 60K—plus some additional cache (memory). It is critical to ensure that one user does not read another user's uncommitted transactions; SQL Server does this with transactions and locks on data pages or entire tables (depending on the query plan).

For data changes, SQL Server uses exclusive locks and holds them until the end of the transaction. For read operations, SQL Server uses shared locks. These are usually held only long enough to read the page, and then released. It is possible to hold read locks until the end of the transaction as well so that all of the rows read are consistent from one point in time.

FRIDAYS ARE SLOW!

A user of an application runs monthly reports. These reports do aggregates over a large table. The report's developer decided to use a SELECT HOLDLOCK option to prevent modifiers from changing the data while the report was running. He didn't pay much attention to indexing for the performance of this report. The report takes 90 minutes. The user decides to run the report on the last Friday morning of the month.

Other users of this application modify the data in the same table. They do not know about the report. Every odd Friday (or so it seems to them) the system crawls to a halt. They try to do an update and the system does not respond to them. They complain. The fact that the report is running is uncovered by the system administrator.

The system administrator looks into improving the time for the report by analyzing the indexing. It now takes 15 minutes. They still may have to run the report some time other than Friday morning, but they have minimized the time for potential lock conflict. It is not unusual to discover these conflicts after a system has been deployed. In all cases, a developer must consider the nature and duration of any locks held. Tasks that introduce substantial likelihood for conflict must be noted and considered.

Open Client

Open Client has two main components: DB-Library and Client-Library. It also includes Net-Library.

DB-Library is a set of functions callable from third-generation programming languages such as C. DB-Library calls allow you to submit queries to SQL Server and process the results. Most client applications use DB-Library to communicate with SQL Server. The DB-Library functions communicate with the server using a protocol called Tabular Data Stream (TDS).

Client-Library was introduced with Sybase System 10. It is also a call-level library and includes more functionality than DB-Library, including the capability to handle cursors and dynamic SQL. New programs should be written with Client-Library.

Net-Library is an interface component of SQL Server, as well as a set of libraries available for use on clients. On SQL Server, Net-Library is a network interface using a given network interprocess communication interface (IPC). All of the SQL Server network-specific considerations are isolated in this layer. SQL Server includes support for named pipes, TCP/IP sockets, SPX, and Banyan Vines. Some of these IPC mechanisms can be used with multiple network protocols.

SQL Server can use these IPC mechanisms simultaneously, allowing client applications using different network protocols to communicate with the same SQL Server.

Open Server

Open Server is a set of C functions allowing you to create applications that look and act like servers. The client application interacts with the Open Server using Open Client calls. Open Server allows developers to provide access to other system services, provide gateways to other database management systems, and provide access to other data sources (real-time stock tickers, nondatabase data sources).

Open servers that interface using stored procedure interfaces are fairly easy to write. For example, an Open Server application providing access to a mail system uses stored procedures on the SQL Server to send a stored procedure request to the mail Open Server whenever an important event occurs (e.g., when inventory is low).

It is often complicated to write Open Server gateways to other database management systems, so typically you purchase them from third-party vendors.

Other Sybase Products

Sybase offers many other products beyond the basic client/server set. A chart (from Sybase marketing materials) of how the pieces fit together is shown in Table 1.2.

A number of the products are summarized in the following section.

Replication Server

Replication Server is a Sybase product targeted for large, complex data environments. It is a multi-threaded Open Client/Open Server application that maintains copies of data throughout a heterogeneous client/server environment. Sites are primary (original sources of data) or subscribers (recipients of copies of the data).

An important function of Replication Server is to separate online transaction processing (OLTP) and decision support system (DSS) activities, which often have conflicting needs. OLTP, at its simplest, is update-intensive and requires high throughput. DSS, on the other hand, relies on

TABLE 1.2 Sybase Products

	OLTP	*Data Warehouse*	*Mass Deployment*
Database	Sybase SQL Server	Sybase SQL Server Sybase MPP Sybase IQ	SQL Anywhere
Middleware	Replication Server DB Gateways Open Server	OmniCONNECT InfoPump	Enterprise Messaging Services SQL Remote
Tools	PowerBuilder S-Designor Watcom Compilers	PowerBuilder InfoMaker SQR	PowerBuilder Desktop

queries, often with joins and complex computations. DSS applications can use a lot of resources and clog the system for OLTP users.

Replication Server has an open architecture that allows it to work with both Sybase SQL Server and other data servers. (For non-Sybase data servers, you use Sybase tools to build an appropriate interface.)

A simple Replication Server installation might include:

♦ A data server with OLTP-dominant transactions (primary site)
♦ A data server with DSS needs (subscriber site)
♦ A Log Transfer Manager (LTM) to get data changes from the primary site (each primary site has one)
♦ A Replication Server to oversee the primary and subscriber sites

The sequence of events in such an installation goes like this:

1. Subscriber sites describe the data they want to receive (a *replication definition*, similar to a SELECT clause), set up tables to hold it, and create *subscriptions* (requests for specific rows, rather like a WHERE clause).
2. Users at the primary site change the data during the course of their work.
3. The LTM reads the primary site log and informs Replication Server that there are new changes.
4. Replication Server tells the primary site server to send copies of the data to the subscriber server.

Subscribers can update the data, but they must do so through the primary site.

Most implementations are more complex than a single primary site and a single subscription site, of course. A primary site can have multiple subscribers and a single site can be primary for some data and a subscriber for other data. The asynchronous event replication capability allows stored procedures in one location to run stored procedures in other locations. See Chapter 7 for a more complete discussion of Replication Server.

MPP

MPP (once called Navigation Server) takes advantage of massively parallel processing systems to deploy a single logical database on multiple SQL Servers. Data is parceled out so that all the SQL Servers in the system can work in parallel, producing very fast operations. Sybase summarizes this approach as *bringing processing to the data, rather than data to the processor.* It is targeted for high query performance, growth flexibility, corporate consolidation, and data warehousing.

Sybase MPP uses

◆ Multiple SQL Servers working "in parallel" for fast operations (SELECT, INSERT, DELETE, CREATE INDEX, etc.).
◆ Data partitioning to physically distribute data among the participating SQL Servers. Individual servers control their own data partitions, which are transparent to the application.

At its simplest, MPP has these pieces: clients, control servers, parallel optimizer, and database engines.

Processing follows this path:

1. Clients submit queries.
2. Control Server receives the queries.
3. A parallel optimizer analyzes the queries, checks data locations, and translates the queries to Parallel SQL.
4. SQL Servers work in parallel, each getting results from its own partition and sending them to Control Server.
5. Control Server receives the results from SQL Servers and forwards them to clients.

OmniSQL

OmniSQL is an Open Server application for accessing heterogeneous data sources, particularly mainframe or legacy data. It supports a seamless connection between SQL Server and other database systems by maintaining a global catalog that maps local to enterprise-wide data and handles differences in datatypes and naming. It also deals with SQL dialects. To the user, there is one system.

OmniSQL includes these pieces:

◆ OmniSQL Server contains the T-SQL parser, optimizer, and catalogs. It handles distributed joins.
◆ OmniSQL Access Module provides access to data sources such as Microsoft SQL Server, DB2, VSAM, Adabas, IMS/DB, Oracle, and so on.
◆ OmniSQL Toolkit allows you to write your own access modules.

Operations on OmniSQL products look roughly like this:

◆ A client submits a request.
◆ The OmniSQL Gateway receives the request, checks the global catalog to find out where the data is, translates the query into the appropriate dialect of SQL, creates and compiles a query plan, and sends the plan to each target location through the appropriate access module.
◆ The data source executes the query and sends the results back to the Gateway.

Sybase IQ

Sybase IQ is tailored for decision support, particularly with ad hoc queries. It

- ♦ Uses a special (bit-wise) indexing system
- ♦ Holds data as bit vectors, making data scans very fast
- ♦ Can work with SMP, multiple engines, and large memory
- ♦ Allows 64-bit processing
- ♦ Uses SQL Server login, administrative and security functions
- ♦ Supports other Sybase products

Because of its architecture, Sybase IQ does not require additional processors or disk.

Powersoft Products

Sybase now owns Powersoft, a database tools company whose products are PowerBuilder, SQL Anywhere, S-Designor, and InfoMaker.

Powersoft products work with multiple relational database management systems.

PowerBuilder is an object-oriented tool that allows you to build screens and forms for efficient user interaction with the database. At present, it is one of the dominant products in the field. Many corporations are using a Sybase-PowerBuilder or Oracle-PowerBuilder combination for creating applications.

SQL Anywhere (formerly Watcom SQL) is a small-footprint, 32-bit RDBMS, compatible with Sybase T-SQL. It is available on PC platforms and is the Sybase work group solution. SQL Anywhere has been announced as a key element in Replication Server mass deployment.

SQL Server Manager

SQL Server Manager is a windows-based interface for the system administrator. It provides on-screen forms for managing common SQL Server administrative tasks, such as

- ♦ Database devices and disk space, including segments
- ♦ Logins and user accounts
- ♦ Permissions
- ♦ Configuration
- ♦ Backup and recovery

SQL manager also controls object definitions and integrity constraints. It handles new System 11 features such as named caches, table partitioning, and new configuration options.

SQL Server Monitor

SQL Monitor is another administrative tool. As the name implies, it monitors SQL Server performance, so that you can tune your applications. It lets you collect performance statistics for SQL Servers across your system and review cache hit rates, spinlock contention rates, and other performance measurements in a graphical GUI interface.

New SQL Server Features

Sybase System 10 and System 11 each introduced some new capabilities, refining the areas previously discussed. System 10 was a "features" release, while System 11 concentrated on performance.

Sybase System 10

System 10 features include support for SQL ANSI (American National Standards Institute) compliance:

♦ Cursors—Sybase resisted cursors (the ability to point to particular rows in result sets) for some time, claiming they did not work well with the relational model. However, users clamored for them and other vendors provided them, so Sybase made them available in this release.

♦ Extensions to the CREATE TABLE command to allow integrated integrity constraints—Sybase provided most of these functions in separate T-SQL commands (CREATE RULE, CREATE DEFAULT, CREATE INDEX). Now you have your choice of using the individual commands, putting everything into the CREATE TABLE command, or mixing methods. See Chapter 8 for a discussion and examples.

♦ Some changes to views—CREATE VIEW now allows you to use DISTINCT and WITH CHECK OPTION. This means that you can eliminate duplicate rows from views and further limit the rows inserted or updated through a view.

♦ Additional datatypes—Sybase added DOUBLE PRECISION, REAL, DECIMAL, and NUMERIC datatypes.

♦ Changes to the GRANT and REVOKE commands—GRANT now includes WITH GRANT OPTION to allow a table owner to pass on the right to grant permissions to other users. REVOKE has a corresponding CASCADE to cancel that right.

Sybase command reference manuals note the level of ANSI compliance for all commands. In most cases, commands meet 1989 standards and are at least "entry-level" compliant with 1992 standards. RDBMS vendors were involved in drafting the standards and generally try to follow them, so incorporating these elements into T-SQL commands makes Sybase applications more portable.

Other additions are major new capabilities:

◆ A Backup Server (created with Open Server) to handle dumps for better flexibility and speed. The Backup Server is part of the regular SQL Server distribution, not a separate product.

◆ The (optional) system database sybsecurity for audit trails, so that you can track specified users, actions, and objects. This means more control—and more work—since you have to monitor the size of the audit queue and sybsecurity and review the audit data.

◆ A threshold manager for monitoring space use so that you get a warning before you run out of space. This is particularly useful on objects that grow steadily (transactions logs, databases like sybsecurity).

◆ The IDENTITY property (available to numeric datatypes) for generating and holding sequential numbers. Users have long asked for this capability. It is useful for creating automatically incrementing numbers.

◆ System roles (System Security Officer and Operator) and the capability to let more than one user exercise these roles and the sa role. Now you can assign specialized functions to the right person or set of persons. In a large system, these roles are very useful.

A third group of features allows increased functionality for existing capabilities:

◆ More user login controls, including account locking, password encryption, and charge-back accounting (CPU and I/O use for SQL Server logins)

◆ New trigger features

◆ Changes to the datatype conversion function

◆ Additional options for the DBCC (database consistency checker) command

A change that represents mostly reorganization is a new system database, sybsystemprocs, to hold all system stored procedures.

Sybase System 11

System 11, internally known as "Cougar," built on these System 10 features and improved them. Major new capabilities include:

♦ User-defined caches allow you to divide the data cache into separate pieces and assign databases or smaller objects to them. When used carefully, this feature can improve performance by cutting down on cache contention.

♦ Data storage changes include MAX_ROWS_PER_PAGE and the new configuration option, PAGE UTILIZATION PERCENT. The first limits the number of rows allowed on data or index pages, thereby reducing competition for locks (and increasing storage needs). The second sets a percent of used to unused pages SQL Server can check when deciding how to allocate space.

♦ Partitioned tables create multiple locations for inserts to a table that does not have a clustered index, and thereby decrease lock contention.

♦ Isolation level 0 supports "dirty reads." This means that while you are running a transaction, other processes can read the data you are accessing in its uncommitted state. They cannot change it until your transaction is completed. Using isolation level 0 can mean better concurrency for some activities. It is not recommended where data consistency is important.

♦ The configuration option HOUSEKEEPER FREE WRITE PERCENT lets you control when SQL Server writes dirty buffers to disk. SQL Server normally does this during idle time and discontinues when total writes increase above some percent (the default is 20 percent meaning that the housekeeper task stops writing when writes grow by more than 20 percent).

♦ Multiple network engines are available for symmetric multiprocessing systems (SMP). It spreads network I/O among the available engines and allows more user connections.

Changes or additions to existing features are:

♦ Transaction log changes allow you to configure some log aspects of user log caches and to find the oldest transactions in each database.

♦ Lock manager changes give you more control over how locks work. Some configuration options are designed for multiple engines only. Others work on all SQL Servers, including options to change the deadlock checking period and modify the granularity of locks by promoting locks from page to table level.

♦ SQL Server configuration is more consistent. Configuration that previously was handled with (the undocumented) DBCC TUNE and **buildmaster -y** commands is now all handled through **sp_configure** options. You can also use configuration files.

♦ Improvements to SHOWPLAN make output from the command more readable and detailed.

♦ Query and data modification changes affect the behavior of some sub-queries and the strategies used for updates.

There are also changes to Backup Server and the IDENTITY property, as well as new text and image global variables.

System 10 and 11 features are covered as they come up throughout the book. Chapter 12 concentrates on new performance and tuning features.

How It Works

Overview

In order to design and deploy SQL Server applications, you need to understand some core technology issues, particularly how SQL Server is architected and how it processes data and data requests. These issues include managing transactions, locking, and processing queries.

Transactions, locking, and query processing are closely related. A *transaction* is a group of one or more SQL commands treated as a unit. SQL Server, by default, handles each single data modification statement (INSERT, UPDATE, or DELETE) as a complete unit of work, sometimes called an *implicit* transaction. When you group modifications together to form a logical unit, you define the *explicit transaction* by bracketing it with BEGIN TRAN and COMMIT TRAN or ROLLBACK TRAN (see Figure 2.1).

Both kinds of transactions exhibit ACID properties (atomicity, consistency, isolation, and durability).

Atomicity: Either all of the transaction's changes are present in the database or none of the transaction changes are present in the database.

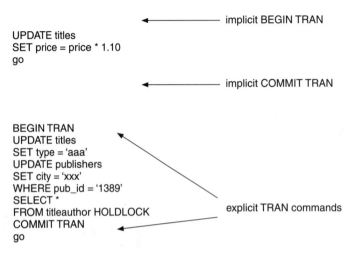

FIGURE 2.1 Implicit and explicit transactions.

Consistency: The transaction must reflect a correct set of changes within the database. This includes business rules implemented using declarative references, triggers, or transaction logic (the use of **BEGIN TRANSACTION, ROLLBACK TRANS-ACTION,** and **COMMIT TRANSACTION** within the application). Locks are part of the mechanism used to implement this in SQL Server.

Isolation: For any pair of transactions, one transaction executes completely, then the other. This is implemented by SQL Server locks.

Durability: Once a **COMMIT TRANSACTION** has been executed for a transaction, the changes must be present, even if the server fails. On SQL Server, this is true unless there is a media failure. In the case of media failure, it is still possible to recover under most circumstances if you have planned ahead.

Locks protect data consistency by isolating transactions. That's good news and bad news. The good news is that a particular transaction is isolated. The bad news is that other transactions may be waiting on the completion of this transaction (blocking) or two transactions may each be trying to get locks the other holds (deadlocking). Poorly constructed transactions and lots of locking can lead to sluggish applications. You can avoid this if you determine the minimum amount of work needed for a transaction, ensure that transactions lock as little as possible, and COMMIT the transaction as soon as possible.

Managing locks means working to get the lowest practical level of locking and the highest feasible level of concurrent access for each transaction. SQL Server makes most locking decisions, but you can influence lock levels by the way you design and administer your application and with a number of SQL Server commands. By paying attention to isolation levels, types of locks, deadlock causes, data segmentation, index design, and command sequence, you can take advantage of SQL Server features to get the best possible performance from your transactions.

Query processing is the realm of the SQL Server optimizer. If you understand the algorithms the SQL Server optimizer uses to process queries, you can make critical changes to the query or the index to improve processing time.

By knowing how transactions, locks, and the optimizer work, and how they interact, you can plan your applications to take advantage of SQL Server features and avoid problems.

Transaction Management

The way you handle transactions can make or break your applications. Each transaction (data modification) is an atomic action: Either it happens completely or not at all. The classic example of a transaction is the transfer of money from one account to another: When you take $1,000 out of your savings account and put it into your checking account, you want the two actions to be performed as one unit, or else you're a thousand dollars short at one point. SQL Server manages this through the use of the transaction log and locks.

Making Transactions Efficient

An efficient transaction has the shortest duration possible. You can accomplish this by making transactions small and execute quickly. When transactions run for a long time, they hold locks for a long time, and other users can't get at the data.

To make a transaction run in the shortest possible time, you can

◆ Remove user actions from the transaction
◆ Limit the logical processing that happens in the transaction
◆ Start and end the transaction inside SQL Server
◆ Optimize query performance

These are simple rules, but easy to forget.

WHERE DID MY CHANGES GO?

An application developer is working on his application. He is testing his new transactions. He runs the application, uses the right keystrokes to make a change in the data, and then goes to another window in the application and verifies that the change happened correctly.

The next day, he brings up the application and discovers that his change is no longer in the database. He heads off to yell at the system administrator and to find out why he loaded a backup copy of the database. The administrator calmly explains that he did not load a backup. . . .

Hm, the developer tries again—makes the change in data, confirms the change. Oh well, he goes on with his work. Next day, the change is gone.

The default behavior of SQL Server is to roll back a transaction if you disconnect without committing it.

For efficient SQL Server transactions:

♦ Use single data modification statements (INSERT, UPDATE, DE-LETE).
♦ Put multistatement transactions inside a stored procedure.
♦ Put dynamic transactions (values determined at runtime) into a single batch, containing the beginning of the transaction, all of the data modifications, error checking, and the commit or rollback logic.

All of these methods limit work done in the transaction, so there is minimal locking and a lower chance of blocking.

Checking Errors in Transactions

SQL Server rolls back a transaction that has very severe errors, but does not automatically roll back a transaction with less severe errors (duplicate rows, null values, and constraint violations). Because of this, you need to check for the error return of each data modification statement in a transaction and take the correct action.

Make transaction error checking efficient by building stored procedures that exit after any error and structuring triggers to issue a ROLLBACK and raise an appropriate error whenever data fails trigger validation. Transaction management is discussed in more detail in Chapter 6.

Locking

Database locking is usually considered an internal and very technical issue, examined only after a project is in trouble. For most applications, SQL Server controls which locks are used and when they are used. It's easy (and wrong) to believe that this means you don't have to think about locking behavior at all. New features allow you to actually define the locking behavior of individual SQL statements and it's tempting to get carried away by this power and establish the specific locking you want in all cases. This is not always a good idea either. The place to start is with a thorough understanding of SQL Server locking behavior so that you'll know when to take the defaults and when to make your own decisions about locking.

The locking behavior of a database engine is critical to almost everything in an application development environment. A technical leader in every Information Systems (IS) department must thoroughly understand it and chart the way for all developers in database use style: reading, writing, and transaction management. These activities should be managed in a systematic and thoroughly defined way. This is especially critical for online transaction processing (OLTP) systems that expect large volumes of transactions and/or large numbers of users. Casual regard for the importance of locking results in performance degradation, deadlocks, and potential failure of an application to deploy.

Locking is a way of controlling access to data in a multiuser system—you don't need it in a single-user system. Locking ensures the critical atomicity, consistency, isolation, and durability properties of transactions.

When you need access to locked data, your success depends on your activity and the type of lock SQL Server has placed on the data. If the style of access that you need is not allowed (prevented by the lock), you will experience blocking or deadlock.

Blocking   means that one process has a lock on an object that another process needs. The second process waits for the first to complete.

Deadlocking   means that each process needs a lock that the other holds. Neither can proceed. SQL Server detects deadlocks and terminates them by killing one of the processes.

SQL Server makes most locking decisions based on the query plan. You can influence locking with

- ♦ The way you structure queries and transactions
- ♦ The use of transaction isolation levels
- ♦ The density of data storage (FILLFACTOR and MAX_ROWS_PER_PAGE)
- ♦ The lock promotion value
- ♦ The deadlock checking period

Before discussing these options, let's review basic locking principles.

How Locks Work

SQL Server locks pages, tables, or extents. A page is 2,048 bytes and the basic storage unit for all data. The locks held are dependent on the query plan. For data modification:

- If the query plan uses indexes, SQL Server locks pages.
- If there are no indexes, SQL Server uses a table scan to locate the rows and locks the whole table.

For SELECT statements, the level of locking depends on the query plan and the isolation level. Extents (sets of eight pages) are locked when SQL Server allocates additional space.

SQL Server tries to use page locks to maintain concurrency. A simple update to a few rows, using an index, calls for one or more page locks.

```
UPDATE titles
SET price = 36.95
WHERE title='Net Etiquette'
go
```

However, when all or most of a table is involved (as in this update of all the rows in the table) SQL Server uses a table lock.

```
UPDATE titles
SET price = price * 1.10
go
```

SQL Server also uses table locks whenever it does a table scan (no indexes available) and when the number of locks used by a single statement is greater than the lock promotion threshold (more about this later).

The larger the lock granularity, the lower the amount of processing required to find and hold the lock. It's easier to find and lock a whole database than to do the same for all the rows in the database. On the other hand, larger locks mean less concurrency. If you lock the database, only you can use it. If you lock a single row, lots of people can work in the database (see Figure 2.2).

Some RDBMSs support row-level locking. Sybase maintains that the overhead required to find and release row-level locks counteracts the concurrency obtained from them. The new MAX_ROWS-PER_PAGE option to CREATE or ALTER TABLE allows you to define data density for pages. In effect, you can use it to get row-level locking, by allowing only one row per page. However, this means wasting a lot of storage space and greatly increasing the number of pages you have to traverse when doing a table scan.

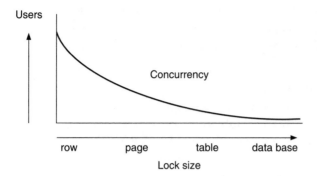

FIGURE 2.2 User concurrency and lock granularity.

Page Locks

There are three kinds of page locks: shared, exclusive, and update. As a rule, SQL Server uses shared locks for reading and exclusive locks for writing (see Figure 2.3).

Shared Locks

In general, SQL Server holds shared locks only while the page is being read and immediately releases them. Each subsequently required page is locked, read, and released. (Isolation levels modify how long a lock is held. More about this later.) When one process has a shared lock, another process can also obtain a shared lock on that page, but no process can get an exclusive lock. If an exclusive lock is in effect, no process can get a shared lock on that page. This model is used for all SELECT statements.

Exclusive Locks

Exclusive locks are used whenever data is being modified (INSERT, UPDATE, DELETE). Exclusive locks are held until the end of the transac-

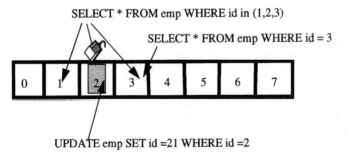

FIGURE 2.3 Shared and exclusive locks.

tion (this is how locks are used to ensure the isolation part of the ACID properties). When data is locked with an exclusive lock, no other process may obtain a lock of any kind on the locked data.

Update Locks

An update lock is obtained when a process is executing an UPDATE against the data as shown in Table 2.1. An update lock allows shared locks, but no other update or exclusive locks. Most UPDATE statements are implemented by obtaining an update lock, reading the page, escalating to an exclusive lock, and making the change.

Table Locks

Table locks include intent locks, shared locks, and exclusive locks.

Intent Locks

SQL Server imposes intent locks when table pages have shared or exclusive locks. This keeps other processes from getting locks on the table until the page locks are released, as shown in Table 2.2.

Shared Locks

A shared table lock is parallel to a shared page lock. It permits other shared locks on the table. SQL Server uses a shared table lock for CREATE NON-CLUSTERED INDEX.

Exclusive Locks

Exclusive table locks are like exclusive page locks, except on a table scale. An exclusive lock prevents any other transaction from access to the data. It is used for CREATE CLUSTERED INDEX commands and some update and delete commands.

TABLE 2.1 SQL Commands, Page Locks, and Access

Command	Lock	Other Processes Can:	
		Select	Modify
SELECT	shared	yes	no
DELETE	exclusive	no	no
INSERT	exclusive	no	no
UPDATE	update	yes	no
	exclusive	no	no

TABLE 2.2 SQL Commands and Intent Locks

Command	*Intent Lock*
SELECT	Intent Shared
INSERT	Intent Exclusive
DELETE	Intent Exclusive
UPDATE	Intent Shared

Lock Summary

Here are the lock types that SQL Server holds:

Shared Page Lock:	Other shared locks are allowed, but no exclusive locks allowed on the page or table.
Exclusive Page Lock:	No other locks are allowed on this page. No table locks are allowed on the table.
Update Page Lock:	Other shared locks are allowed, but no exclusive (or update) locks allowed.
Shared Table Lock:	Other shared locks are allowed, but no exclusive locks at the table level or individual exclusive page locks within the table.
Exclusive Table Lock:	No other locks are allowed at the table level or on any page in the table.
Shared Intent Lock (Table):	At least one page in the table has a shared lock. This lock is recorded as a convenience for SQL Server. It does not imply any additional locking beyond the page lock that is held. It makes it easier for the server to determine whether a specific table lock is allowed for some other process. In particular, no exclusive table lock would be allowed.
Exclusive Intent Lock (Table):	At least one page in the table has an exclusive lock. This lock is recorded as a convenience for the server. It does not imply any additional locking beyond the page lock that is held. It makes it easier for the server to determine whether a specific table lock is allowed for some other process. In particular, no other shared or exclusive table lock would be allowed.

Exclusive Extent Lock: This lock indicates that an additional extent (eight pages) needed to be allocated for this object.

Looking at Locks

You can use the system stored procedure **sp_lock** to examine current locks. With no parameters, you see all current locks. If you add an spid parameter (system process id, available from **sp_who**) the display shows only locks for that process.

On one connection:

```
USE pubs2
go
BEGIN TRAN
UPDATE titles
SET type = 'aaa'
UPDATE publishers
SET city='xxx'
WHERE pub_id = '1389'
SELECT *
FROM titleauthor HOLDLOCK
WHERE royaltyper = 10
go
```

On another connection, run **sp_who** to find your system process id (here spid 1):

spid	status	loginame	hostname	blk	dbname	cmd
1	recv sleep	bowman	BOWMAN	0	pubs2	AWAITING COMMAND
2	sleeping	NULL		0	master	NETWORK HANDLER
3	sleeping	NULL		0	master	MIRROR HANDLER
4	sleeping	NULL		0	master	DEADLOCK TUNE
5	sleeping	NULL		0	master	HOUSEKEEPER
6	sleeping	NULL		0	master	SHUTDOWN HANDLER
7	sleeping	NULL		0	master	CHECKPOINT SLEEP
8	recv sleep	bowman	BOWMAN	0	pubs2	AWAITING COMMAND
9	running	bowman	BOWMAN	0	master	SELECT

Still on the second connection, look at the locks your transaction generated:

```
EXEC sp_lock 1
go
```

```
spid     locktype      table_id     page     dbname  class
-------  -----------   -----------  -------  -------  ----------------
      1  Ex_intent       48003202         0   pubs2  Non Cursor Lock
      1  Ex_page         48003202       545   pubs2  Non Cursor Lock
      1  Sh_table       176003658         0   pubs2  Non Cursor Lock
      1  Ex_table       208003772         0   pubs2  Non Cursor Lock
```

You can translate the **table_ids** to find the names of the locked tables.

```
SELECT object_name(48003202)
SELECT object_name(176003658)
SELECT object_name(208003772)
go
```

They turn out to be pretty much what you expect.

```
publishers
titleauthor
titles
```

The **locktype** column shows the types of locks you have. Table locks have a table or intent suffix and a page number of zero. A **locktype** suffix of -blk means the lock is blocking another.

Blocking and Deadlocking

When one transaction has a lock that is in conflict with a request from another user, the second user waits. Consider the following example:

```
User 1 -     BEGIN TRAN
             UPDATE WHERE id = 'xxx'
User 2 -     UPDATE WHERE id = 'xxx'
```

User 2 waits until User 1 issues a COMMIT or ROLLBACK. In this case, if you looked at the results of EXEC **sp_who,** the row for User 2 would have an entry in the **blk** column indicating User 1's block. SQL Server does nothing to resolve this conflict and User 2 waits until User 1 issues a COMMIT or a ROLLBACK.

If each of two transactions holds a lock on a page that the other transaction wants, there is a deadlock. Although SQL Server automatically detects this case and rolls back one of the transactions, deadlocks should still be avoided. Often, when there is a deadlock, the application that owns the rolled back transaction will rerun the transaction. This reflects wasted effort by the server (and possibly other blocking). You can do much to minimize the threat of locking and deadlock:

♦ Shorten transactions and transaction times

- Use the resources in the same sequence in all transactions where possible
- Minimize indexing (and therefore index locking) on vulnerable tables

Without analysis, deadlocks will surprise you when you start to test or deploy with many users. Testing with few users will not usually illustrate the deadlock problem.

```
User 1 -     BEGIN TRAN
             UPDATE WHERE id = 'xxx'
User 2 -     BEGIN TRAN
             UPDATE WHERE id = 'yyy'
User 1 -     UPDATE WHERE id = 'yyy'
User 2 -     UPDATE WHERE id = 'xxx'
```

In this case, the SQL Server will pick one of the two users and ROLLBACK that transaction.

Special Locking Situations

In addition to INSERT, UPDATE, DELETE, and SELECT statements, there are other statements that acquire locks. You need to pay attention to possible conflicts when running the following commands:

1. The **CREATE CLUSTERED INDEX** command obtains an exclusive table lock. Any user accessing this table will be blocked until the statement has finished executing.
2. The **CREATE NONCLUSTERED INDEX** command obtains a shared table lock. Any user executing a data modification statement against this table will be blocked until the statement has finished executing.
3. The **UPDATE STATISTICS** command also creates a shared table lock. Any user executing a data modification statement against this table will be blocked until the statement is finished executing.

Influencing Locks

The most important way to affect locks is by carefully constructing your transactions. Other factors are transaction isolation level, page density, and lock promotion.

Planning Transactions

You can influence locking by the way you plan queries.

- Make sure that your change requests (INSERT, UPDATE, DELETE) use indexes. Otherwise, the whole table is tied up with an exclusive lock. (The section on query processing shows you how to check the query plan to find out what indexes the optimizer is using.)

♦ Minimize the number of modifications in a transaction. Determine whether multiple modifications are really dependent on each other. If not, make them separate transactions. Shorter transactions mean shorter locks and more concurrency.

♦ Use a stored procedure for your transaction. This ensures that your transaction is as short as possible by eliminating the network communication, parsing, and optimization.

♦ Some transactions cannot be defined ahead of time. They must be dynamically generated in the application. In this case, you cannot use a single stored procedure. If it is not possible (or practical) to put your transaction in a stored procedure, at least make sure that it is completed in a single batch. Again, this will eliminate any network communication time from the transaction.

♦ If you are using a third-party application development tool, make sure that you understand how the tool is processing transactions. When using some development tools, each change may be submitted as a separate batch. You may have to override this default behavior in order to minimize the duration of transactions (and hence locks).

♦ In transactions, always refer to objects in the same order.

♦ Do not allow user interactions inside transactions.

Using Transaction Isolation Levels

Isolation levels specify how a transaction interacts with other transactions running at the same time. The ANSI standard notes four isolation levels (0–3) and SQL Server supports three of them (0, 1, 3). These isolation levels only affect the behavior of SELECT statements.

Isolation level 0 allows the maximum concurrency; that is, it has the least impact on other users. Isolation level 1 reduces concurrency somewhat, but avoids the possibility of reading changes which have not yet been committed. Isolation level 3 allows for much less concurrency. It is more likely to block or be blocked by concurrent access to the same data.

Isolation level 0 (READ UNCOMMITTED) allows one transaction to read modifications made, but not yet committed, by another transaction. This is often called a *dirty read*. Using this isolation level will probably improve performance where data consistency is not important (snapshots of current data in volatile tables, for example). However, for most applications, this level will cause accuracy problems: You'll read changes that were not (and may never be) committed. If your application encounters errors, you must resubmit your query or transaction. Isolation level 0 is rarely needed and may give inconsistent results for many queries. We recommend against its use in most queries or applications. NOHOLDLOCK is equivalent to this isolation level.

Isolation level 1 (READ COMMITTED) is the SQL Server default. At this isolation level, a transaction can only read the rows changed by another transaction *after* that other transaction has committed. This isolation level does not guarantee repeatable reads.

Isolation level 2 (REPEATABLE READS) prevents nonrepeatable reads. If one transaction reads data, a second transaction changes the data and commits, and the first reads again, the data will be different and the results not the same. SQL Server does not support isolation level 2 as a separate option. It is incorporated into isolation level 3.

Isolation level 3 (SERIALIZABLE) ensures that inside a transaction, running the same query twice will yield the same answer (repeatable reads). It also ensures that while a query is running other transactions will not modify some of the rows that this query is reading (producing *phantoms*). In particular, the following query will yield a result that is consistent.

```
SELECT sum(amount)
FROM account
go
```

At lower isolation levels, it is possible that another transaction can modify multiple rows in this table while the query is running. With READ COMMITTED, you may get a result that is inconsistent. With READ UNCOMMITED, you may include changes that are not yet committed or you may get an error. Although isolation level 3 guarantees the greatest consistency of data, it also holds locks for a longer time (all shared locks are held for the duration of this query or for the entire transaction if the application explicitly starts a transaction). This reduces concurrency and is equivalent to using SELECT with HOLDLOCK on all of your queries.

Setting Isolation Levels

You can check the current level of isolation with

```
SELECT @@isolation
go
```

You can enforce isolation levels in these ways:

♦ Select an isolation level for the current connection using the SET TRANSACTION ISOLATION LEVEL command.

```
SET TRANSACTION ISOLATION LEVEL 3
go
```

♦ Choose an appropriate isolation level for a given SELECT statement using the AT ISOLATION keyword.

```
SELECT *
FROM titles AT ISOLATION SERIALIZABLE
go
```

♦ Use the keywords HOLDLOCK, NOHOLDLOCK, or SHARED in an individual query. (SHARED is available in DECLARE CURSOR statements only.)

```
SELECT *
FROM titles HOLDLOCK
go
```

Table 2.3 shows how the different commands compare.

Isolation Hierarchy

1. SET TRANSACTION ISOLATION LEVEL 0 has the highest precedence.
2. SELECT . . . HOLDLOCK, NOHOLDLOCK, and SHARED overrule SELECT . . . AT ISOLATION and SET TRANSACTION ISOLATION LEVEL (except for isolation level 0).
3. SELECT . . . AT ISOLATION comes next.
4. At the bottom of the heap is SET TRANSACTION ISOLATION LEVEL 1 (or 3).

Effects of Isolation Levels on Locks

SELECT HOLDLOCK or SERIALIZABLE transactions hold the shared lock for the duration of the SELECT statement's execution or, if the SELECT is embedded in a transaction, will hold the lock until the completion of the transaction.

TABLE 2.3 Isolation Level Commands

ANSI Isolation Level	*SET TRANSACTION ISOLATION LEVEL*	*SELECT . . . AT ISOLATION*	*Keyword*
0	0	READ UNCOMMITTED	NOHOLDLOCK
1	**1 (Sybase default)**	**READ COMMITTED (Sybase default)**	
2			
3 (ANSI default)	3	SERIALIZABLE	HOLDLOCK

Setting Page Density

FILLFACTOR and MAX_ROWS_PER_PAGE are options you can use when you create indexes or create or alter tables to control the amount of free space on index and data pages. Very low values lead to data pages with few rows, so that page-level locks function almost as row-level locks.

- ◆ FILLFACTOR is a short term solution: It sets an initial density, but SQL Server does not maintain it over time.
- ◆ MAX_ROWS_PER_PAGE, a new feature with System 11, establishes page density on a permanent basis.

FILLFACTOR and MAX_ROWS_PER_PAGE have their uses, but they can be expensive. They require more memory, disk space, pages to read in queries and in DBCC commands, pages in dump database, and locks. See Chapter 8 for a more extensive discussion.

Promoting Locks

The lock promotion threshold determines how many page locks a single statement can generate before SQL Server imposes a table lock. If SQL Server continues obtaining more page locks for this one command, the likelihood of a conflict, including a possible deadlock, increases.

Before System 11, SQL Server obtained a table lock when a single command held more than 200 page locks against a table. You could modify this value with the **sp_configure** locks command. System 11 has the same default, but gives you more control over it, letting you change the lock threshold on a table, database, or SQL Server basis with the new system stored procedure **sp_setpglockpromote**. You can set

- ◆ The minimum number of locks for an escalation (below which no escalation is attempted)
- ◆ The maximum number of locks (above which escalations are always attempted)
- ◆ The percentage of locks (used between the minimum and maximum to determine when to escalate)

For example, to set the low value to 200, the high to 300, and the percentage to 50 for the pubs2 database, use a command like this:

```
sp_setpglockpromote 'database', pubs2, 300, 200, 50
go
```

You can view the server-wide lock escalation values with **sp_configure**.

One of the most important uses is for very large tables with many pages. A higher threshold can make queries more efficient. Increasing the likelihood of table locks (by lowering the maximum below the default of 200) can lead to more lock contention. You should only consider it when your application requires it—giving a user exclusive access to a particular table.

Checking Deadlocks

SQL Server checks for deadlocks on a regular schedule. The default (minimum) is every 500 milliseconds. You can change this value with **sp_configure "deadlock checking period"**. If your application is unlikely to have deadlocks (being heavy on queries and light on updates, or particularly well designed, for example) you can increase the deadlock checking period and cut down on overhead.

A Conclusion

Knowledge, planning, and study can help. What will help even more is to design a systematic way of processing all data manipulation statements. A defined protocol can give developers proven tools and methods with which to implement their transactions and greatly improve the rate of success for deployment of new systems which, of course, will reduce costs. This is one of the many topics for which the consideration of client/server systems (client, network, and server) changes the way we should construct applications. The old ways will not work. The new ways are a challenge, but one that can be understood and used.

Query Processing

SQL Server processes SQL statements to create an efficient execution plan, as shown in Figure 2.4. The query is parsed, then it is standardized or normalized, and finally it is optimized. Optimization is the process of building an execution plan that will use the fewest system resources.

Parsing

Parsing prepares the query for normalization. SQL Server scans the syntax and divides the query into recognizable components. The resulting clauses or phrases are stored in a structure called a *query tree* (examples to follow).

Normalization

In normalization, the overall strategy is to *flatten* the query tree by analyzing the query mathematically (relational databases are set-theoretic). Flattening the query tree

- ♦ Breaks conjunctive selects down into cascading selects
- ♦ Moves the cascading selects down the tree to reduce the number of rows returned
- ♦ Moves projections (lists of columns) down the tree to eliminate unnecessary attributes
- ♦ Processes operations (converts BETWEENs to >= and <=)
- ♦ Converts subqueries into joins, if possible

The normalized query tree is optimizer input. To examine these trees, consider three tables:

```
Employees      Projects      Tasks
E_Num(PK)      P_Num(PK)     E_Num(FK)
E_Name         P_Name        P_Num(FK)
                             T_Title
                             T_Time
```

A query using all three tables looks like this:

```
SELECT E_Name
FROM Employees E, Projects P, Tasks T
WHERE T.E_Num = E.E_Num
AND T.P_Num = P.P_Num
AND E.E_Name <> 'A. Programmer'
AND P.P_Name = 'SQL SERVER'
AND T.T_Time = 12 OR T.T_Time = 24.
```

The initial query tree is shown in Figure 2.5.

Although not completely optimal, an improved version is shown in Figure 2.6. Note how the flattening process changes the query tree.

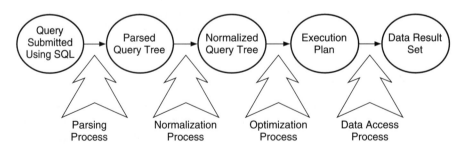

FIGURE 2.4 The optimizer and the overall plan.

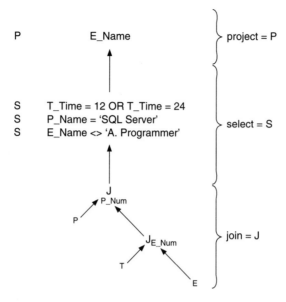

FIGURE 2.5 Query tree from previously defined SELECT statement.

Optimization

During the optimization, SQL Server tries to find the best access path to satisfy the query. The optimizer has knowledge of the tables, their indexes, the size of the tables, and the distribution of values within the indexes of the table. It considers many different access strategies (including some that may not have occurred to you).

The query optimizer is cost-based. It constructs an execution plan based upon the lowest cost in terms of disk accesses. It uses statistical data to evaluate different alternatives and may choose to do a table scan instead of using an index, if the table scan looks more efficient.

There are three main phases to query optimization. The number of tables within a query determine the tasks performed in the different optimization phases.

	Number of Tables	
	Single	*Multiple*
Query Analysis—Phase One		
◆ Analyze the query for search arguments	yes	yes
◆ Locate disjunctions, (qualifications with OR clauses)	yes	yes
◆ Locate join clauses		yes

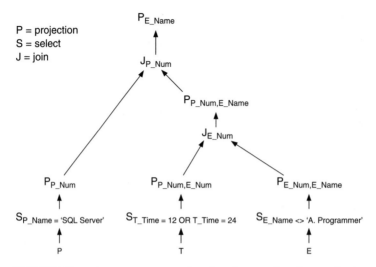

P = projection
S = select
J = join

FIGURE 2.6 Rewritten query tree showing the moving down of selects.

Index Selection—Phase Two

♦ Rank indexes by usefulness	yes	yes
♦ Match search arguments to indexes	yes	yes
♦ Find best index for each join clause		yes

Join Selection—Phase Three

♦ Permute tables and indexes for join order evaluation		yes
♦ Evaluate reformatting strategy		yes

Query Analysis—Phase One

Phase one of the SQL Server query optimizer is to analyze the query, scanning and breaking it down into clauses to identify *Search* arguments, *OR* clauses, and *Join* clauses.

Search Arguments

Search arguments (see Table 2.4) are WHERE clause conditions that limit the search. They have this general format:

```
<column> <inclusion operator> <expression>[AND...]
```

All search argument columns must be in the same table. A search argument must be conjunctive, that is, all terms are linked with AND.

TABLE 2.4 Search Arguments

Column	*Operator*	*Expression*	
price	=	50.00	
price	>	50.00	
price	>=	50.00	
price	<	50.00	
price	<=	50.00	
price	BETWEEN	25.00	AND 50.00
title	LIKE	'Net%'	
title	ISNULL		

```
WHERE price> 20.00 AND title LIKE 'Net%'
WHERE pub_id = '1389'
WHERE price = 25 * 3
```

BETWEEN and LIKE are both converted.

```
BETWEEN 25 and 50      becomes   >= 25 AND < 50
LIKE 'Net%'            becomes   >= 'Net' and < 'Neu'
```

If LIKE does not include at least the first character, it is not a valid search argument.

Some arguments are *not* search arguments; that is, they do not limit the search. However, if there are other search arguments, the query may take advantage of them. So the presence of a non-search argument clause doesn't imply that an index won't be used for the query—it just won't be used for that clause. Following are some examples of **WHERE** clause conditions that don't qualify as search conditions.

◆ Comparisons between columns:

```
WHERE QuantityShipped = QuantitySold
```

Since both columns are in the same table, an index is not meaningful.

◆ Computations where the data must be retrieved and the calculation done before the comparison is made.

```
WHERE MonthlyRent * 1.2 > 1500
```

◆ Functions on columns.

```
WHERE substring (lname, 1,5) = 'James'
```

◆ Negative operators (NOT, NOT IN(), !, and <>).

```
WHERE price !>25.00
```

◆ Incompatible datatypes.

Sometimes you can apply simple logic to convert a clause to search argument form. When using numeric values, change $A <> 0$ to $A > 0$ if you don't have any negatives in the table.

OR Clauses

As part of the analysis phase, the optimizer recognizes OR clauses. The optimizer converts IN clauses to OR clauses.

```
SELECT *
FROM authors
WHERE au_lname IN ('James', 'Hemingway')
```

becomes

```
SELECT *
FROM authors
WHERE au_lname ='James' OR au_lname = 'Hemingway'
```

The optimizer resolves OR caluses with either a table scan or the special OR strategy.

Joins

The optimizer also identifies join clauses. These are **WHERE** clauses that include columns from two tables, separated by an operator.

```
table1.colA <operator> table2.colB
```

The operator may be any of the comparison operators ($=$, $>$, $>=$, $<$, $<=$, $!=$, $!>$, $!<$) or the outer join operator ($*=$ or $=*$).

Index Selection—Phase Two

SQL Server supports two types of indexes, clustered and nonclustered. A clustered index has data stored at the *leaf* level in sorted order. A nonclustered index has *pointer pages* at the leaf level. A clustered index is termed a *sparse* index, since at its lowest level there is a pointer to each page of data. A nonclustered index is termed a *dense* index, since at its lowest level, there is a pointer to every row of data. You can have at most one clustered index per table and up to 249 nonclustered indexes.

If you do not have a clustered index on a table, then that table is a heap. All new rows are inserted at the end of the table. The data pages of a table are connected together in a linked list.

The optimizer has a number of choices in determining how to find query results. The first approach is a *table scan*. The optimizer finds the first page, and then reads all of the data pages, following the pointers that link them together.

Figure 2.7 shows a clustered index on a table. Another approach is to evaluate indexes, looking for the fastest access. The most obvious candidate is a WHERE clause search argument that includes at least the first column of an index. For example, the optimizer would consider using an index on last name and first name for a **WHERE lastname='Smith'** query. Using the index would probably mean reading fewer data pages than doing a table scan.

Search arguments are not the only thing that cause the optimizer to consider a given index. If SQL Server is asked to count the number of rows (SELECT count(*) FROM authors), it may choose to read all of the leaf pages of a nonclustered index. That is more efficient than doing a table scan.

STUPID OPTIMIZER (TRICKS?)

We regularly hear from Sybase customers (often, new Sybase customers) who complain that the optimizer is stupid. When pressed for details, they tell us that the optimizer refuses to use their indexes. It keeps coming up with a query plan that says "Table Scan."

A "Table Scan" is a great plan when:

1. There are only one or two pages in the table.
2. You are trying to select all the rows with the string "XYZ" in the middle of a column.
3. You want all of the "Males" in the table, and you only have a nonclustered index on the "sex" column.
4. You have no WHERE clause.
5. . . .

Join Selection—Phase Three

The join analysis (see the next section) will select the most useful index and the best strategy for JOIN clauses. The selection is cost-based and its goal is the least I/O. Cache size is included as a factor.

Reviewing Query Plans

SQL Server provides a tool for reading query plans, the SHOWPLAN option of the SET command. It's often convenient to couple it with the NOEXEC option. That way, you can submit a query and examine its plan without actually running it. You use it like this:

```
SET SHOWPLAN, NOEXEC on
go
```

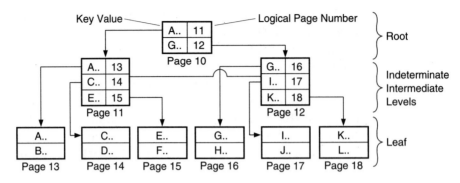

FIGURE 2.7 Clustered index detail.

```
SELECT au_lname
FROM authors
ORDER BY au_lname
go

QUERY PLAN FOR STATEMENT 1 (at line 1).
    STEP 1
        The type of query is SELECT.
        FROM TABLE
            authors
        Nested iteration.
        Index : aunmind
        Ascending scan.
        Positioning at index start.
        Index contains all needed columns. Base table will not be read.
        Using I/O Size 2 Kbytes.
        With LRU Buffer Replacement Strategy.
```

The output is cryptic, but useful. It tells you the type of query, tables used (FROM TABLE and TO TABLE), and whether indexes or table scans are used.

Running SHOWPLAN on queries with puzzling performance (or results) is an excellent way to check your assumptions about the optimizer and learn how SQL Server processes queries.

Query Optimizer Processing Strategies

Processing strategies include index analysis, OR strategy, and join strategy.

Index Analysis

The query optimizer can always use a table scan to process a query. It considers various indexes and attempts to find the one that will allow it to process the query with the least I/Os. In order to evaluate the cost of an index, it considers the following values that it has available in the index statistics:

Density   The average percentage of duplicate rows. A unique index will have a density of 1/number of rows in the table and is highly selective.

All Density   For composite indexes, the density is available for each index segment. For a three-column composite index, density is available for the first column, the first and second columns combined, and for all columns combined.

From the index statistics and, if necessary, the densities, the optimizer calculates how selective a given index is for this query. Selectivity can be expressed as the ratio of the number of rows accessed to the total number of rows in the table. Low selectivity may return many rows while high selectivity will return very few rows. With index statistics, the optimizer knows (or has a very good estimate) how many rows will match the clause. This is particularly important when evaluating a nonclustered index.

When isn't an index used?

♦ If there is no index, the optimizer must do a table scan.
♦ If the table is small, the optimizer may decide that it is faster to use a table scan.
♦ If the nonclustered index is not very selective, the optimizer may decide that a table scan will be faster.
♦ If there are no index statistics or the statistics aren't being used, the optimizer may do a table scan. This occurs when:

   1. A local variable is used, so the value is unknown.
   2. UPDATE STATISTICS have never been run and there were no rows in the table when the index was created.
   3. The optimizer can't evaluate the value being compared to the column. This may happen if the datatype of the column is different from the datatype of the value to which it is being compared.

With an index and no statistics, the optimizer assigns default values for selectivity. Having poor statistics can be a major factor in rejecting an index. The optimizer makes the following assumptions about selectivity when statistics are not available or cannot be used.

Operator	*Default Selectivity*
=	10%
Closed Interval (e.g. BETWEEN)	25%
Open Interval (e.g. >)	33%

If there is an equality match on all of the columns of a unique index, it realizes that at most one row will match.

OR Processing Strategy

An OR (or IN) clause is resource-intensive since each component is a SELECT statement and the result is equivalent to a UNION statement. For this reason, each column component of an OR clause should have an index and all columns must be in the same table. Otherwise, the optimizer will do a table scan or treat the OR as a join.

The OR processing strategy builds a *dynamic index* in **tempdb,** which starts as a work table with row identifiers for all qualifying rows, gets sorted, and has all duplicates removed.

The resulting dynamic index is used to retrieve rows from the original table. An example of an OR processing strategy is shown in Figure 2.8.

The optimizer may elect to do a table scan even though both OR components have an index. If the optimizer thinks that it is faster doing a table scan to satisfy one of the components of an OR, then it will do all of the comparisons in a single pass of the table scan. If any portion of the OR clause causes a table scan, even though an index is available, the table scan will be used in the execution plan rather than the OR processing strategy.

SQL Server maintains shared locks on all pages during the whole OR process. Avoid isolation level 3 and HOLDLOCK for queries that contain OR clauses, or other users may have access problems.

JOIN Strategies

When analyzing joins, the optimizer

◆ Picks an index for each table. If a table has no useful index, it is a candidate for *reformatting*—building a temporary index.
◆ Decides the order of joins (in sets of up to four tables at a time) after weighing the cost of each combination. The first table is the *outer* table, the second the *inner* table, and so on to the innermost table.

All join strategies use nested iterations. Reformatting is simply a special form of this technique.

SQL Server loops through the join tables in a nested iteration; it reads the outer table once to find the qualifying rows, the second (inner) table once for each qualifying row in the first table, and the third table once for every read in the second table multiplied by the number of reads in the first table.

Figure 2.9 shows what a nested interation would look like in the pubs2 database.

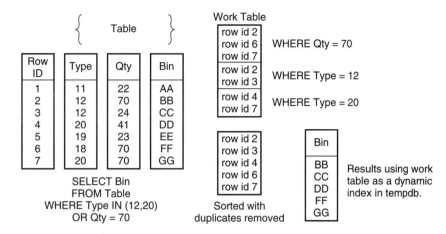

FIGURE 2.8 An example of OR processing strategy.

For joins, the optimizer uses only one index per table. The outer table index is typically used for a search argument, to find the rows that match the WHERE clause conditions. The next inner table index helps find the corresponding rows in that table. If no index exists or the index is not usable, then the optimizer may reformat the table, creating a temporary index on the table.

The optimizer evaluates the number of tables, indexes, joins, and number of rows to determine the optimal order for the nested iteration. The iteration proceeds as follows:

For each row in the outermost table

Find every qualifying row in the next outermost table

Determine whether the matching row meets the WHERE criteria

For each qualifying row in the innermost table

Solve constant query

Because the outer table is read just once and the inner tables many times, the optimizer considers the access cost. For example, it might pick a large unindexed table to be the first or outer table and a smaller indexed table as the inner table. Because it will traverse the inner table many times, the index will be more useful here than in the outer table.

Reformatting Strategy

The optimizer considers reformatting when there is no useful index on the inner table. This involves creating a worktable with qualifying columns and rows, and adding a temporary clustered index on the join column. The optimizer compares the cost of creating the worktable to that of repeatedly scanning the table.

Special Strategies

The optimizer uses special strategies for aggregates, ORDER BY, GROUP BY, and views.

Aggregates

Aggregates include COUNT, SUM, MAX, MIN, and AVG. They are always done in two steps: The first step finds the data; the second step presents it.

If you search for MIN(column) or MAX(column) and you have a clustered index on the column, the query optimizer uses it. Since data is in clustered index order, the optimizer need only find the first (or last) value on the root level of the index to locate the minimum or maximum value.

```
        SELECT min(au_id)
        FROM authors
        go
STEP 1
    The type of query is SELECT.
    Evaluate Ungrouped MINIMUM AGGREGATE.
    FROM TABLE
        authors
    Nested iteration.
    Using Clustered Index.
    Index : auidind
    Ascending scan.
    Positioning at start of table.
    Scanning only up to the first qualifying row.
    Using I/O Size 2 Kbytes.
    With LRU Buffer Replacement Strategy.

STEP 2
    The type of query is SELECT.
```

However, if your query calls for *both* MIN() and MAX(), the optimizer does not use the clustered index—it chooses a table scan instead.

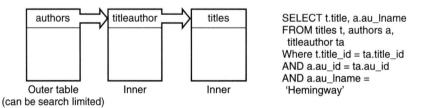

```
SELECT t.title, a.au_lname
FROM titles t, authors a,
    titleauthor ta
Where t.title_id = ta.title_id
AND a.au_id = ta.au_id
AND a.au_lname =
'Hemingway'
```

FIGURE 2.9 Nested iteration in the pubs2 database.

```
        SELECT min(au_id), max(au_id)
        FROM authors
        go
STEP 1
        The type of query is SELECT.
        Evaluate Ungrouped MAXIMUM AGGREGATE.
        Evaluate Ungrouped MINIMUM AGGREGATE.
        FROM TABLE
            authors
        Nested iteration.
        Table Scan.
        Ascending scan.
        Positioning at start of table.
        Using I/O Size 2 Kbytes.
        With LRU Buffer Replacement Strategy.

    STEP 2
        The type of query is SELECT.
```

A covering index (a nonclustered index that contains all of the columns required to fulfill the query) is ideal for an aggregate. When there isn't a WHERE clause and there is either a clustered or a nonclustered index, processing starts at the leaf level. When a nonclustered index covers the query, the root is accessed and the leaf level scanned.

Consider the following query and its query plan.

```
        SELECT COUNT(uid)
        FROM sysobjects
        go

STEP 1
        The type of query is SELECT.
        Evaluate Ungrouped COUNT AGGREGATE.
        FROM TABLE
            sysobjects
        Nested iteration.
        Index : ncsysobjects
        Ascending scan.
        Positioning at index start.
        Index contains all needed columns. Base table will not be read.
        Using I/O Size 2 Kbytes.
        With LRU Buffer Replacement Strategy.

    STEP 2
        The type of query is SELECT
```

Order By

The ORDER BY clause is usually resource-intensive. If you want rows in a given order, ask SQL Server to do it (and maybe, just maybe, there will be a nifty index). If you then decide (after the rows are on the client) that you want a different order—sort them on the client rather than selecting them again.

The optimizer will consider a clustered index or a nonclustered index that covers the sort. Otherwise, it will create a work table.

Group By

The optimizer always creates a work table for a GROUP BY clause, even if an index exists. The GROUP BY operation is resource-intensive, but is still an operation which should be done on the server. If you can use a GROUP BY on the server, it will likely *dramatically* reduce the number of rows in the result set. A server is a great place to do this summarization. It is resource-intensive—but it is often exactly what you want.

Views

Views are useful to the SQL Server user, but present problems to the optimizer. A view masks the underlying database structure. When using the view for data access, you request information from a view even though there may be a much simpler data access path. The optimizer ends up looking at all the tables in the view, even if they are not needed for results.

For example, the titleview view in the pubs2 database is based on three tables: titles, authors, and titleauthor. A query accessing two columns in the view (both from the titles table) produces this query plan:

```
     SELECT title, price
     FROM titleview
     go
QUERY PLAN FOR STATEMENT 1 (at line 1).
   STEP 1
        The type of query is SELECT.
        FROM TABLE
            titles
        Nested iteration.
        Table Scan.
        Ascending scan.
        Positioning at start of table.
        Using I/O Size 2 Kbytes.
        With LRU Buffer Replacement Strategy.
        FROM TABLE
            titleauthor
        Nested iteration.
        Table Scan.
        Ascending scan.
        Positioning at start of table.
        Using I/O Size 2 Kbytes.
```

```
With LRU Buffer Replacement Strategy.
FROM TABLE
    authors
Nested iteration.
Table Scan.
Ascending scan.
Positioning at start of table.
Using I/O Size 2 Kbytes.
With LRU Buffer Replacement Strategy.
```

The optimizer accesses all three tables, even though the columns in the select list come from only one table (titles).

If you run the same query directly on the titles table, the query plan is much simpler.

```
SELECT title, price
FROM titles
    go
QUERY PLAN FOR STATEMENT 1 (at line 1).
    STEP 1
        The type of query is SELECT.
        FROM TABLE
            titles
        Nested iteration.
        Table Scan.
        Ascending scan.
        Positioning at start of table.
        Using I/O Size 2 Kbytes.
        With LRU Buffer Replacement Strategy.
```

The results of the two queries are the same. The optimizer must consider all the tables in the view, even though the results come from only one table: It can't assume that it can ignore the join.

Picking Your Own Index Strategy

If you're not satisfied with the strategy the optimizer chooses, you have several alternatives:

◆ Evaluate the current indexes and create new ones if necessary.
◆ Use **UPDATE STATISTICS** to recalculate the distribution pages for current indexes. If the distribution pages are out of date, the optimizer will not make good choices

```
UPDATE STATISTICS authors
go
```

◆ Force the use of different indexes in your query by using the **INDEX** clause in your SELECT statement.

```
SELECT au_lname
FROM authors (INDEX aunmind)
WHERE au_lname = 'White'
go
```

♦ Change the order of tables in a join with the Transact-SQL SET FORCE-PLAN ON statement. It makes the optimizer process joins in **FROM** clause order. However, FORCEPLAN is not recommended. You are asserting that you are smarter than the optimizer. You also have the problem that the optimizer changes with each **SQL SERVER** update, and your technique may fail on a later version. FORCEPLAN is an option of the **SET** command.

```
SET FORCEPLAN on
go
```

♦ Increase or decrease the number of tables SQL Server examines as a group when choosing join order with the **SET TABLE COUNT** command. The default is four tables. Increasing the value is expensive: It can slow the optimizer. If you have a query with more than four tables, and suspect the optimizer is making a mistake in ordering the joins, you can use a command like this to change the number of tables compared to six (or any other number).

```
SET TABLE COUNT 6
go
```

You can also modify the I/O and cache strategies with the SET PREFETCH ON command and the **sp_cachestrategy** stored procedure, respectively. See Chapter 12 for more information.

Index Statistics

SQL Server stores index information in the distribution page, which contains a distribution table and a density table. Each index has a distribution page if either there were rows in the table when the index was created or the object owner or dbo refreshes index statistics with the UPDATE STATISTICS command.

You can find out if statistics exist for a particular index by checking the distribution column of sysindexes. A value of 0 means there are no statistics.

Here's a query that checks all non-system indexes in the pubs2 database (their names end in "ind"):

```
SELECT name, distribution
FROM sysindexes
WHERE name LIKE '%ind'
go
```

```
name                             distribution
-------------------------------  ------------
auidind                                     0
aunmind                                     0
pubind                                      0
titleidind                                  0
salesind                                    0
titleidind                                  0
salesdetailind                              0
taind                                       0
auidind                                     0
titleidind                                  0
titleidind                                562
titleind                                  466
```

Update Statistics Command

To create or freshen index statistics, use the UPDATE STATISTICS command. If you give the table name as a parameter, all indexes for that table are updated. For a more specific target, give both the table name and the index name as parameters.

This command updates statistics for all indexes in the authors table.

```
UPDATE STATISTICS authors
go
```

If you check sysindexes again, you'll see new values for the authors indexes. The value in the distribution column is the number of the index's distribution page. There is only one distribution page per index.

```
name                          distribution
----------------------------  ------------
auidind                                378
aunmind                                266
```

Distribution Tables

Distribution statistics are stored as an *even* distribution. The data is divided into *n* equal steps with each *nth* value recorded. You can figure how many steps you'll find on each page with these formulas:

```
Fixed-length keys:     keys/page = 2016 - (2 * number of keys) / key size + 2
Variable-length keys:  keys/page = 2016 - (2 * number of keys) / key size + 7
```

For example, consider a table with 22 rows as shown in Figure 2.10. Assume that there is one 245-byte fixed-length key.

```
8.15=2016 - (2 *1) / 247
```

The results show that SQL Server can fit eight values on the distribution page, so it breaks the table into seven pieces and puts the eight values (including the min and the max) in the distribution table.

From this distribution table, the optimizer can conclude that a WHERE clause like "WHERE key BETWEEN 19 and 26" would return about 3/7 of the rows. It could also conclude that a WHERE clause like "WHERE key > 200" probably would return few rows (it can't assume that no rows will match, since some rows may have been inserted since the distribution page was updated).

Density Tables

Density is the average number of duplicates in the index. The optimizer uses this value in joins to determine how many rows will match a given value. It is expressed as a percentage. If all the non-null values are the same, the density is 100. If it is a unique column, then the value is $1/N$ (where N is the number of rows).

User Tools

The UPDATE STATISTICS command is your only tool for maintaining index statistics. Several, however, are available for checking indexes, including SET options and DBCC TRACEON options.

SET Command

You're already familiar with three SET options: SHOWPLAN, NOEXEC, and SET TABLE COUNT. Other SET commands provide extra information about command processing across the current connection.

SET PARSEONLY—The syntax of a query statement can be checked without generating a query tree or an execution plan. Use it as a tool for query building. To use this feature execute: SET PARSEONLY ON. Use the OFF parameter if normal query processing is desired.

SET STATISTICS IO—If this feature is enabled, it displays the number of scans, the number of logical reads (cache pages accessed), and the number of physical disk I/O reads for each table in the query. To enable this feature execute: SET STATISTICS IO ON. To disable it, use the OFF parameter.

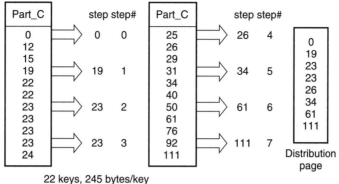

FIGURE 2.10 Distribution page detail.

SET STATISTICS TIME—When set, this displays the time in milliseconds required to parse and compile each command. This feature is enabled with SET STATISTICS TIME ON. The parameter OFF disables this feature.

DBCC TRACEON

SQL Server has four DBCC TRACEON/TRACEOFF flags you can use for analyzing index selection and join clauses:

302 Display index selection information.

310 Show optimizer analysis output.

3604 Send DBCC output to the screen.

3605 Send DBCC output to the *errorlog*.

Here is a query and DBCC trace flag 302 information. The main thing to look for in the output is how the WHERE clauses are handled—each search clause and join should be evaluated. Look for the **Scoring the SEARCH CLAUSE** and **Scoring the JOIN CLAUSE** lines. Since DBCC TRACEON 302 output is quite cryptic, you'll probably use it only when other attempts to understand the query plan have failed.

```
USE pubs2
go
DBCC TRACEON (3604, 302)
go
SELECT t.title, ta.au_id
FROM titles t, titleauthor ta
WHERE t.title_id = ta.title_id
```

```
AND ta.royaltyper > 50
go
DBCC TRACEOFF (3604, 302)
go
```
```
*******************************
Entering q_score_index() for table 'titleauthor' (objectid 176003658,
varno =
1).
The table has 25 rows and 1 pages.
```
Scoring the SEARCH CLAUSE:
   royaltyper GT

```
Base cost: indid: 0 rows: 25 pages: 1 prefetch: N
       I/O size: 2 cacheid: 0 replace: LRU
```

```
Cheapest index is index 0, costing 1 pages and
       generating 8 rows per scan, using no data prefetch (size 2)
       on dcacheid 0 with LRU replacement
Search argument selectivity is 0.330000.
*******************************
*******************************
Entering q_score_index() for table 'titles' (objectid 208003772, varno
= 0).
The table has 18 rows and 3 pages.
```
Scoring the JOIN CLAUSE:
   title_id EQ title_id

```
Base cost: indid: 0 rows: 18 pages: 3 prefetch: N
       I/O size: 2 cacheid: 0 replace: LRU
Unique clustered index found--return rows 1 pages 2
```

```
Cheapest index is index 1, costing 2 pages and
       generating 1 rows per scan, using no data prefetch (size 2)
       on dcacheid 0 with LRU replacement
Join selectivity is 18.000000.
*******************************
*******************************
Entering q_score_index() for table 'titleauthor' (objectid 176003658,
varno =
1).
The table has 25 rows and 1 pages.
```
Scoring the JOIN CLAUSE:
   title_id EQ title_id

```
Base cost: indid: 0 rows: 25 pages: 1 prefetch: N
       I/O size: 2 cacheid: 0 replace: LRU
Relop bits are: 4
Estimate: indid 3, selectivity 0.055556, rows 1 pages 2
Cheapest index is index 3, costing 2 pages and
       generating 1 rows per scan, using no data prefetch (size 2)
```

```
        on dcacheid 0 with LRU replacement
Join selectivity is 18.000000.


*******************************
```

DBCC trace 310 output is similar. We only recommend that you force the use of specific indexes as a tool in investigating a problem query. In most cases, there are other actions you can take to ensure the use of the appropriate index. Some of the steps you can consider are updating statistics, making sure that the appropriate index really exists, making sure that you are using the same datatype in your queries, and minimizing the use of variables in your WHERE clauses.

3

Project Lifecycle

The software development endeavor is a complex one. Traditionally the industry has evolved methods and structures with which to understand, organize, and control the development process. Many of these techniques and structures continue to be useful and important while developing with the client/server architecture supported by Sybase. Out of existing strategies and methods, the industry has evolved successful implementation methods and ways of structuring the vast number of technical disciplines involved in the new architectures.

An implementation methodology must map and organize the key elements of project development: technical capabilities, technical facilities, personnel, and time. It needs to define a clear sequence of steps, a complete list of deliverables, explanations of how, explanations of why, guidelines for controlling the process, and a complete descriptive structure of the system. This chapter will not provide a complete presentation of a methodology, but will attempt to outline some of the issues that must be addressed.

Four major elements will be discussed:

1. The first considers the technologies involved in client/server development and the use of these technologies. These are called disciplines.
2. The second is applying the concept of time to the process which will be discussed as project management sequences with an emphasis on the advantages and challenges of iterative development.
3. Management issues are the third issue. What is involved in controlling the process?
4. The fourth component is the use of standards with respect to process and the software deliverables.

This is not intended to be a thorough discussion of any of these topics, but an introduction to lay the groundwork for understanding the complexities of the platforms and processes involved in SQL Server development.

I NEVER KNEW THERE WOULD BE THIS MUCH DATA...

A consultant (not affiliated with any of the authors of this book—we got involved just in time for the punch line in this story) recommended a hardware platform to a company that was going to implement a database application (keeping track of procedures performed by about 250,000 dentists in the United States). After the hardware was installed, and the database started to shape up, performance was abysmal. The application was seriously pushing the capacity of the system.

In a meeting to review what had happened and discuss possible action plans, the consultant said, somewhat under fire: "I never knew there would be this much data." As if the number of teeth in the country had changed...

Disciplines, Skills, and Tasks

Disciplines, skills, and tasks are a structured way to look at the myriads of complex technologies and issues in the development process. One of the problems with this environment is its extreme complexity. Client/server was not designed to make the software engineer's or administrator's job easier. (It enables complex, distributed systems based on heterogeneous platforms.) Much of the information available is from vendors and clarifies a particular topic or product. For someone new to the environment, it is almost impossible to distinguish how the technologies relate to each other, much less how to use them. Not every technology is required (or desired) in each implementation effort.

Disciplines

A discipline is a group of tightly related technologies which provide a portion of a client/server system or of the client/server development process. It is used to group the technologies we encounter in the marketplace (shows, vendors, magazines). A detailed understanding of each of these disciplines is required to sort out which are important to your process and your system. As you evaluate new technology, you can better understand where the value lies and how you might make use of a particular technological innovation. Remember, this is just a way of looking at technology; as technology changes, though the technique still applies, the details will change.

In addition, these disciplines help us to categorize skills and tasks. There are an enormous set of skills required to accomplish the detailed tasks involved in the development and support processes. These disciplines help us to view the skill sets and tasks required. As you adopt a technology, you must acquire the knowledge to use that technology through additional personnel or training. *Training and continuous acquisition of new skills is a critical component of the corporate investment.*

The disciplines group into three principal arenas: infrastructure, software development, and support and control.

Infrastructure Arena

Infrastructure includes the technologies that are required to provide the underlying structure and architecture for a physical system. The structure of your developed system is based on the architecture and services that you install as the backbone. This can vary from simple two-tiered client/server (database server, network, and client application as shown in Figure 3.1) to a much more complex architecture with transaction monitors, complex communications, replication, and a more extensive array of services (see Figure 3.2 for an example). The number and nature of the products used will be dependent on the tasks you wish to accomplish with your systems. As the capabilities increase so does the complexity.

Disciplines associated with infrastructure are: hardware, operating systems, networks, network operating systems, DBMS, data warehouses, communications, Web and Internet services, and other purchased services.

These are the primary underpinnings of a complex system. You may have more than one version of each of these in a heterogeneous collection of clients and servers. That is what makes client/server and the concept of open systems so challenging.

Software Development Arena

This arena includes those technologies that are part of the specific system or application development cycle. They contribute directly or indirectly to the development process. These disciplines have dynamically changed the process of building software in the last decade.

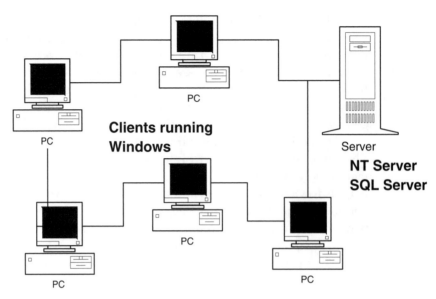

Clients running Windows

PC

PC

PC

PC

PC

Server

NT Server
SQL Server

FIGURE 3.1 Two-tiered client/server system.

Disciplines associated with software development are:

◆ Database Management Systems
  ◆ Relational Database Management Systems (RDBMS)
  ◆ Object-Oriented Database Management Systems (OODBMS)
◆ Graphical User Interfaces
◆ Object-Oriented Technology
◆ Client/Server Development: Cooperative Processing
◆ Analysis and Design
◆ Programming

Many of these are recognizable from reading the media and listening to vendors. Some are not. Cooperative Processing architecture is a field that is sorely neglected by many vendors. (How do you make it all work together?) As you evaluate a new technology, you must understand how it explicitly comes to bear on the development cycle. There are many aspects to each of the disciplines and it is critical to understand how each applies directly to the project lifecycle.

Support and Control Arena

Many new technologies and new versions of old technologies support the development process. All of these things have always been a part of the development process. Because the platforms and technologies used for

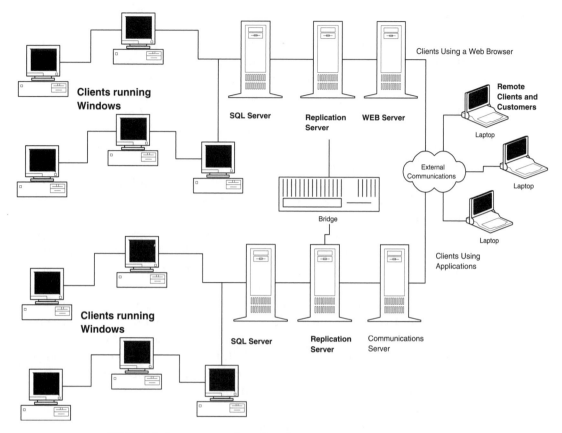

FIGURE 3.2 A more complex client/server system.

development have changed, the techniques and tools for support have changed as well. Project management and control are very critical elements in the success of a project. These disciplines need particular attention if you are to be successful.

Disciplines associated with support and control are:

♦ Project Management
♦ Development Methodologies
♦ Documentation (User and Internal)
♦ Version Control and Configuration Management
♦ Testing
♦ Technical Review
♦ Deployment and Distribution

Many of these disciplines are well established, but need adjusting to deal with new design concepts, methods, and new technologies.

Skills for Each Discipline

While not providing a complete enumeration of all possible skills and tasks involved in the development of a client/server system, some of the skills for each of the disciplines will be discussed. A map can be constructed of the relationship of disciplines, skills, tasks, and time (see Figure 3.3). This is the basic project plan, a musical score for your client/server orchestration.

A skill is something that someone on a project must possess. That is, you must hire or train a person to accommodate each skill required by your system. A complete understanding of the disciplines and skills allows you to plan training and hiring. In addition, disciplines and skills are selectively enhanced by the adoption of tools or methods purchased or developed.

There are some standard tasks that must be accomplished for many of these disciplines. They deal with acquiring the hardware or software, understanding it, and getting ready to use it (research, training, evaluation, acquisition, installation, and operational management). In most systems, you must first understand the current system's architecture with respect to the discipline. To plan for the future you must study the discipline and the marketplace, evaluate products, choose a product solution, and train personnel. You must acquire the item and install it. It is important to understand your system requirements within the constraints of your process or organization. It is not necessary to understand all of the possible technologies to construct a small discrete system.

For example, you have heard of object-oriented technology. You think you need it. You try to get it. But, what are you getting? Object-oriented technology is not something you buy. It is a large, complex array of technologies, tools, and skills that apply to different aspects of software analysis, design, and implementation. It is not enough to know that you want to adopt object-oriented techniques. You have to understand how they apply to your process and which elements of the technology you want to adopt.

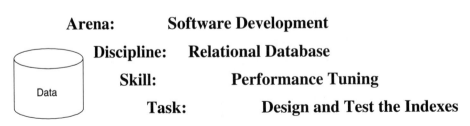

Arena:	**Software Development**
Discipline:	**Relational Database**
Skill:	**Performance Tuning**
Task:	**Design and Test the Indexes**

FIGURE 3.3 Hierarchy of disciplines, skills, and tasks.

Hardware

The hardware required to support a client/server installation is quite extensive. In the early phases of this market it was called downsizing because it was viewed as a way to move off the mainframe on to smaller, less expensive hardware. In reality, costs can go up or down. In all cases, the promise of open systems is that you can interoperate various systems of various sizes. Everything in the system can be "right-sized" for your requirements.

Hardware, of course, includes computers of various sizes: servers and client hardware. It also includes network hardware and protocols, interfaces between networks (routers, bridges), externally supplied network services (T1, ISDN, etc.), printers, fax machines, storage devices (disks, optical devices, jukeboxes, tape drives), modems, memory configurations (solid state memory). The list is endless and getting longer.

Skills needed for the hardware discipline are: hardware installation and integration, system administration, routing and communications for LAN/WAN, and external communications.

Operating Systems

Operating Systems are the core software platform on which you will build your system. Choosing one is a more important decision than selecting the hardware in many cases. It is critical that you understand the functionality and interoperability of the various operating systems. In addition, existing requirements and established protocols can create limitations in operation system choices.

Skills needed for the operating systems discipline are: operating system installation, system administration, monitoring, security, and performance and tuning.

Networks and Network Operating Systems (NOS)

The basis of client/server architecture is the network and the software ability to parse application logic into multiple processes that can be deployed on various platforms connected by a network. Networks are the hardware and software that enable the communication between systems. They provide communication, messaging, security services, and location transparency (see Figure 3.4).

Skills needed for the network disciplines are:

♦ Network installation
♦ Network Operating System installation
♦ System administration

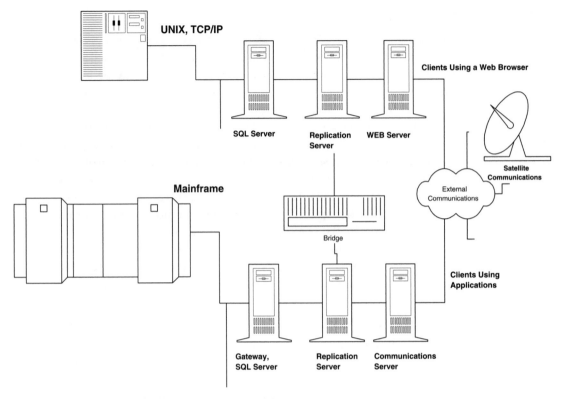

FIGURE 3.4 Complexities of networks.

- ♦ Security
- ♦ Interoperability
- ♦ Performance and tuning
- ♦ External communications (Internet, Web, etc.)

Database Management Systems

Most client/server systems use a relational database system for primary data storage. This is the current leading technology for managing data. While its success has been a key factor in the growth of client/server computing, it is not an architectural requirement for client/server computing. Some client/server systems can be deployed without database management at all. In the future, we may see the growth of other primary data management systems including object-oriented databases or object-relational databases.

Understanding, installing, programming, and managing a relational database system like SQL Server will be one of the major focuses of the development process. Skills needed for data management discipline are:

- Entity/Relationship analysis and design
- Data normalization
- RDBMS installation
- RDBMS programming
- SQL standards
- RDBMS performance and tuning
- RDBMS system administration
- All of the above for OODBMS and ORBBMS

This discipline contains vast areas of required expertise and much of the training and experience base must be vendor-specific. A detailed understanding of the behavior of the system's optimizer and transaction management behavior is critical to writing successful SQL in an application.

Graphical User Interfaces (GUIs)

The deployment of applications in client/server is often associated with graphical client applications (see Figure 3.5). The advent of stronger graphical development tools has moved client/server strongly to the area of graphical applications. Not all client/server application development is graphical, because there is still a strong contingent of batch and report processing that is not user-interface based. Most user-interface software constructed is graphical and based on Windows 3.1, Windows 95, Macintosh, UNIX Motif, OS/2, and other contenders. Some applications are required to run on more than one graphical operating system. This places additional design and implementation constraints on the application.

The graphical development platform is a critical decision factor based on the hardware and operating system requirements for users. This is a large and complex discipline, usually requiring new training and new tools. There are management and design issues associated with graphical user interfaces including graphical design, user interviews and reviews, iterative development, and usability. Design methods associated with these aspects are variously named, but deal with the constant (and historical) issue of accurately understanding the user's requirements and desires and correctly reflecting them in software design. New methods are possible because of the power of the current graphical application development tools. It is possible to build versions of the software and allow constant and frequent review by the user to improve and expand the design of the software. This development has led to improved software deliveries though the development cycle is more complex to manage.

Skills needed for graphical user interface disciplines are:

- Graphical user interface design
- Graphical user interface implementation

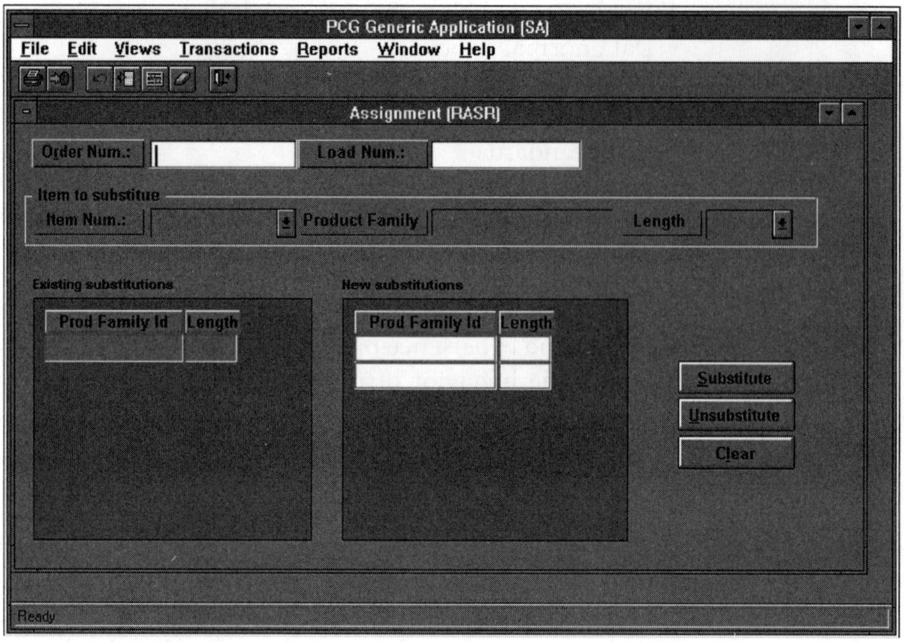

FIGURE 3.5 Illustration of a GUI.

- ♦ Cross-platform design and implementation
- ♦ Iterative development
- ♦ User interview techniques
- ♦ Usability testing
- ♦ Graphic design
- ♦ Joint application development (JAD)
- ♦ Rapid application development (RAD)

Object-oriented Technology

Object-oriented Technology (OO) is another discipline that has become associated with client/server development, though they are independent technologies. Object-oriented technology applies to many areas of the software development cycle. It can be used in analysis, design, and/or implementation. It is not required to use it in all of the phases to take advantage of the technology in any one of the phases.

Object-oriented technologies deserve a thorough study to understand how they can be utilized by your development process. Key aspects of OO include: classes and objects, inheritance, structures, polymorphic behavior, and more. Understood and used well, object-oriented technology can provide great advantages, but it is a technology that requires serious investment in training, study, and experience.

In addition to understanding object-oriented technology itself, there are special techniques and systems required to manage the corporate use and reuse of objects and object-based systems. Planning and designing for reuse and managing the successful reuse of classes is a new and different task in corporations, sometimes requiring new development groups and management responsibilities.

There is one more use of the term objects, in distributed objects. A distributed object architecture defines the style, standards, and protocols for communications and behaviors between distributed software components. OLE 2.0 and CORBA are contending standards in this area. Application developers can reuse objects (often referred to as software components) provided by vendors in their applications and can construct reusable distributed objects to build client/server applications that are more distributed and segmented. This provides interoperability throughout an application's environment and provides the application developer with expanded capabilities in the reuse of developed and vendor-supplied complex objects. This is a new area of development that will grow in the future.

Skills needed for object-oriented disciplines are:

- ♦ OO analysis
- ♦ OO design
- ♦ OO implementation
- ♦ OO to entity/relationship conversion
- ♦ OO object management process
- ♦ OO database management systems
- ♦ Distributed objects
    - ♦ OLE 2.0/COM
    - ♦ CORBA
    - ♦ OpenDoc

Cooperative Processing

The heart of client/server development is the concept of cooperative processing. The key to client/server architecture is the support for the parsing of applications into discrete processes that communicate with each other through messaging protocols. These application partitions can be individually deployed on appropriate hardware and operating system platforms that provide communication through a network. In addition, these systems are created to provide open interoperability—the ability for the layers of products to communicate through industry standards that are used among vendor's products.

The simplistic version of a client/server system is a single server application (often a relational database system like SQL Server) and a client application (often a Windows application). Even in this simple version of a client/server system, one can discern the advantages of the client/server architecture and the advantages that one can derive from using a very task-specific operating system like Windows on the client and NT on the server. In addition, the hardware can be application-specific and can be scaled appropriately at every point in the process.

One of the difficulties in deploying systems on this architecture is understanding the implications of the internal capabilities and behaviors in the systems being deployed. For example, it is critical to understand the connection, locking, and communication behavior of a server to properly implement the communication to it from a client application. When you design a client/server application, you must choose (design) how, when, and where to program any particular behavior. It is necessary to *design* these cooperative processing elements of your applications. This design work is very reusable throughout a system. Failure to design these cooperative elements usually leads to serious failures in the production application.

Classical (if you can use the term classical for a concept that is barely a decade old) client/server deployment is two-tiered. That means that a client application is communicating directly with one or more server applications. In this architecture, each application process is parsed into two components, part of which is executed on each tier. There has been a movement in the industry to define a more distributed architecture. In a multi-tiered environment much of the business logic of the application is moved to a third, middle tier. The concept is used to create application and database independence in the business logic.

Skills needed for cooperative processing disciplines are:

♦ Two-tier Client/Server
♦ Multi-tier Client/Server
♦ Open Servers and Gateways
♦ Transaction Analysis and Design
♦ Performance and Tuning

Analysis and Design

Analysis and design have always been components of the development process. The nature of analysis and design has changed over the years. Analysis and design techniques need to be applied to all of the software component architectures and the system specifications at all levels: the enterprise, the application domain, the database, the processes, and the user interface. Various methods of analysis and design are appropriate for client/server. Experience, appropriateness, and technical capabilities should be used to choose methodologies. Don't be afraid to use more than one. Application components are very different and different analysis and design methods may be appropriate.

It is important to try to identify a primary design methodology with which everyone is familiar: the development team, management, and the user community. It is possible to build a primary and unifying model of the system to guide and control the development processes.

One of the most important tools for analysis, design, and testing is reviewing the system with the user. User review needs to be institutionalized as a technique for understanding and designing a system. To accurately reflect the business requirements of the system, the users should be involved throughout the analysis and design of a system. This is accomplished with joint application design sessions and one-on-one interviews and reviews. This provides a method of assurance that you are building the correct system.

Skills needed for analysis and design disciplines are:

- ♦ Entity/relationship analysis
- ♦ Structured analysis
- ♦ State/transition modeling
- ♦ Object-oriented analysis
- ♦ Object-oriented design
- ♦ Business expertise
- ♦ Facilitation (JAD)
- ♦ Rapid Application Development (RAD)
- ♦ Software design
- ♦ User review

Programming

The number and types of languages and development environments is growing. You should try to restrict the number of languages and environments that you use to the minimum that will support your needs. The system's chosen operating systems, development, and database platforms will dictate the particular implementation methodologies (languages and development environments).

We must acknowledge that the nature of programming has changed. It is not a procedural and linear process anymore. Object oriented language development requires a more sophisticated level of design when architecting reusable software components. A project plan must make allowances in the development methodology, sequencing, and timing to successfully support the development of reusable software components.

Skills needed for programming disciplines are:

- ◆ 4GLS
- ◆ 3GLS: C, C++, COBOL, and so on
- ◆ Scripting languages
- ◆ Macro languages
- ◆ Software design
- ◆ Software implementation
- ◆ Design, development, and management of reusable components

Project Management

Project management is the most important aspect of software development. As a discipline it comprises many, many skills. Because the technology is so complex, it is requisite that a client/server project manager be quite technically experienced and understand the reality of the development process and the problems and solutions proposed by staff.

A client/server project has an enormous number of small and complex tasks that must be organized and integrated. The development schedule must be flexible and must be juggled (This is a technical term!) at regular intervals. Technical expertise is required to allow a manager to be successful in these maneuvers.

DUPLICATE ROWS

A programmer stomps into the room. Says he is running a query and the results he is getting indicate that there are duplicate rows.

Programmer: "When I run my query, it behaves as if there are duplicate rows."

Naive Manager: "I think there must be duplicate rows."

Programmer: "There can't be duplicate rows; I have a unique index."

Naive Manager: "I think there must be duplicate rows."

Programmer: "Well, I looked at my index and I forgot to make it unique, but the process ensures that there are never duplicate rows."

Naive Manager: "I think there must be duplicate rows."

Programmer: "I ran that subtraction operation and sure enough, there are duplicate rows."

Naive Manager: "I think there must be duplicate rows."

Project design is the task of deciding how to organize the development cycle and how to structure the dynamic dependencies inherent in the project. These stem from the complex development environment, the high level of user involvement, the quick turn-around for any given single task, the skills of the development team, and the constraints imposed by the organization or technical environment. A manager can only microschedule within a short time frame. Some tasks, or iterative development processes, can barely be scheduled at all, but will be timeboxed (i.e., "We will continue with this cycle for a certain number of days/weeks/months."). What a developer will be doing on a given day in the future will depend directly on how today's work is going and where it leads (see Figure 3.6).

Project control (the desired result of project management) requires detailed reporting and analysis to understand progress, direction, and productivity of the project. Scheduling is not useful without tracking and analysis. The loop of information back to the developer about his work must be completed to steer the project team on the correct course. The project manager has the hardest job on the team. It requires skill and experience for success.

Skills needed for project management disciplines are:

♦ Personnel management
♦ Communication skills
♦ Negotiation skills
♦ Project design
♦ Technical design and implementation
♦ Scheduling
♦ Tracking
♦ Reporting
♦ Juggling

FIGURE 3.6 Juggle everything and predict the future.

Development Methodologies

Methodologies are reusable systems that contain lists of tasks, deliverables, sequences, explanations, examples, and tools. To improve development cycles over a period of time it is necessary to evolve strong reusable methods for accomplishing tasks. Key areas for systematization are the development process itself, testing, and designing. Methods are used to enable a group to produce consistent and high quality results. The best methods come from experience; it is important to remember to reuse what works and throw out what doesn't. Methods need to evolve and be constantly reviewed for continuing applicability.

Many methods have been developed to support analysis and design methodologies: entity/relationship, structured (dataflow diagrams), object-oriented, and so on. Choosing and institutionalizing (tools, training, and support) one or more of these systems can vastly improve productivity and quality.

The development process itself is a prime target for a methodology. In the client/server area, it is of utmost importance because of the complexity of the development process. Many projects fail because too many of the required skills and tasks were unknown to the planners of the development cycle. This is an expected problem when addressing a new technological area. It is necessary to train or buy experience when planning first projects in client/server; or it is necessary to allow for the fact that you are learning and to make management and corporate allowances for that. Most organizations allow for some leeway and freedom on a small first pilot, but then expect the next "real" project to be in full control. This usually isn't the case. A method should constantly evolve with the tools, technologies, the skills of the participants, and previous experience.

Skills needed for development methodology disciplines are: know-how in developing a client/server system (experience) and development, testing, analysis, and design methods.

Documentation

Documentation is an important underpinning of the development lifecycle. At every step of the way, the document is the tie that binds one state of the process to the next. It is very important to insist that documentation be done, and create standards concerning when, where, and how it should be done. When designing documentation systems, look at the system as a whole and how the documentation will consistently flow from phase to phase, from analysis through design through implementation. Never consider a document as an isolated component, but as part of a consistent thread of information about the growing detailed knowledge that is being developed. Build systems that implement this thread (connection) between all of the documents. Our methodology uses an object model as a key, primary, and unifying design document. Such a unifying model will hold the map to all other design documents and tie them back to the abstract business model developed in the analysis phase.

The discipline of user documentation has changed with the advent of graphical user interfaces for our end-user applications. We are required to write manuals, but more importantly, we are required to embed context-sensitive online help into our systems. Technical writers are ever more in demand and have to possess new skills for developing effective help systems.

Skills needed for documentation disciplines are: analysis, design, software, and user documentation; technical writing; and document management.

Version Control and Configuration Management

Version Control and *Configuration Management* are standard disciplines that must move to new technology platforms. They need to be developed before a project begins or immediately thereafter. *Librarianship* is a term used for the responsibilities of organizing, filing, archiving, and restoring of documents, software, and systems. It is often neglected, but is always critical when a major system fails.

Configuration Management is more important than ever in the client/server environment. Any given client/server system has a complex pattern of hardware and software interoperability. Changes in any given piece can cause a system to fail. Tracking the correct combinations of operating systems, networks, databases, tools, and interoperability layers is complex and technical work, and much has to be done to control this environment.

Skills needed for version control and configuration management disciplines are: librarianship, documentation and software version control, and configuration management.

Testing

Testing is a major set of tasks that comes in many flavors. Complex systems require varying types and scopes of testing. Each software element must be individually tested (unit tested) for accuracy of performance and robustness. Each element must be tested for usability. In addition, subsystems and entire systems must be tested as a whole. Testing must pertain to usability, data manipulation accuracy, behavior correctness, robustness, and consistency.

Many tools exist to assist us in these processes. In addition to tools, testing requires discipline, method, measurement, tracking, and consistency. Skills needed for testing disciplines are:

- ♦ Design test systems
- ♦ Testing and reporting
- ♦ Fault tracking and repair
- ♦ Usability testing
- ♦ Unit testing
- ♦ System testing

TESTING

I took over management of a project that was producing an interactive debugger for C. At that time I didn't know C. There were concerns about the quality of the product, so I took the tool home on weekends and tried various things. The first weekend, the product crashed. It actually crashed many times. When I described the failures to the programmers, they said, "That's not a bug; you entered invalid input!" And I said, "A user shouldn't be able to 'crash' the product." I had to say that several times before I got their attention.

You can't just test with the values you think are interesting.

Technical Review

It is critical to have a technical review process in your software development cycle. It enables early checking/testing of methods and techniques, and the ability to keep everyone on a similar development tack. It also provides a mechanism for a more experienced developer to guide a less experienced developer. The junior developer can learn by reviewing the experienced developer's code and by having his reviewed.

Skills needed for technical review disciplines are: evaluation methodologies, standard procedures, facilitation of meetings, mentoring, and problem resolution.

Roles and Responsibilities

Many roles and responsibilities must be covered, even on a small project. Team members may play multiple roles; that is, they may take responsibility for multiple facets of the development process. The term *wizard* refers to those very experienced people who can solve problems quickly. These environments are so complex that much time can be saved by identifying an expert or wizard in certain areas to use until you have acquired this expertise on the team. The most important job is to identify the disciplines your system will encompass, the skills required, and the tasks that need to be accomplished. Map those skills to the available team—find out what you are missing before you begin. Figure out where and how you are going to obtain that skill.

Infrastructure Roles:

- ♦ Hardware system administrators
- ♦ Operating system administrators

- ◆ Network administrators
- ◆ Database administrators
- ◆ Interoperability wizard
- ◆ Performance and tuning wizards
- ◆ Communications administrators

Software Development Roles:

- ◆ Project manager
- ◆ Technical manager
- ◆ Technical reviewers
- ◆ Database designer
- ◆ Database builder(s)
- ◆ Database performance and tuning wizard
- ◆ Application designer
- ◆ Application builder(s)
- ◆ Application tuning wizard

Support and Control Roles:

- ◆ Librarian
- ◆ User representative/s
- ◆ Quality assurance (tester)
- ◆ Technical writer

Timing

A task is an action item that is part of a skill set within a discipline. The development process incorporates an enumerated list of tasks (what to do); those tasks are scheduled and accomplished over a period of time. There are an infinite number of ways to organize the tasks over time. Most of those ways will lead to failure.

Many issues are involved in organizing tasks:

- ◆ Task dependencies
- ◆ Availability of staff with the correct skills
- ◆ Requirements for deliverables
- ◆ Creating proof-of-concept solutions
- ◆ Prototyping
- ◆ Iterative design loops
- ◆ Risk management

In addition, there are usually corporate or organizational requirements to prove progress and to confirm delivery dates and estimates. All of these factors bear in the organization of time and sequence that will be useful in the development lifecycle.

Much has been made of changing styles of management in software development. A phased waterfall approach had been replaced by one or more *spiral* technologies in the "fashion" of development. A traditional waterfall development methodology steps through rigorous phases which have finite deliverables. No application code was written until the entire system was completely designed and specified. Once coding began, no design changes were allowed. Large systems were developed using this approach, but often the final application did not meet the system's goals which had changed since the analysis was complete. Iterative, or spiral, development methods allow the system to be designed, implemented, and tested by producing ever-improving versions of the software. This has been enabled by the great improvements and power in development languages and tools.

In reality, complex software development uses aspects of both styles. Complex systems must step through a series of design, implementation, and test phases, but must use iterative (spiral) development techniques in key phases of the development cycle. Rapid application development (RAD) is a set of techniques for very rapid deployment of relatively small and discrete applications. To use RAD you must already have a corporate infrastructure and an architecture of reusable components in place. In addition, RAD is most effective on small to moderate projects (maximum of 4–6 experts and 4–6 months) or modules of a larger system. When a system is larger than this, management and corporate requirements usually demand that the project is constructed in a phased approach keeping many of the productive elements of RAD.

Most development methods for large projects (or for inexperienced development groups) use a series of phases which each have a specific list of tasks and deliverables that progress toward project completion. Many tasks can be moved from one phase to another if you understand the dependencies involved. The complete list of tasks involved must include the construction of a complete infrastructure for client/server systems and establish the reusable systems and components required to build subsequent applications with rapid techniques. The use of defined sequences of tasks does not imply that everything is 100 percent complete before you move on, or that one cannot return to a previous phase task on a given area of the application if that is required. In fact, if the analysis information proves not to be complete, it is a *requirement* that you pass through the analysis and design phases on that piece of the application to make sure you've covered the bases and documented the new information.

Many of the tasks in the development plan require iterative development processes and make use of *timeboxing* (limiting the development process or the number of iterative loops by fixing a time to quit). Not all processes can be timeboxed. Some things (like building the triggers) have to be complete. But the overall scope of a project, the effort devoted to user review and design, the effort devoted to analysis, can and must be limited to a reasonable and cost-efficient expenditure.

Another key reason for phasing the development cycle is to meet organizational requirements for reporting on progress and expenditures. Some projects are by nature fairly large and it is necessary to track the ratio of effort to progress (work to percent complete) and to re-evaluate estimates during the lifecycle of the project. Phases should be designed to do this. They should group tasks into meaningful, dependent phases that provide a point of delivery (not necessarily formal). At these moments, it is possible to take stock of progress and with increased knowledge make predictions on the costs and risks of subsequent phases of the project.

It is also important to assess and document risk at each of these points in the project lifecycle. Risk is the existence of the unknown: unknown business problem, unknown technology, unknown solution, or unknown user requirements. These are problems that have no currently known solution and have the possibility of becoming large problems or time sinks. They are called *black holes*. Just identifying them gives your estimates and projections new meaning because you can allow for the fact that some of these things will take a significant amount of time.

Once your infrastructure is in place, new applications or changes to existing applications can be managed within a rapid development framework. The extensive learning and experience developed in creating a complete client/server infrastructure will give you the experienced team required to build a system much more quickly at each subsequent turn.

Iterative and Parallel Development

Two key facets of the development process are iterative development and parallel development.

Goals of Iterative Development

Iterative development is a process of building something, holding a user review, a technical review, and improving and extending it based on the review feedback. You go through the cycle again, until the result is close enough to be effective, you run out of time, or it's perfect! It is often represented as a prototyping method of development, but in reality, for the current state of the art of software development, the entire lifecycle proceeds in iterative stages.

Iterative development is used because it produces better and more applicable software solutions. The user community is not involved only once at the beginning and once at the end when it is delivered software. The community is a continual part of the process. This process, while challenging to manage, produces software that is more precisely what the user requires at the time of the deployment. Many strategic systems that are being developed cannot be defined by the user completely before development starts. New business systems and strategic solutions are invented and created through this partnership of the developer and the business user.

Iteration is applied at many levels to the development lifecycle. First, a large system should be modularized as much as possible. If it is possible to deploy part of a system, the system should be broken down into smaller applications that are delivered in sequence. Sometimes you can deploy the inventory system before you deploy the sales or shipping systems. This allows you to pass through the entire lifecycle of software development for each module with all of the reusable components and experience gained on the previous module. Iteration leverages learning and gets a team up quickly on the entire process (see Figure 3.7). In addition, you only have to train one division of the corporate users at a time.

In addition, each task accomplished throughout the lifecycle has its own iterations: development, test, review, development, test and review. But it can't go on forever. It is necessary to stop at some point. The total time is dictated by business implications, cost effectiveness, timeliness, and efficiency. *The design, development, and testing cycles of software development are actually one single stage of iteration toward a more perfect solution. Delineation of phases in this period of the lifecycle are done for business and management reasons: risk control, cost control, cost projections, and management review.*

Parallel Development

Parallel development is the ability to move forward on more than one tactical front (area of development) at a time. At a minimum, there are five fronts on which effort needs to be made simultaneously: infrastructure, support and control, database implementation (software development), user-interface applications (software development), and batch components (software development).

While developments on these fronts interact and share information, there are vast areas in which they are independent of the others. Understanding dependencies, or more importantly, finding nondependencies is one of a manager's key tools in creating a project plan or schedule. Finding and creating parallelism in the lifecycle can improve delivery schedules by

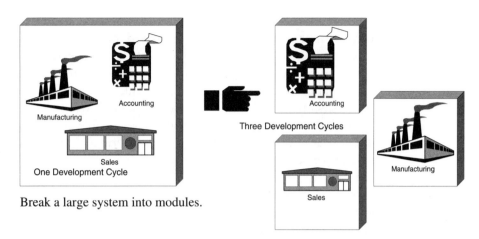

Break a large system into modules.

FIGURE 3.7 Iteration leverages learning.

allowing you to put more people on the project. Experience improves this ability.

Project Management Sequencing

This is not a complete, detailed task list for client/server development, but a suggested way to break the tasks into meaningful phases and a suggested starting list. Detailed task lists will vary depending on the software tools and platforms you use. It is important to structure tasks to support key development requirements:

1. Task dependencies
2. Estimating future costs
3. Deliverables
4. Constant forward progress
5. Proof of progress and concepts
6. Iterative development
7. Risk assessment
8. Available staffing

Many of the tasks involved for the database implementation side of a client/server system will be enumerated. These tasks are pertinent to building a database system with SQL Server. There are many other tasks dependent on the application architecture and tools involved in your process. These phases and their contents are relatively arbitrary. There can be fewer phases. In a small project, design, development, and testing can be one iterative sequence. With a very experienced team and a relatively small project, the entire process can be collapsed into a rapid application development process. Larger projects and less experienced teams will benefit from a more structured way of stepping through the process.

The phases are: specification, analysis, design enumeration, design, implementation, testing and deployment, and maintenance and support. The tasks involved will be discussed in the following sections.

These lists are a general guide. They evolve every day with the introduction of new tools, technology, and experience. They illustrate a method using seven distinct phases. This set of phases and tasks applies to a moderate or large project that is a first project to formally adopt and use client/server, object-oriented development, and a new client/server infrastructure. It will accomplish the development of the infrastructure and architecture creating a reusable corporate architecture which will allow for more rapid development in subsequent projects.

EXAMPLE: THE ALEXANDER MANUFACTURING PROJECT

The Alexander Manufacturing Company manufactures widgets. They are a subsidiary of a large corporate entity. Over the last 10 years the parent company has supported all of the subsidiaries on a large centralized mainframe. The subsidiaries are spread over a large geographic area and use wide-area network technology for communications. Two years ago, the mainframe became overloaded as the subsidiaries grew. In addition, the mainframe was considered to be too expensive. The Alexander Manufacturing Company was told that it had 18 months to remove all of its systems from the mainframe. This action would save Alexander Manufacturing $350,000 per year and would free the mainframe for other growing corporate requirements.

Specification

A specification phase defines the business problem addressed and the enterprise and system components involved in the process. Statements of business problems should address existing systems, business processes served, goals of a new system, project parameters such as expected costs (investment), expected time of delivery, and the who's who of corporate involvement (user community, financial sponsor, information systems sponsor, likely development team, etc.).

Infrastructure

- ◆ Analyze hardware systems and requirements
- ◆ Analyze architectural requirements
- ◆ Review platform possibilities

Software Development

- ◆ Define business requirements
- ◆ Define business goals

Support and Control
- ♦ Review staffing requirements
- ♦ Identify management
- ♦ Define management expectations

ALEXMAN (CONTINUED)

The MIS director of Alexander Manufacturing (AlexMan) determined that the systems should be redeployed on client/server. The MIS group consisted of two system administrators and three developers. Half of these services supported the work done on the mainframe. The other half supported the user systems and small spreadsheet applications.

The MIS director, the CFO, and the COO of AlexMan worked to define the business case for the project. They produced preliminary reports on costs, savings, and benefits of a new system. The administrative group started to accumulate information on hardware, system requirements, and possible platform choices. The MIS director identified a leader from the parent organization to hire/borrow for the duration to help manage the project and together they defined potential staffing requirements and solutions. They produced an estimate of costs for the next phase and a detailed list of risk factors that they could envision.

The documents produced were presented to a steering committee from the parent company and partner companies for review, risk assessment, recommendations, and approval for moving into the next phase. Once approved, the project was on its way.

Analysis

The Analysis Phase of a project captures a high-level picture of the business problem at hand, defines the scope or extent of the problem to be addressed, and creates a model of the business problem from the standpoint of the business and/or users of the system. This business model should enumerate all entities (or objects) and all processes (or methods) required for the system. In addition, many of the tasks involved in the designing, selection, and installation of infrastructure items must begin here.

There are three areas of work to be done at this moment:

1. Infrastructure documentation and conceptualization
2. Enterprise or system analysis
3. Conceptualization for support and control systems

These areas of work are all iterative using joint application development (JAD), research, interviews, and review.

Infrastructure
- ♦ Proceed with hardware research
- ♦ Select development tool
- ♦ Select relational database platform
- ♦ Design primary architecture

Software Development

- ♦ Define the mission of the system to be deployed
- ♦ Define the mission of the project
- ♦ Key word list
- ♦ Joint application development sessions
- ♦ Create an enterprise model
- ♦ Research and document user scenarios
- ♦ Document list of tasks the system should support
- ♦ OO analysis
- ♦ Publish data dictionary

Support and Control

- ♦ Risk assessment
- ♦ Select system software
- ♦ Create a training plan
- ♦ Estimates for design enumeration

ALEXMAN (CONTINUED)

The group had no experience with client/server and hired an outside consulting firm, Consultants R Us (CRU), to lead the entire organization through the process. The first action was a joint application development (JAD) workshop that lasted three days. It included the heads of all the major departments in the corporation (Sales, Manufacturing, Shipping, Inventory, and Production Planning), major users, and the MIS staff. This group became the primary review committee. The CRU lead analyst led the meeting jointly with another senior analyst. The attendees learned about the process they were about to go through, and then proceeded to create the following design documents: illustration of the business, business object model, key terms definitions, goals of the new system, and lists of key tasks that must be supported by the system. They also made estimates/guesses about the final costs of the system and came to an agreement that the system was possible and critical, and that they should move forward.

The analysis team proceeded with modeling the system with user interviews and questionnaires. In addition, the review committee met periodically to review the designs, answer questions, and keep the analysts on track.

The administrative group proceeded with hardware and operating system platform research and testing. At the end of this phase, they had a pretty good idea which platforms they would choose. A preliminary physical architecture design was produced with cost estimates for implementation. In addition, this group began a checklist of risk factors that they could append to and share with the other groups.

The manager of the project began to choose and develop a design team for the project, put management tools in place, and plan for training. At this time the system had a preliminary architecture and scope (size and areas of responsibility). An estimate was made for the costs of the next phase.

The steering committee met to review all of the reports and plans. They were concerned about the growing complexity of the system and their lack of client/server development experience. They cautioned the group to carefully track risk factors and make sure they were getting experienced help where needed. They were particularly concerned about the cost overruns they had heard about in software development for client/server. They stressed that they wanted the team to develop strong controls to measure and track the progress they were making. As the next design phase started, they wanted regular reports on progress and costs.

Design Enumeration

Design enumeration is a phase designed to help scope the total size of the project at the earliest moment. It is properly part of the design task, but focuses on enumerating the nature and number of each software element to be constructed. This enumerated list, combined with a complete list of global tasks, gives you the best possible opportunity to estimate the total cost of a system. Of course, every step forward will get you more accurate numbers (You'll really have it down when you finish!), but this phase is deliberately separated from the design phase so you'll know how many software objects you need to design, and therefore how much design time you need. Any decisions need to be considered tentative and changeable, but with experience you should be able to be relatively accurate.

The use of object-oriented implementation technologies will change this and subsequent phases significantly. If you need to design reusable objects and architectures, you will have to allow for this here and in the design phase as a separate and ongoing set of tasks, some of which can only be complete after prototyping (a major design phase task), and more complete system design. But if you know it is coming, you can allow for it in your estimates and planning.

Infrastructure

- ♦ Purchase or acquire infrastructure components
- ♦ Complete training sequences for all components
- ♦ Install all infrastructure components
- ♦ Install all tools

Software Development

- ♦ Extend the business object model or enterprise model
- ♦ Review reusable components already developed
- ♦ Document business rules
- ♦ Design cooperative processing model
- ♦ Iterate enumeration of each task to be supported by the system
- ♦ Tentatively design implementation model for each task (user interface objects, stored procedures, 3GL components, etc.)
- ♦ Establish programming standards
- ♦ Database

    Translate business object model to preliminary database implementation

    Define table volumes

    Define datatypes

    Design and implement domains (defaults, rules, user-defined datatypes)

Build preliminary database

Compile preliminary test data

Design a data conversion process for existing data

♦ Applications or user interface

Enumerate and rate for difficulty all user interface components

Estimate effort and time to design each component

Identify trouble spots

Design prototype

Window flow diagram or hierarchical map of the application

Establish user interface standards

♦ Batch or task components

Enumerate and rate for difficulty all user batch or task components

Estimate effort and time to design each component

Identify trouble spots

Support and Control

♦ Technical review
♦ Project management
♦ Select supporting software
♦ Design testing systems
♦ Implement the development environment
♦ Modularize the system
♦ Sequence modules
♦ Sequence design phase
♦ Estimates for design

ALEXMAN (CONTINUED)

At this point the project was in full swing. Besides the MIS group and the user community, four experienced application designers were added to the team. The MIS group focused on the data model, database design, and associated issues. In addition, they documented the complex batch requirements with which they were so familiar. Another complexity they addressed was the problem of moving from the old to the new system (transferring data, running in parallel, and cutting over).

The design team worked extensively on building the architectural infrastructure (cooperative processing model, development standards, reusable components) and the design of application components to support the user scenarios developed previously. At the end of this phase they had a detailed design of the number and nature of application components and could more accurately size the design and implementation process.

The administrative group began the process of acquiring and installing the infrastructure. This was a slow process in a manufacturing plant. Several false starts were made with network hardware decisions to optimize the speed and minimize the maintenance of the system. The administrative group went to appropriate training for administering and tuning their systems.

The management group finalized the selection of programming and management tools, made plans for testing the systems, managed the coordination of technical reviews, user reviews, and meetings. They worked on modularizing the system and decided on a system by functional area (Sales, Manufacturing, Shipping, Inventory, and Production Planning). They realized that they could not switch any of the functional areas over to the new system independently. Because of the tight integration of their information, the switch from the mainframe would have to be done all at once. The addition of experienced team members helped reduce the risk factors somewhat. The modularization was still a great asset. Each of the modules had its own production schedule and user group, and each could be managed independently. This reduced contention and improved parallelization on the project.

All groups produced a list of risk factors that they had identified: potentials for network failures, a new area of the business that was not fully understood, and a technical complexity with bar code readers integrated with the Windows applications, and so on. Management was concerned with the likelihood that the application was so large that they would need more developers and began a plan for integrating more members of the team.

With a detailed list of the "bill of materials" (identification of all software components) for the system and a complete list of other global tasks required, the team was able to jointly develop a detailed estimate for the design phase. In addition, they made some preliminary guesses at the cost of implementation. When they finished they were concerned about how big it was, but pleased to note that their estimate had only grown about 40 percent. They also believed that with all of the information they had developed that their number was much more accurate.

The steering committee approved the budget for the next phase.

Design

The design phase involves the design all of the software elements and systems, databases, and infrastructure support. One of the key tasks is prototyping key aspects of the application. Prototype all aspects of the application that have risk associated with them: They need lots of user review, the user is sensitive to his application, the technical problems are not understood, you are going to use many versions of this solution, you haven't built anything like this, you don't understand the business problem, the user is defining the solution to his problem as he goes, and so on. Design other things on paper or not at all, only enumerate them.

During the design phase much of the database implementation is completed. The database implementation should always be somewhat ahead of the user interface and task programming if possible. This makes the other lines of development easier and more productive.

Infrastructure

- ♦ Continue installation of infrastructure
- ♦ Support the new environment
- ♦ Tune the environment
- ♦ Plan for installation and support for deployment

Software Development

- ♦ Document cooperative processing solutions
- ♦ Implement cooperative processing solutions as required

- ◆ Database

  Categorize all transactions the system will support

  Implement domains

  Implement business rules

  Define trigger model to be used

  Iterate implementations of database

  Compile test data

- ◆ Applications

  Review reusable components

  Design inheritance hierarchy

  Design each ancestor

  Extend and maintain the window flow diagram

  Design key windows

  Prototype key application areas

  Design user documentation

  Address and resolve all difficult problems

  Finalize reusable framework and reusable components

- ◆ Batch or task components

  Design each report

  Design each batch task

  Address and resolve all difficult problems

Support and Control

- ◆ Implement version control
- ◆ Implement testing software
- ◆ Implement testing systems
- ◆ Implement application repository
- ◆ Modularize the system
- ◆ Sequence modules
- ◆ Sequence implementation phase
- ◆ Technical review
- ◆ Project management
- ◆ Estimate for construction of all elements

ALEXMAN (CONTINUED)

The administrative group now had the complete development environment installed and were ready to support it. In addition, they were finishing their plans for final installation of the production system. They had a noncritical path for the installation of extensive connectivity hardware throughout the factory and started early so that it would not become a critical path.

The design team broke up into groups for each of the functional areas. The prototype was specified. All areas of the application that entailed risk were chosen to be included in the prototype. This included application areas that had technical difficulties, usability problems, components for users with specialized requirements (difficult users), things that hadn't been tried before, components that would be reused extensively, or new technologies. The prototype is essentially starting development early on those things that may need more time, research, or testing. In addition to the prototype, the functionality and definition of all the application components were detailed. This entailed documentation, research, and technical review. All of the application modules were defined in "story boards" that could be reviewed by the users in great detail. Design groups met with the user community at least weekly.

A technical leader was identified to design, integrate, and control the reusable components for the application. He worked with all of the design teams throughout this phase to design components that would work for all of the application modules.

The database design team delivered ever more accurate implementations of the database. Changes that came out of design work were worked into the database design and it was redeployed regularly. All of the transactions (INSERT, UPDATE, DELETE) were defined and studied to optimize their design for performance and concurrence. Test data was generated for use by the prototyping team.

Except for system testing, the management team was in full swing. All developers were delivering product, prototypes, and design documents on a regular basis. Coordination of resources was a major task. Regular user reviews were scheduled, along with technical reviews and management meetings. Systems were developed to minimize meetings for status only. E-mail and voice-mail were used for that extensively.

At the end of the phase, the steering committee and the user community were invited to a demonstration of the prototyped systems. Everyone was jazzed at the progress the entire organization had made. The steering committee approved the budget for the next phase. The implementation budget had to go to a higher authority—the CFO of the parent company. This caused a three and a half week delay when the project was without budget. Some of the outside contractors had to be sent away for three weeks, which was problematic—would they be there when things started up again? The internal folks struggled to keep things going. All worked out, but it was decided that next time the phase would be planned in such a way to consider a possible funding delay. This could be done by producing the estimate for the next phase before completing all of the design work. It was judged that this could be done by leaving wrap-up design work and documentation until after the estimates. This work would occupy everyone while the funding process was taking its appointed time. All phase-completion periods are planned this way now.

Implementation

Implementation is the phase where most of the construction and unit testing is conducted. It is a continuation of what has been happening in the preceding phase. In a prototyping environment, it is very difficult to draw the line between design, implementation, and testing. The general focus changes gradually from conceptualizing the application to constructing it. In the middle of each phase you can recognize where you are, but at the edges it is very arbitrary where you draw the line. The key difference between design and implementation phases is that during implementation you know *how* you are going to build the system, while in the design phase you are figuring that out.

It is critical to understand that each of these tasks is iterative and will require complex scheduling with regard to user reviews, technical review, and the number of iterations required to get satisfactory results.

Infrastructure

- ◆ Continue installation of infrastructure
- ◆ Support the new environment
- ◆ Tune the environment
- ◆ Plan for installation and support for deployment
- ◆ Design system administration systems
- ◆ Begin installation for deployment

Software Development

- ◆ Write user documentation
- ◆ Test the system
- ◆ Database

Create indexing strategies and implement indexes

Monitor index effectiveness

Iterate implementations of database as required by changes

Compile volume test data

Write the required triggers

Write the required stored procedures

Test all components

- ◆ Applications

Implement inheritance hierarchy and reusable components

Maintain window flow diagram

Implement all windows and user interface components

Implement all transactions

Test each component

- ◆ Batch or task components

Implement data conversion

Implement each report

Implement each batch/task

Test each component

Support and Control

- ◆ Maintain application repository
- ◆ Provide librarian services
- ◆ Sequence testing phase
- ◆ Begin Sub-system testing as soon as possible

♦ Maintain project plan
♦ Technical review
♦ Project management
♦ Estimate for testing and deployment

ALEXMAN (CONTINUED)

This phase was a continuation of the design phase. All of the systems were constructed and tested. Constant user reviews were continued throughout the phase. Users were used to test certain applications as well.

A problem arose. Developers would indicate to their management that they were done with a certain portion of the application. When the manager put a user to work testing it, it would crash more than rarely. It was discovered that the developer had a different meaning for the word "done" than the manager. The amount and nature of the testing that the developer was expected to do had not been clearly defined. The group met and carefully defined the amount and nature of the testing that the developer was expected to do before he declared a component "done." This improved the quality of the deliveries. It was also decided that the developer should fix any problems in his code immediately (as opposed to putting them on a list to be fixed later). This made the developers a little more sensitive to leaving problems in their code and they were more likely to remember the coding situation than if it had been left until later.

Database tuning began at this time using the applications and stored procedures being developed. Final projections on database sizing were used to finalize the order of the final production hardware.

The management group put together a small team of junior developers and users to execute testing of sub-systems (integrated components) as they came together. This provided usability testing (did the users like it?) and preliminary testing of robustness and accuracy. The testing tool allowed them to begin to develop regression testing scripts that could be amalgamated later for a complete regression testing system.

The implementation phase was reviewed by the steering committee in the middle of the process. Though costs were fairly in line with estimates, the time schedule had slipped. The CFO was quite concerned with the slippage and whether the team had really improved its estimating capabilities so that the new schedule was accurate. The group reviewed the information that was being used to make the judgments and determined that it was as good as they could do. The good news was that though early components had run over, the last three delivered components had come in under their estimates. Everyone noted the concern and the system development proceeded. Of course, turning back at this point was hardly an option. They were not failing, nor excessively over budget. The user community was very pleased with the applications they had seen.

Testing and Deployment

Testing and Deployment can vary in formality. Thorough testing should be employed throughout the implementation phase. Each developer should have a method by which he tests his portion of the application before it is considered done. System and sub-systems should be tested as soon as they are ready. Corporations requiring a formal testing phase need to document and standardize tools, processes, and results tracking. Regression test suites should be constructed to enable rapid regression testing at each new release of the product. Testing in this environment is complex. It will involve a set of tools to test the different types of software and system components involved.

Infrastructure

- ♦ Support the environment
- ♦ Tune the environment
- ♦ Installation for deployment
- ♦ Implement system administration systems
- ♦ Build delivery system
- ♦ Test delivery system

Software Development

- ♦ Unit test each component
- ♦ System and sub-system testing
- ♦ Finalize all documentation
- ♦ Fix problems
- ♦ Consolidate and document reusable software components

Support and Control

- ♦ Track problems
- ♦ Collect enhancement requests
- ♦ Provide librarian services
- ♦ Evaluate project
- ♦ Technical review
- ♦ Project management

ALEXMAN (CONTINUED)

This phase really began during the implementation phase as application components became available. As lead developers finished their components, they were assigned to formalize the testing of other components. Some developers were no longer needed and were put on other projects. A small team of senior testers and user testers was developed to integrate and use the test suites. The developers still on the project were assigned problems to fix and reintegrate into the application. User documentation was completed and tested along with the usability testing.

The technical leader studied the final application and extracted from it the best and most reusable components for inclusion in their growing reusable framework. As available, the team reviewed and/or helped improve the framework architecture.

The administration group finalized testing of the installed hardware and then began deploying the application for testing over the network. They also finalized the development of the support structure of the system: deployment, backup/recovery, help desk services, and technical firefighting.

The core MIS team moved the system through the cut-over procedures and brought the system up. The old system was still in place. Another pass of testing ran as if the system was up. There were some difficulties. When they were addressed they went through the process again and brought the final system up for parallel execution with the old system. This proceeded with only a few data glitches that the programmers were able to fix as the system moved forward. After eight weeks of parallel processing, it was felt that the system was stable.

Key developers were available for emergency repairs throughout this period; they had some long days when they had trouble with some of the batch processes. One key user also had serious problems that were traced to an unusual setting in his Windows environment which took days to trace. A new system was developed to test differences (diffs) in the .ini files on Windows clients.

Management produced wrap-up reports. The project had gone 18 percent over budget and delivered 12 weeks later than originally planned. The system also produced a corporate reusable hardware and software architecture which the company feels it can leverage throughout the parent and peer subsidiaries.

Maintenance and Support

Maintenance and support of existing applications is an ongoing task. How it proceeds depends on the corporate model for this activity. In more formal organizations, this entire process is passed from the development team to a support group. This requires high quality and formal documentation and controls. In some organizations, the development team continues to support the software. If this is the case, you must allow for this as the team is assigned new projects. Proper preparation throughout the development lifecycle ensures the groundwork for the continued support and enhancement of a system.

ALEXMAN (CONTINUED)

The original AlexMan organization was not very big. It was basically a support organization. With this success under their belts, the MIS group began to have designs on building other systems to enhance the business capabilities of the company. As they tried to do this, they were hampered by the fact that they had one team to support the new application and develop new systems. With the staff reduced to the internal group, they did not have enough bandwidth to engage new opportunities. The management was able to go to the parent company and the steering committee and convince them that they should hire new staff to support the application, so that the entire company could leverage the investment in education, experience, and skill of the development team. Over a period of time, they did this and created a small, highly talented swat team of developers that are used to kick-start development efforts throughout the company.

This was a successful project. At least, that's how the story goes. Client/server projects can be successful, but they need constant care and attention, a lot of talent, some experience, and dedication to the end results.

Management Issues

Software development is a difficult process to manage and always has been. It has become increasingly more difficult with the advent of client/server. Corporations have been sold on how easy it is to deploy systems and therefore are not amenable to investing an adequate amount of resources to the project. Proper investment in adequate and high quality management is the most powerful investment a development organization can make. The highest leverage in software development is in an investment in management skills and tools.

Project management will probably take between 10 and 15 percent of the time for everything else. Unless a project is very small (fewer than three developers) a project will gain from a full-time project manager. If it is large (more than six), think about more management or at least break the group into teams with team leaders.

There are key tasks that must be accomplished by project management:

◆ Create an effective schedule
◆ Keep developers productive
◆ Understand technological problems and roadblocks
◆ Help developers to keep moving
◆ Juggle what really happened as opposed to what you planned to happen
◆ Move quickly

One of the most critical issues is that the project manager must be technical. It is not possible to manage in this environment without a thorough technical understanding of the primary platforms and development issues. Good technical skills along with good problem-solving skills will lead to expeditious and accurate decision-making. A project manager must also understand the business reasons for software. Software is not just an interesting technical challenge, but is a business tool. A manager must understand the financial importance and cost efficiencies required to make a software organization support the business goals of a corporation.

LIKE THERAPY?

Will good project management elininate all development and deployment problems? Not a chance. But it will make you face them and deal with them.

Opportunities

Management is full of opportunities. A manager's job is to manage a team that delivers a high quality product at a reasonable price. Like a pilot, a manager has to be ready, able, and willing to make course corrections on a moment's notice to ensure timely delivery of the system. Opportunities are those points where something is not optimal (sometimes something's *really* wrong) and a correction can improve effectiveness of the team. It is paramount that a manager search out, recognize, and act on these opportunities.

Problems in the project lifecycle come from varying sources. In all cases, they require management to comprehend, analyze, predict, resolve, and act. In the software development area, a project can fail for many reasons.

1. The software does not work as required.
2. It was not completed in the time allowed.
3. It doesn't meet technical specifications for speed, architecture, usability, etc.
4. The specifications were wrong or have changed.

Review this list of opportunity identification questions and see if you can find a next step or resolution.

Wrong Staff

> Is the developer on the task skilled enough?
>
> Do I have a more able developer?
>
> Could someone else be more effective? How would that affect the project?
>
> Can the original staff be put on a more effective task for their capabilities?

Inadequate Training

> Have we provided adequate training?
>
> Can we stop and get the training now to get up-to-speed?
>
> How would that affect the project?
>
> Can we get a mentor for the developer to speed up the process?

Wrong Timing

> Would this task be easier or more effective at another time in the sequence?
>
> Is a required predecessor not yet complete?

Wrong Solution

> Is the design of the solution being implemented the best and most efficient solution?
>
> Is it the one that was designed?
>
> Is there an inferior solution that is sufficient and can be done in time?

Wrong Estimate

> Does the estimate reflect correctly the component requirements?
>
> Do the lead developers concur with the estimate?
>
> Why is the development going over the estimate?
>
> If the overage is appropriate, can we explain it and document new estimates?

Changing Specifications

Are we doing more than we originally planned?

Are we doing a more user-friendly, but more costly solution?

Do we have information which was not available or accounted for in our estimates?

Did we forget that there were cost constraints at some point in our process?

Look for what's going wrong during the development process. Something is *always* going wrong somewhere.

Responsibilities

When building project plans and implementing a project, it is important for all team members to know what their responsibilities are and how they are to proceed when they encounter a problem. A list of responsibilities and guidelines for processes are an important part of the agreement between management and the development team.

Here is a sample list of responsibilities for the developer responsible for implementing each software component during the implementation phase:

- ♦ Review and amend (if necessary) the component design
- ♦ Review and amend (if necessary) the component estimate
- ♦ Prepare a component work plan
- ♦ Obtain management and technical sign-off for work plan
- ♦ Coordinate with other developers as required
- ♦ Construct component
- ♦ Unit test component
- ♦ Document component
- ♦ Maintain design documentation
- ♦ Obtain technical review and sign-off for component
- ♦ Accurate recording of effort (hours) and progress (% complete)
- ♦ Regular reporting on progress to management
- ♦ Notification of management of unsuspected problems

The management responsibilities for the same phase include the following:

- ♦ Assigning and scheduling all tasks
- ♦ Tracking effort and progress on a weekly basis
- ♦ Generating reports on effort and progress on a weekly basis
- ♦ Providing appropriate technical review personnel on a timely basis
- ♦ Obtaining resources for developers on a timely basis

- ♦ Coordinating requirements from the customer
- ♦ Provide all required reports to customers
- ♦ Evaluating effort to progress ratios for management adjustments:

  Appropriateness of developer—Training

  Appropriateness of design

  Appropriateness of estimate

  Appropriateness of scheduling or sequencing

- ♦ Notification of customer in the case of any failure of effort to progress

Standards

Standards are an important part of developing a corporate methodology, affecting many areas. This chapter discusses architecture and user interface standards. Programming standards are covered in Chapter 4.

Architectural and cooperative processing standards are difficult to develop, but are the most important standards for ensuring successful deployment of client/server systems.

Architecture Standards

There are key architectural issues that are critical to the successful deployment of a client/server solution. If a corporation or project team does not knowledgably design solutions for these technical issues, the likelihood is that the application can fail to be successful for any number of reasons.

A client/server technical issue is one where the client, the server and the communication between them affect the *usability* of an application, the *control* that the programmer has over the application, and the *performance* of the application. For example, how should you validate data in a SQL Server application? Tools are available from the server and the client development environment. Which should you use and when?

One of the most critical areas in an online transaction processing (OLTP) application, is the execution of transactions. Transaction management is the heart and soul of an OLTP system. You also may have the problems of size: hundreds of users and thousands of transactions. It is critical that a programmer (and a corporation) understand the implications of transactions and the locks that the Server uses to manage them. Once you have understood the issues and how the tools work, you can design reusable solutions that can deliver the quality of usability and performance required by your system.

Developing corporate standards around these issues is vitally important. Imagine that you have an OLTP system being developed by *n* programmers. You have *not* created a standard for how to implement data modifications. Each develops his own style; some are better and some are not so good. You have n styles. As you go into production, the performance of the application is not adequate and the system generates deadlocks. How do you fix this? Whose transactions have caused the problem? The problem transactions might have been adequate by themselves, but they interact poorly with other programmers' transactions. The problems could be widespread throughout the application and very difficult to fix. Planning ahead and designing architecturally correct solutions always pays off.

The key issues are connection management, error handling, data access, data validation, transaction management, concurrency management, distributed processing, and security. You'll find details on these topics in other chapters.

User Interface Standards

There are many books on graphical user interface design. Here's a brief outline of why and how to standardize. It is important to remember the basic principles of good interface design.

- ◆ The user should be in control during the execution of the application. The user should be able to decide how to proceed and always have the option of changing his mind. The application should use modal behavior (the user *has* to do a particular action) as little as possible. The user should be able to, at some level, customize the application to his preferences.
- ◆ The interface should be consistent within itself and with other applications in use by the user community. Consistency should be reflected in design, layout, color, and most importantly, in behavior. Common actions should be reflected in common implementations. Metaphors for data manipulation should be constantly and consistently reused. Allow users to leverage what they learn in using applications with all new applications.
- ◆ Users should be able to reflect their activities directly in the software. They should be able to directly view and manipulate their information. The metaphors in the application should present intuitive ways for the user to interface with his information.
- ◆ The interface should be direct in its response to the user. The software should reflect all user actions directly with visible and informational

feedback. The application should visually respond to the user and reflect its actions visually.

◆ The interface should allow the user to change his mind and make errors. Primary decisions should allow for cancellation.

◆ The user interface should be pleasing to look at and should have as little clutter as possible with respect to the user interface. Appropriate aggregations of information should be defined according to the tasks, capabilities, and desires of the user community. (Occasionally, you will build a cluttered-looking screen, because the task at hand and the users demand that a large amount of information is present at one time so that they can make quick decisions. This is a business- and utility-based decision.)

Designing an Application Interface

To design an application interface, start with existing application standards and existing guidelines for the graphical user interface. For example, there are published guidelines for building Windows 3.1 and Windows 95 applications. In addition, the developer must use and study existing applications.

An application interface is designed for a particular task and a particular set of users. It is necessary to study the user's tasks and work with the users to design a system that will serve them. It is an iterative process.

◆ Understand the overall goals of the system; study any analysis, modeling, and design work that has been done for the system.

◆ Review all existing applications in use by the user community for reusable components and design concepts.

◆ Know your platform.

◆ Classify the users into groups that define required functionality.

◆ Work with user representatives to enumerate the nature, sequence, control required, and importance of each task or task sequence. Understand their requirements for flexibility, availability of information, sequencing, and transaction management.

◆ Build a storyboard of the application area which includes menus, windows with controls on them, navigation metaphors (menus, tabs, toolbars, etc.). Work with the user in iterative design cycles, improving the storyboard until the user likes it.

◆ For any critical or problem areas, build a working prototype from the storyboard. Solve difficult problems. Review with the user.

◆ Extend the storyboard/prototype into an application working iteratively with the user providing review and testing. This is a continuous iterative process until the application is complete.

There are many more tasks in building a system; we have isolated just the steps dealing with the user interface design and implementation. This process can be formalized with complete usability testing.

Reusable Frameworks

An application framework is a set of application objects that work together to implement application-specific and business-specific behavior. In many development environments, there are commercial application frameworks available. It is also standard to build application frameworks within a corporation to gain reusability, control, and standardization of coding practices.

In a graphical environment like Windows, the application objects consist of windows of differing styles, menus, other control objects, or widgets. They have specialization with regard to specific metaphors, graphical representation, and behavior. It is standard to have frameworks to support standard windowing models like single document interface (SDI) and multiple document interface (MDI). In addition, other standard behaviors are supported in controls.

In an object-oriented environment, it is possible to extend these objects and create related classes of objects. Graphical development is ideally suited to object-oriented development and implementation because of the nature of the graphical operating systems. Object-oriented development of graphical frameworks is one of the most productive and powerful types of reuse available in the development architectures. Standard use of frameworks, purchased or developed, is an important part of standardizing the corporate investment in software development. It provides standardization, better quality, and reuse of software investments.

Corporate frameworks would implement behavioral and coding standards like error handling, security, transaction control, data validation, query methods, and so on. In addition, frameworks can implement corporate graphical standards such as color, fonts, layouts, and so on. At the lowest level of inheritance, the objects in the framework can be application- or business-specific. That is, they can be intelligent about reusable corporate entities (or objects) like "customers" and embed the methods and attributes of these entities into reusable application objects.

It is important to view the development of a corporate application framework as an investment, and allow adequate resources and time to this process. It will pay off, but as in all investment, the payoff happens over time. Development of a framework will actually lengthen the development of a first project. Use of a framework on later projects will save time and money. In addition, it will improve maintenance costs.

4

Setting Up Programming Standards

Overview

Programming standards are guidelines for programmers. They give your code a unified look and feel, and a consistent usage. This means you can

♦ Improve the structure and organization of code
♦ Make it easier for the developer and the maintenance staff to read the code
♦ Remove confusing or obfuscating inconsistencies

NAMING CONVENTIONS AND BANDWIDTH

Scene:
    Jim, working on site late into the evening.
    Mary in the office trying to wrap up for the day.

Ring, ring. . . .
Mary: "Hello, this is Mary."
Jim: "Hi. I'm having trouble setting up to run this code for you. Can you go over this module with me?"

Mary: "Okay. Let me get it." Rustle, rustle. "Okay."

Jim: "I'm trying to run this script and I can't manage to find the data."

Mary: "Well, it's in the PPOProvider table. I can't imagine why you can't find it."

Jim: "When I run the query to select the name column from the ppoprovider table, it says that it doesn't exist."

Mary: ". . . Oh, I know. I bet you're in the wrong database. Can you check the equ88 database? Or pru88?"

Jim: "It'll take a minute to get there . . . No, that doesn't seem to work either. Are you sure that these databases were completely built and loaded?"

Mary: "Yes, I did it this morning. I wonder if Steve took them off the system this afternoon."

Jim: "No the database is here; it's just that the ppoprovider table isn't here. Is that the right name?"

Mary: "P-P-O-P-r-o-v-i-d-e-r. The Name is just 'Name.' "

Jim: "That's what I'm typing . . . p-p-o-p-r-o-v-i-d-e-r. I don't get it."

It's going to be a long night.

Programming language standards are easier to develop than architecture standards and are usually where corporations start. Architecture standards are much more critical to the success of a project than the coding standards, but coding standards are still very important.

You can create standards for structuring and laying out code, naming variables and other objects, making comments, and handling documentation.

Standards are often particular to a specific language, though many of the standard issues can be addressed at a general level. This chapter starts with general standards, and then provides some specifics for using SQL.

General Programming Standards

You can apply general programming standards to almost any language. Each corporation, development team, and environment extends and customizes these principles to meet particular requirements.

Formatted or Structured Code

Format or structure program code to make the program control-of-flow clear. It should be easy for an outsider to read the code and follow the logic. This means using tabs (indents) to show how sections of code relate to each other.

```
IF ( condition1 )
        BEGIN
                IF ( condition2 )
                BEGIN
                        statements for execution...
                        .
```

```
               END
               statements for execution
                   .              .
       END
```

As word processors and editors treat a TAB differently, replace each TAB with the actual ASCII value of three spaces.

The general rules are:

♦ Indent one tab under every IF/BEGIN, FOR, DO, WHILE (or similar construct).
♦ For long conditional sections or loops, or for nested conditionals or loops, add a short comment following the terminator specifying which IF, FOR, DO, or BEGIN it belongs to. ELSE statements may require additional comments during complex logic.
♦ Declare and initialize all variables at the beginning of a script or piece of code.
♦ For variable datatypes, declare system datatypes (string, integer, long) first, followed by object types.
♦ In object-oriented languages, specify the *object* portion of the function call before the function name itself, not in the parameter list.

```
this.GetText ( )
dw_figs.GetItemNumber ( )
```

♦ Always add a space before **and** after the opening parenthesis, and after each comma, and after the final parameter listed. Do this even if no parameters are passed to the function. *This is vital if your code is to be readable.*

```
this.GetItemNumber ( row, column1 )
Date ( Today ( ) )
this.GetText ( )
```

Naming Conventions

Each language has its own naming conventions. It is more important to be consistent in your use of conventions than to follow a set of rules exactly. The goal is to improve productivity, creating a consistent environment with easily understood indicators, structures, and documentation. For example:

♦ Don't use underscores with mixed case. Capital letters (in mixed case names) and underscores (in lowercase names) serve the same purpose: They separate words. Using the two together gets overly elaborate.

```
Get_Item_Tag
GetItemTag
get_item_tag
```

- For mixed-case languages, use an uppercase letter to start each variable or object name and as the first letter of each word in the name.

```
GetItemTag
AssignSeqNum
```

- Use underscores with names that are all lowercase.

```
get_item_tag
assign_seq_num
```

- Separate prefixes from names with underscore ("_") characters.

```
r_rulename
ud_datatype
```

- Within a variable or object name, break up whole words with underscores.

```
f_this_function
g_global_variable
```

- Where possible, favor whole names over abbreviations for the significant part of a name. That is, abbreviate the prefix (g for global, f for function) or type (int for integer, char for character), but leave the name whole.

```
Patrick instead of PTK
Jellyfish instead of JFSH
```

- All objects and variables should be named *explicitly*. Do *not* use the default names in languages that support default variables or structures.
- Variable Scope Conventions: Assigning a prefix for a local variable or function argument is optional. Use a prefix in either case when a datatype prefix will also be used (see Table 4.1).

Comments

Accompany all major processes within a program with a comment header and annotate important single commands as well.

TABLE 4.1 Variable Scope Prefixes

Variable Scope	*Convention*	*Example*
Global	g_	g_this_var
Shared	s_	s_that_var
Instance	i_	i_this_here_var
Local	l_	li_row_count
Function Arguments	a_	astr_parameter

The general rules are:

◆ *Every* individual or standalone piece of code (function, stored procedure, trigger) should have a header specific to its type of object and the language you are working in.
◆ Remember, your comments are for developers who maintain the code. Write concisely but liberally about what is about to happen and why.
◆ In between minor processes—simple function calls, variable initializations—add blank lines (one or two) to add "breathing room" to your code. This should also be done in between SQL SELECT, INSERT, UPDATE, and DELETE statements.
◆ Include comments to identify modifications made to the code. Include the date of the modifications.

Documentation

Here, *documentation* means formatting and commenting on source code. Documentation deliverables for a project should have their own standard templates.

All of the following language software components should have a documentation format as well as coding standards.

◆ C or C++

.c files

.h files.

Function header for C functions

◆ Other 3GL languages: COBOL, FORTRAN, Pascal, etc.
◆ Other object-oriented languages: Smalltalk, C++, etc.
◆ T-SQL

Triggers

Stored procedures

SQL batch files

◆ DOS batch files
◆ UNIX script files
◆ Development environment languages

Event header scripts

Object functions

Global functions

Transact-SQL

The primary language for programming SQL Server is Transact-SQL (T-SQL). Transact-SQL is an SQL language consistent with the 1989 and 1992 ANSI standards. (Sybase documents indicate the level of ANSI compliance for each command.) T-SQL also includes many Sybase-specific extensions. The language includes all statements required for:

- Object creation (Data Definition Language or DDL)
- Data manipulation (Data Manipulation Language or DML)
- Logical constructs
- Specialized functions
- Triggers
- Stored procedures
- Remote procedure calls

Within the SQL Server environment, T-SQL is a full-programming language. Since all of the SQL Server-based functionality created for an application will be written in Transact-SQL, it is an important language and needs programming standards.

Formatting and Structuring Code

Here are some example rules for formatting and structuring your Transact-SQL code. Feel free to adjust them to your requirements.

Variables

Declare and initialize all variables at the beginning of a batch. You can use a separate DECLARE for each variable

```
DECLARE @log_seq_no        tinyint
DECLARE @log_seq_last      smallint
```

or a single statement for a series of variables.

```
DECLARE @log_seq_count     tinyint,
        @scale_segment_no   tinyint
```

In either case, align the variable names on the left and the datatypes on the right.

Control-of-flow

Structure code so that control-of-flow statements are easily readable.

♦ Indent one tab space (defined as three spaces) following each IF or BEGIN. (All IF statements require BEGIN and END, even if there is only one statement between them.)

♦ Left align BEGIN and END keywords with their associated keywords (IF, ELSE, WHILE).

♦ Include short comments in nested conditions or long BEGIN-END structures indicating which condition they apply to.

```
IF (condition1)
BEGIN /*Condition 1*/
      IF (condition2)
      BEGIN /*Condition 2 */
           SQL statements...
      END /* Condition 2 */
      SQL statements...
END /* Condition 1 */
```

SELECT

♦ Place the SELECT statement itself at the leftmost position.

♦ Indent subsequent lines of the SELECT columns and other lists to a common indent.

```
SELECT cli.lsp_species_group_code,cli.lsp_grade_group_code,
       cli.diam_range_code, cli.conf_line_grade_seq_no
```

♦ Left align all other SQL keywords (except AND and OR) associated with the SELECT under the SELECT.

```
SELECT @lsp_grade_code = lsp_grade_code,
       @gross_segment_diameter = gross_segment_diameter
FROM   segment_to_confirmation sc, grade_map gm
WHERE  sc.certificate_key = @certificate_key
```

♦ Because a single SELECT statement can include a number of clauses (WHERE, HAVING, ORDER BY, GROUP BY), it is important that structure be maintained within each individual SELECT.

```
SELECT @lsp_grade_code = lsp_grade_code,
       @gross_segment_diameter = gross_segment_diameter
FROM   segment_to_confirmation sc, grade_map gm
WHERE  sc.certificate_key = @certificate_key
  AND sc.scale_ticket_no = @scale_ticket_no
  AND ( sc.log_seq_no = @log_seq_no
  OR  sc.scale_segment_no = @scale_segment_no)
```

FROM

When structuring the FROM clause, try to list the tables in a logical sequence. Table aliases require some special rules:

♦ Generally limit aliases to no more than three characters.

```
FROM titles t, authors a, titleauthors ta
```

♦ Each project should define standard aliases for each table.
♦ Avoid the use of a preface of "temp" for working tables maintained in the permanent database.
♦ For multiple joins to one table (including self-joins), use aliases with a number or role name.
♦ When aliasing table names, use the alias (as opposed to the full table name) exclusively and consistently throughout the T-SQL statement.

```
SELECT t.title_id, a.au_lname
  FROM titles t, authors a, titleauthors ta
 WHERE t. title_id = ta.title_id
   AND a. au_id = ta.au_id
```

WHERE

♦ When structuring a WHERE clause, try to order the joins by table, so that it is easy to read the join sequence.
♦ List the joins at the beginning of the WHERE clause.
♦ List all the domain restrictions (**column = "constant"**) or (**column = @variable**) at the *end* of the WHERE clause.
♦ Right-align all ANDs and ORs underneath the WHERE clause, so it is clear they belong to that WHERE clause.

```
SELECT @lsp_grade_code = lsp_grade_code,
       @gross_segment_diameter = gross_segment_diameter
FROM   segment_to_confirmation sc, grade_map gm
WHERE  sc.certificate_key = @certificate_key
  AND  sc.scale_ticket_no = @scale_ticket_no
  AND  ( sc.log_seq_no = @log_seq_no
  OR     sc.scale_segment_no = @scale_segment_no)
```

♦ With any combined use of AND and OR, use parentheses to explicitly identify associations.

```
SELECT @lsp_grade_code = lsp_grade_code,
       @gross_segment_diameter = gross_segment_diameter
FROM   segment_to_confirmation sc, grade_map gm
WHERE  sc.certificate_key = @certificate_key
  AND sc.scale_ticket_no = @scale_ticket_no
  AND ( sc.log_seq_no = @log_seq_no
  OR    sc.scale_segment_no = @scale_segment_no )
```

Subqueries

On creating a subquery for a SELECT, there are two acceptable alternatives for structuring the subquery, depending on the length of the subquery SELECT statement.

♦ For long subqueries, follow all the rules for structuring the SELECT in the subquery, so it is clear what belongs to the subquery and what belongs to the outer query.

```
SELECT titlename
FROM   titles
WHERE  author_id in ( SELECT author_id
                      FROM authors
                      WHERE date_hired > getdate () )
```

♦ For shorter subqueries, string the subquery SELECT out in one line under the main SELECT WHERE clause.

```
SELECT titlename
FROM   titles
WHERE  author_id in
       (SELECT author_id FROM authors WHERE au_id = '1')
```

INSERT

♦ List the table name being inserted into on the line with the INSERT.

```
INSERT tickets
```

♦ Always list the columns to which data is being added for a given INSERT.

```
INSERT tickets
       (
       column1, column2, column3,
       column4, column7, column9
       )
```

♦ Place the parentheses at the beginning and end of the list on separate lines below and above the list itself. You can list multiple columns on one line.

```
INSERT tickets
       (
       column1, column2, column3,
       column4, column7, column9
       )
```

♦ Left-align the VALUES list with the INSET statement. If you list three columns on the first line, list three values in the first line of the VALUES clause, and so on.

```
INSERT tickets
    (
    column1, column2, column3,
    column4, column7, column9
    )
VALUES
    (
```

```
    value1, value2, value3,
    value4, value7, value9
    )
```

♦ If you include a SELECT in the INSERT, left-align the SELECT with the keyword INSERT and follow the usual rules for structuring a SELECT.

```
INSERT tickets
    (
    column1, column2, column3,
    column4, column7, column9
    )
SELECT column1, column2, column3,
       column4, column7, column9
FROM   old_tickets
WHERE  . . .
```

UPDATE

Left-align all keywords associated with the UPDATE statement. Tab and left-align object name lists.

```
UPDATE contract
SET    date_expired = getdate()
FROM   contract cnt
WHERE  cnt.date_created = getdate()
```

If you are updating multiple columns at once, left-align each column name and assignment with the topmost column, and give each its own line.

```
UPDATE contract
SET    col1 = val1,
       col2 = val2,
       col3 = val3 . . .
```

If you have a subquery in the WHERE clause, follow the rules for structuring a SELECT.

DELETE

Left-align all keywords associated with the DELETE under the DELETE keyword.

```
DELETE titles
FROM   titles ttl, authors au
WHERE  ttl.author_id = au.author_id
```

If a subquery is included in the WHERE clause, follow the stipulations for structuring a SELECT previously provided.

T-SQL Naming Conventions

By definition, an object name in T-SQL must

- Start with an alphabetic character or an underbar (_). Exceptions are temporary table names, which begin with the pound sign (#), and local variable names, which begin with the at sign (@).
- Be between 1 and 30 characters long (except temporary table names, which have a maximum length of 13 characters).
- Not be SQL Server reserved words.

You can test the acceptability of an object name before you use it with the **valid_name()** function. It returns 0 for an invalid name and some other number for a valid one.

```
select valid_name ('index')
go
----------
        0
select valid_name ('index_no')
go
----------
         1
```

If you need to be compliant with ANSI SQL standards for 1989 or 1992: limit object names to 18 characters, do not use lowercase letters, and do not begin an object name with #.

Otherwise, these standards work well:

- Use uppercase letters for all T-SQL keywords/statements (SELECT, INSERT, CREATE, DROP).
- Use lowercase letters for all object names (including databases and user names) and don't begin them with underscores.
- Avoid, where possible, both cryptic abbreviations and long object names. Go for the name that conveys information and is easy to type.

```
sls_trk
sales_tracking
sales_tracking_system_table
```

SINGULAR OR PLURAL?

It doesn't matter if table names are singular (the title table) or plural (the title table), but they all ought to be the same. I designed an example database where all the tables except one had plural names. I never noticed it until I started getting complaints; then I realized I usually typed that table name as plural, got errors, and typed it again.

Comments

Use comments liberally to explain your code. Sybase supports two kinds of comments.

- ♦ Long comments begin with /* and end with */. They can include any number of lines.

```
/* This is a comment */
/* This is a long, long comment. It goes on for several lines,
explaining everything with great thoroughness. But it is extremely
helpful--it tells you everything you need to know, as you peer at a
complex piece of code. The comment ends here. */
/* One convention is to start lines after the first line
** with a set of double asterisks. This is just to make it
** stand out. */
```

- ♦ You can also start a comment with a double hyphen and a space and end it with a new line.

```
-- This is a comment.
-- You can create long comments by starting each succeeding line with
-- a double hyphen.
```

Align header comments left. Indent block comments and embed in code where they are used.

Documentation

Design document header sections for triggers and stored procedures. Fill them out when the object is created and update them each time it is modified.

- ♦ Introduce and end large blocks of comment text, in a header or embedded in the code, by a single line of *s, followed by a blank line.

```
/*********************************************************

This is the header section for the . . .


*********************************************************/
```

- ♦ Block comments for a trigger or a stored procedure should follow the AS keyword.

```
CREATE PROC p_authors_insert
AS
/*********************************************************


Procedure Name: this is the name of the stored
                procedure in the database


Date Created:   date when first submitted to server
.........
*********************************************************/
```

♦ The comment header for a trigger should have, roughly centered on the first line, the table name and action which fires the trigger. Again, this should go after the AS keyword. The header should include a listing of each event in the trigger. The text of each of these events comment is repeating with the code of each event. The order that the validations are listed here should be the same order that they are executed in the trigger.

♦ The comments for a trigger should list, briefly, the validations being performed and the actions taken in each case. Again, these are repeated in the trigger header.

```
CREATE TRIGGER ti_authors
AS
/*********************************************************


                     Author INSERT
- Disallow insert if the inserted author_id does not exist in
title_authors. RAISERROR and ROLLBACK.


*********************************************************/
```

♦ Stored procedures should have comment headers like this:

```
/*********************************************************


Procedure Name:         this is the name of the stored
                        procedure in the database


Date Created:           date when first submitted to server


Original Programmer:    developer's name


Last Updated:           date of most recent update


Updated By:             name of developer for most recent update
```

Called From: *Script, procedure or executable * which*
                      calls this stored procedure.

Database(s) Used: *list of databases referenced.*

Description: *description of procedure logic, in*
                      structured English.
**/

C H A P T E R 5

Thinking Relationally

Relational Processing

Programming a relational database is a science, isn't it? Or is it really more of an art? Few of us who use relational databases to solve business problems are truly versed in the mathematics of the relational model, which is scientific. If we were, we might be able to more accurately predict the optimal way to process any given business problem. Instead we study the tables, look at the desired results, and with our experience we come up with a *process* that produces the correct results.

But some ways of writing a solution are better than others with respect to the reusability of the solution pattern, developer time, maintenance time, flexibility, and, last but not least, performance. How do we choose how to design a solution?

Designing relational instead of procedural solutions is one critical step in better utilizing the technology at hand. Relational databases are designed to manage *sets* of data. They are not optimal for managing lots of individual *rows* of data (the area where procedural processing excels). Can we take any, or perhaps every, problem and design a solution that uses data sets instead of data rows?

Certain solutions are fairly obvious. Everyone would write:

```
UPDATE all the rows that....
```

instead of using a cursor and looping:

```
for each row: UPDATE
```

But what happens when the process gets very complicated? What solutions come to mind for the programmer? Many of the developers that we have dealt with move to a procedural solution when the going gets very tough. Why? Because it is the technique with which they have the most experience and training. Some of this experience and training comes from the prerelational days; many computer science graduates leave college with little or no relational training. We all need mentoring and study to develop the skills necessary to solve complex problems in a relational way.

Relational versus Procedural

A procedural language describes how to get something done. A nonprocedural language describes what you want the end result to be and leaves it to the system to figure out how to do it. Procedural languages include COBOL, FORTRAN, BASIC, and C. SQL is naturally a nonprocedural language, but you can use it to do procedural processing.

Procedural processing looks vaguely like this: For each row,

- Based on logic and the data in the row apply Operation 1, and/or
- Based on logic and the data in the row apply Operation 2, and/or
- Based on logic and the data in the row apply Operation 3, and/or
- and so on.

That is, find each row and loop through the possible operations on that row.

A relational view of the same problem would look more like this:

- Apply Operation A to all of the qualifying rows, then
- Apply Operation B to all of the qualifying rows, then
- Apply Operation C to all of the qualifying rows, then
- and so on.

That is, instead of looping through the rows and applying operations, step through the operations and apply them to all the rows that qualify for that operation. Operations 1 through 3 are not necessarily the same as Operations A through C. It is often necessary to recast the operation into relational terms.

Often the operation has to be decomposed when being applied to the whole set. For example, what was considered Operation A may require an Operation A.1 for NULL values and an Operation A.2 for non-NULL values. (Occasionally, these different operations can be written to utilize one table scan, that is, be done at the same time.) The two set operations will still likely out-perform the row operation especially for large data sets. You may be required to create temporary data sets to control a midpoint in the processing. The ability to store interim data sets (the results of partial steps toward a solution) may improve your ability to design a relational solution.

Why would a relational solution be better? Well, for a very small data set, equal programming skills, and equal resulting code clarity, the procedural and relational solutions might be comparable. But if you have a medium to large data set, or if the row looping operations are nested, the processing time of the relational method can be much faster (orders of magnitude). If you have learned to conceptualize set operations, the processing logic may also be clearer to other programmers.

Of course, there are some limits to replacing all procedural processing with relational processing. If the number of operations generated by decomposition begins to approach the number of rows, you might be loosing ground toward your goal of improving performance and clarity. Some problems really are procedural. It happens. Remember that a relational database is optimized for set operations. Let it do its job.

Master-Detail Example

Let's explore a problem whose shape and nature is very common because it is constructed on a three-tiered master-detail relationship. This relationship is a natural structure in the entity-relationship model, and therefore common in our relational databases.

Take a manufacturing operation that creates products and call the individual items pieces. These pieces are grouped after manufacturing into pallets; a group of pallets is tracked by the system in an object called a batch. A batch relates to many pallets and a pallet relates to many pieces (see Figure 5.1). You have a process that looks at all of the batches for a month and for each batch, for each pallet, and for each piece processes records. In this discussion, it is not really important what you do to them. (This could just as easily be an accounting or a personnel problem—anything.)

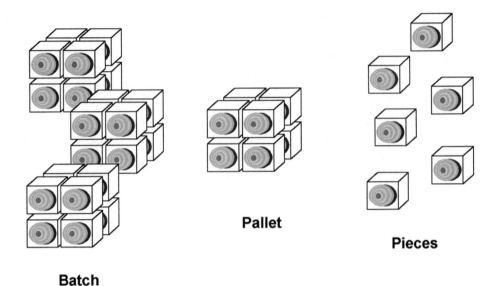

Pallet

Pieces

Batch

FIGURE 5.1 A batch is composed of many pallets; a pallet is composed of many pieces.

The Procedural Solution

This problem looks procedural to many, many programmers, often because the people who actually work with the batches, pallets, and pieces have explained it this way. That's how they think of the processing sequence. The procedural solution outline looks like this:

> Get the list of batches
> For each batch
>> Process the batch record
>> Get the list of pallets
>> For each pallet
>> Process the pallet record
>> Get the list of pieces
>> For each piece
>>> Process the piece record

This approach requires three cursors working against the data structures. You are essentially writing row-at-a-time processing. Is this bad? Well, it certainly works and can give the correct answer. If the data sets are small, the performance may be acceptable. In this particular case, the programmer was originally told that he would process about 30 batches at a time. The performance wasn't great, but it was acceptable given the constraints, and he developed a very clear understanding of the process.

Incidentally, we discovered that infrequently the accountants reprocessed 1,000 batches at a time. Suddenly, the solution was totally unacceptable. It couldn't finish in a reasonable period (say, over the weekend). (Actual mileage always varies. The point is that there is a significant increase in processing time as the number of batches grows. It may even be a geometric growth depending on the techniques available for getting the matching pallets and pieces.)

The Relational Solution

The good news is that developing the procedural solution through design, research, and testing smoked out the process and we now have a very good idea what the process is suppose to do. (This is not to imply that you should write the procedural solution as an exercise, but we're trying to look on the bright side. The rewrite is not too time-consuming.)

Now, when you have been looking at a problem from a procedural view, the next step—looking at it relationally—is sometimes tough. Let's walk through it.

A simple starting relational version might be:

♦ Process all the batches
♦ Process all the pallets; join to batches as required
♦ Process all the pieces; join to pallets and batches as required

This may be too simple. There may be conditional logic required to separate some distinct sets of batches, pallets, and pieces. So, you decompose the operations as required.

♦ Process all the batches where X (where X is qualifying information embedded in joins and in conditional qualifications)
♦ Process all the batches where Y
♦ Process all the pallets where Z
♦ And so on

The processes will be different for each of the conditions to process the data correctly. Too much decomposition is bad, but it would have to be excessive. (To resolve borderline problems you would have to thoroughly study access paths, optimization techniques, caching efficiency, and logical I/O required to properly optimize.) When decomposing the operations produces a high number of suboperations, the logic may get difficult to read and you may do too many scans through the data. You may have a procedural problem. But, remember, there are fewer procedural problems than we think.

It is also possible to gain performance by partially shifting to a more relational solution. For example, process the highest level with a cursor and move the other processes to set operations. Sometimes a particular level in the master-detail relationship will require a cursor. Even so, the rest can be optimized by moving to a relational solution.

Scalability

The most important quality that you can gain with this rewrite is improved performance. Many things contribute to the performance improvements.

- ♦ The individual count of SQL statements executed grows linearly when you issue multiple cursors against the inner loops of the processing as the number of batches grows. With the relational solution the number of individual SQL statements executed does not change.
- ♦ Transact–SQL is an interpreted language and processing conditional logic and cursors in an interpreted language affects code execution time.
- ♦ In pre-cursor implementations of our Transact-SQL programs, some of the gyrations programmers used to isolate a single row (for example, "set row count 1" and "select data where the key value is the minimum value greater that the previous value") are inefficient.
- ♦ The server has more optimization leverage in large operations than with many small operations. That is, the server's ability to optimize access to a large single data set is better (due to index structures, buffering, etc.) than getting the large data set a row at a time.

In most cases, the procedural solution will hit a wall with performance as the data sets processed get larger. This will often catch a development team that tests against unrealistically small test data sets. The relational solution might out perform the procedural solution for small volumes, but the difference will grow as the volumes increase. Actual volumes and time are relative and what works is always a factor of the demands for your specific problem.

While the principles here are very important and applicable in most situations, there are examples where cursor processing can be faster than what seems like set processing (but isn't really). An example is a nested query that ends up selecting a value for each row (correlated queries) where the nested query is doing a large and repetitive analysis. You need to understand the performance aspects of any given solution to apply performance improving metrics to it.

BIG PROCEDURE

Prior to System 10, there was a limit on the size of text in a stored procedure. It couldn't be bigger than about 65K. That always seemed like a rather large number to me, but one of our customers complained that SQL Server wouldn't handle his procedure.

We looked at it, and discovered that breaking it up would be advantageous for all the reasons that "Structured Programming" gurus give when they advise using modules. There were pieces that were actually used several times. We could turn those into stored procedures that were called by an "outer" procedure. When we pulled those pieces out, we started getting a better idea of what the procedure was doing.

Examining the code more closely, we found lots of loops and cursor-like operations that could be handled as relational sets. We ended up completely restructuring the stored procedure. The customer protested at first, but soon got interested in the process of converting procedural to relational.

The net result was a procedure that was easier to understand, much smaller, and faster.

As a kind of by-product, the customer got some new ideas—or had old ones refreshed.

Elapsed Time Example

This is the story of one problem's path to an efficient relational solution. The names of the participants have been hidden to protect the innocent.

The problem doesn't sound too hard when you say it briefly in passing: For any two datetime values, calculate the difference in days and fractions of a day between the dates, not including time for weekends or holidays. Well, actually, do this for 400,000 records at a time, once a week. Either of the datetimes might actually be on a weekend or holiday.

The business accepts a unit of work from a customer, records the starting datetime and, when finished, records the completion datetime. The time can vary between a few hours to several weeks. The business problem is to report to the customer the actual working days that it took to process each of the services provided.

A previous implementation of the process walked through the service records and for each record calculated the difference by stepping through each day, identifying and subtracting out the weekends, and then checking to see if a vacation day came inbetween. It then recorded the result for this record and moved on. It was very slow. It was prone to small errors. The data had been moved into a relational database and the process needed to be rewritten.

The developer had trouble seeing how to rewrite the problem in any other way and got an experienced programmer, a mentor, to help.

The first step is to clarify all of the technical requirements of the solution:

♦ Calculate the difference between two datetimes for a very large set of records that was growing rapidly.

♦ The difference should be in days and hours.
♦ Subtract all weekends.
♦ Subtract identified holiday dates.
♦ The beginning date or the end date might be on a weekend or holiday.
♦ The beginning date and the end date might be the same day.
♦ Any number of weeks can be between the two dates.
♦ The large set of records must be run frequently.
♦ The calculation must be accurate, not an estimate.

The Procedural Solution

A procedural solution might look like this:

Open a cursor to loop through all of the records
For each record
    Initialize a variable to hold the total hours for this record
    Identify the first day (a partial day)
        If it is not a Saturday or Sunday
            If it is not a holiday
                If it is the same day as the last day
                    Get the difference into total hours and exit
              Else
                  Calculate the hours for this day
        Add hours for this day to total hours
    Loop through the 2nd to Nth – 1 day (where N represents the last day; all complete days)
    For each day
        If it is not a Saturday or Sunday
            If it is not a holiday
                Add 24 to the total hours
    Identify the last day (a partial day)
        If it is not a Saturday or Sunday
            If it is not a holiday
                Calculate the hours for this day
        Add hours for this day to total hours
    Convert hours to days and hours
    Record the record with the time difference

This provides a clear explanation of the process and a clear enumeration of the programmer's understanding of the problem. It is also very clear for a user review which is critical in complex calculations like this. It will not, however, provide acceptable performance.

The Relational Solution

As the table gets bigger, the performance will continue to deteriorate. So, instead of going through the rows and applying operations, let's see if we can design operations that work against all of the records at once.

The previous outline shows that there are basic components of the hourly total that can be calculated on all of the records:

♦ Hours for the first day (partial day)
♦ Hours for the middle days (whole days)
♦ Hours for the last day (partial day)

In addition, we know that we have special cases:

♦ The first day is on a weekend or holiday
♦ The last day is on a weekend or holiday
♦ The first day and the last day are the same

So let's outline the series of statements that will calculate all of these components and special cases against all (or much) of the data.

One of the key issues is the identification of all of the weekends and holidays. The first solution only solved part of the problem, but developed an algorithm to subtract weekends between any two dates in a single query. This is due to the fact that weekends are regular and are a factor of the total number of days and the number of days per week (two weekend days per seven-day week).

The problem with this solution is that it doesn't take care of holidays which are not a factor of the length of a week. There is another solution: Put the holidays in a table (offdays), and while you are at it, put the weekends there, too. (The offdays table is quite small, approximately 120 records for each year.) This enables you to write joins against this table with the dates in the primary record. The entries into the table for the weekends can be done once a year with a process that loops through each day of the year and adds the record to the table if it is a Saturday or Sunday. (Wow, a procedural process. But it's okay; we only do it once a year and we only loop through 365 days.) Then the holidays get added to the table from the corporate published set of holidays.

1. Create a temporary table (temp) to hold the keys, date1 and date-last, and the calculated parts of the total (date1hours, date-lasthours, midhours, offhours, totalhours).

2. Insert into the temp table the record keys and the two dates for all records. (This gives you a smaller sized record and table to scan.)

3. Update temp setting total hours to the hourly difference between date1 and datelast where date1 and datelast are the same day and the date is not an offday.

4. Update temp setting total hours to 0 where date1 and datelast are the same day and the date is an offday.

5. Update temp setting date1hours to be 0 where date1 is in the off-days table (and date1 and datelast are not the same date).

6. Update temp setting date1hours to be the partial day where date1 is not in the offdays table (and date1 and datelast are not the same date).

7. Update temp setting datelasthours to be 0 where datelast is in the offdays table (and date1 and datelast are not the same date).

8. Update temp setting datelasthours to be the partial day where datelast is not in the offdays table (and date1 and datelast are not the same date).

9. Update temp setting midhours to be the hours inclusive between the second day and the second to last day (and date1 and datelast are not the same date).

10. Update temp setting offhours to be 24 times the number of off days inclusive between the second day and the second to last day—joining offdays to temp—(where date1 and datelast are not the same date).

11. Update temp setting totalhours date1hours + datelasthours + midhours – offhours and convert to days and hours (where date1 and datelast are not the same date).

Several of these operations can be joined into single passes using characteristics functions and subqueries. While this process seems to be quite a few table scans across the table, the performance advantages improve as the table gets bigger which is quite different from the procedural solution.

After this solution was constructed, additional challenges arose. In reality, subtracting the holidays or the weekends is optional depending on what report the user is running. This required some parameterization of the process and a simplification for the alternate reports. Also, sometimes weekends are declared to be workdays and then should be counted. Fortunately, the solution takes care of this. They are simply removed from the off-days table.

Relational Mentoring

The approach in the master-detail and time-elapsed examples works with many application problems and can be applied to complex and exotic problems. Here's another problem you can solve either procedurally or relationally, though the relational solution is much faster.

> For a column with three values A, B, C, and a key that has multiple rows (duplicate key values, not the primary key): For each key value find the count of keys that have one or more A values, the count of keys that have one or more B values but no A values, and the count of keys that have one or more C values but no A or B values. All distinct sets.

Even as I describe this, it looks like set operations. But the problem didn't look that way in the first place because procedural thinking is natural to us. Thinking relationally is harder and less natural, and you must learn to do it.

How do you learn to solve problems relationally? The same way you get to Carnegie Hall, "Practice, Practice, Practice!" The best way is to find, hire, or train a Mentor (create a *titled* position). This experienced program designer can then work with others to extend their understanding of efficient design techniques. It is important to train the developers in many of the more sophisticated relational operations: group by, use of temp tables, outer joins, and correlated queries. After that, concepts of mathematical transformations and characteristic functions provide a continuing learning path. Mastery of these techniques puts the proper tools into the hands of the developer.

Rules of Thumb

It's a good idea to define a set of guidelines for T-SQL usage. Certain configurations flag possible problems for managers which they see when reviewing early design plans. They assign a senior technical review person (Mentor) to review the solution.

In pre-cursor days, the big flag was SET ROW COUNT. It should not be allowed in any T-SQL program without a sign-off from a senior technical person. It is often an indication that the programmer cannot think of a relational solution which may exist. SET ROW COUNT is sometimes useful; the senior technical reviewer will recognize and authorize the usage.

Other language elements also require technical review:

◆ Again, always, cursors on large data sets should be checked, particularly nested cursors (or any technique that steps through rows one at a time like WHILE).

- ♦ A sequence of statements that each scan an entire table might be collapsed into a single pass through the use of a SQL technique like characteristic functions.
- ♦ Correlated queries on large data sets are probably doing procedural processing and should be evaluated for other possible techniques.
- ♦ Negative operators (NOT IN, <>, NOT EXIST) should be checked for alternative ways to state the problem.
- ♦ Non-equijoins are rare in practice and require experience to use properly and should be reviewed.
- ♦ Cross products are extremely rare and should be reviewed.
- ♦ GROUP BY statements that take advantage of the Sybase extension that allows columns on the SELECT clause that are not in the GROUP BY can cause critical data errors and require review and testing.

The most important of these is the use of cursors and particularly nested cursors. Have these reviewed. You need to require technical review anyway; this gives the technical reviewer the chance to explore the problem with the developer and provide education along the way. Very difficult problems can almost always benefit from multiple minds working on the solution. The final solution may have the best from both developers and be far better that any one programmer might design.

CODE REVIEW FROM HELL

Everyone has coffee, no one has notes. The senior people think the code looks bad, but they're not really sure why, so they zero in on the structuring and the grammar in the comments (abysmal!) and ignore the logic (for now). The junior people are uncomfortable, and the author of the module in question is considering moving to New Zealand.

Been there?

It's a lot less painful with rules of thumb. The author can apply them to the code before the review and, if that doesn't find all the weird places (it probably won't), the group can locate the rest with a minimum of personality dislocation.

New ways of thinking promote new ways of solving problems. Moving to more relational solutions can buy you measurable improvements in your applications. For those of you who like technical challenges and learning, there is still much to learn about the optimal use of the SQL language. It can continue to challenge you in interesting ways. For those of you interested in cost efficiency and performance, you must remember that a continuing investment in education and mentoring can improve the overall efficiency of an organization and the success of its applications.

C H A P T E R

6

Client/Server

Tiered Architecture

Tiered architecture refers to the parsing of application solutions into multiple processes (client, server, middleware, etc.) and the number and design of those processes. Simple client/server implementations use a two-tiered architecture; more complex architectures use additional tiers for varying architectural reasons.

Parsing of application logic and processing are dependent on the use of standard communication application programming interfaces (APIs) that enable peer-to-peer, client/server, and server-to-server communications.

Two-Tiered Architecture

The classic client/server architecture consists of a server process (most often a relational database) and a client process, and the communication between them. This architecture is used to isolate the presentation of information to the client process and the data storage and manipulation to the server process. To properly leverage the client/server architecture the two processes would be deployed on independent and scalable platforms using appropriate hardware and operating systems for the system requirements.

Many implementations of two-tiered architectures also provide programmable servers. Application logic can be embedded into a logical layer that happens to reside in the server in stored procedures, triggers, and views. This logical layer provides a layer of data independence for the application. The data structures can be modified without major changes to the application due to the programmed layer. This architecture provides for multiple logical layers without the need or advantages of implementing a third physical tier. These solutions are appropriate for many applications.

In a two-tiered system transaction management is server-based, that is, internal to a single server implementation. It is possible to write heterogeneous transactions, but they must be controlled from a client application with two-phase commit protocols.

You must establish the interfaces between the application's client and server components in a way that minimizes communication between the client and server computers and takes advantage of the hardware resources. Otherwise, performance diminishes as time and resources get used by this communication.

The client portion of the application receives data from the server, presents the data to the user, and provides screen interactions for requesting, manipulating, and validating data. The application's server portion:

- Processes, stores, and retrieves the physical data.
- Maps logical data structures to the physical media.
- Restricts the data to be moved.
- Ensures that multiple users don't interfere with each other's actions against the data.
- Maintains various business rules.
- Executes transaction logic.

Multitiered Architectures

Extension of basic client/server architecture to a multi-tiered environment (see Figure 6.1) is commonly done for one or more of the following reasons:

- Requirements to execute queries or transactions in a heterogeneous database environment.
- Creating logical isolations of functionality and logic into a middle tier that is not tied to a particular database or development environment vendor and therefore more reusable and flexible.
- Modularization of components in generic, compiled languages.
- Development and deployment of reusable and sharable components.

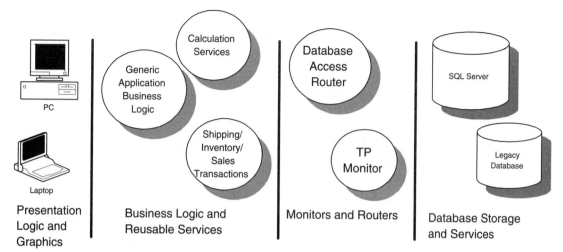

PC

Laptop

Presentation Logic and Graphics

Business Logic and Reusable Services

Monitors and Routers

Database Storage and Services

Logically and Physically Distinct Components

FIGURE 6.1 Multi-tiered architecture.

♦ Enabling systems to scale to a very large number of users through the use of routers (TP monitors) to balance the number of processes and enable better use of symmetric multiprocessing.

♦ Improving scalability by creating flexibility in moving resulting functionality from one to another platform in the architecture.

♦ Interfacing with object request brokers to enable execution of methods on object servers.

♦ Functional advantages such as messaging, data subscription services, event management, and alerts.

A more complex view and usage of client/server architecture will become more pervasive as the tools and technologies improve. This usage will also develop as corporations become more comfortable with their existing client/server systems and feel capable of entertaining even more complexity.

Open Servers

Many implementations of client/server solutions are data-centric: They are based on storing and manipulating data. An underutilized component of a client/server system is that of open services. The architecture supports the construction of servers with the Open Server product from Sybase. This product is a library of functions (an application programming interface or API) to enable the construction of server processes. The message protocols and basic architecture of a server are built into the API structures. It enables the construction of extensions to the basic SQL Server services and gateways into external data sources.

Open Servers are constructed in two basic styles:

♦ They can process language events, which means that they parse and process command strings sent from the client application.
♦ They can process procedure events, wherein they interpret a remote procedure call (RPC) and execute an appropriate event handler for that procedure. The remote procedure call architecture is easier to construct and is further strengthened by the support of RPCs between server processes. A SQL Server can call the Open Server with an RPC or it can pass the RPC from a client to another server.

Some of the functionality that can be provided with Open Server includes:

♦ External gathering of real-time data
♦ External communications
♦ Broadcasting messages that result from the logic in a trigger
♦ Gateways into external or legacy data systems
♦ Anything you can build in C

Client/Server Architectural Model

A client/server architectural model is a standard for how to build high quality cooperative processing within your chosen architecture. It is critical that corporations architect a suite of technical solutions for their business processes. It may consist of database servers, GUI development tools, report writers, batch processing tools, real-time processors and monitors, networks, gateways, and communication protocols.

Whatever tool set you choose, you must develop standards for:

♦ How the tools will be used
♦ How communications will proceed
♦ How databases will be designed
♦ How client applications will behave

Many corporations and departments worry about standards. Often these standards are about how to name things or how a GUI application should function or look. These are important. But few corporations understand that, more importantly, they need standards on interoperating:

♦ How are we going to implement *cooperative processing*?
♦ Where will each part of the solution be implemented and why?

What are cooperative processes? When you build a complex system from multiple processes, they must interoperate (send messages and pass information). One hopes that the processes work cooperatively. That is, they solve an application problem in the most efficient way possible. They must communicate efficiently and process information in a way that leverages the best features of each of the individual processes. A client/server architectural model defines the way a particular server and development tool should interact to execute a system and formalizes the best design decisions.

The decisions made in this model lay the groundwork for a solid and successful implementation of a system. The issues involved should be addressed before any major development work is begun on a strategic system. It requires a thorough understanding of your development platform, your server platform, and the strategic requirements of the application system to be deployed.

Once understood and defined, a programmer's manual can be developed with specific instructions for implementation of these client/server features. Some of the decisions can be built into reusable tools and objects that represent correct usages. Once a model is deployed, all subsequent application development can use it with only minor modifications.

The Key Architectural Issues to Standardize

There are key architectural problems that have to be addressed by all client/server developers. These are the issues to be standardized in a client/server architectural model. The advantage of identifying and classifying these problems is that a corporation can categorize and standardize solutions and know the ramifications of all the choices made.

The cooperative processing issues to address include:

♦ Connection management
♦ Error handling
♦ Data access
♦ Data validation
♦ Transaction management
♦ Concurrency control
♦ Distributed processing
♦ Security

Connection Management

When a client process needs to communicate with a server process, it is required to establish a connection. A connection is a structure established in the client application and at the server process. Communications between these processes use a standard client/server protocol called Tabular Data Stream (TDS). There are important resource and performance issues with regard to establishing connections—for example, the number of connections the server can support and how fast the application can respond to the user. In addition, there are options to set attributes of a connection that govern its behavior. It is important to design connection behavior and usage to optimize the control you have over application behavior. This allows you to fine-tune the server load and the application response time to meet your application requirements.

When an application establishes a connection, it can set properties of the connection that affect its behavior. Some of these properties are set in the communication protocol API (DB-Library or CT-Library). Some of them are set with Transact-SQL (T-SQL) after the connection is established.

RAT HOLE

A programmer walks into a room and says, "I have a problem with my DLLs." After a LONG exchange, we confirm that the DLLs seem to be correct. Then we ask, "What was your error message?" The response was that he was trying to access a database and the USE statement was failing. His theory was, if he can't even use the database, then the connectivity stuff must be messed up.

I sit down and connect to the database just fine. He takes over the keyboard and it doesn't work:

```
Attempt to locate entry in sysdatabases for database 'PUBS' by name failed -
no entry found under that name. Make sure that name is entered properly.
```

Yes, database names are case-sensitive. Hours were wasted on a bad assumption about where the problem was.

Establishing a Connection

As previously stated, a connection is established between a client and a server when the client issues a request. Before issuing the request, the login structure must be populated with appropriate property values for the connection, including server name, database name, user name, user password, and so forth. This may be done directly with the API in a 3GL language or, in many development environments, this service is encapsulated into functionality or objects in the development tool. In any case, the native API behavior is under the covers.

The client application creates the connection structure and the programmer populates it. When the client application requests the connection from the server, the server creates a similar structure (server process or spid) at the server, reads the properties sent from the client, validates the user and password, and sets up the state of the connection.

A server can, of course, have many connections with client applications. A client application can have more than one connection to a given server and can hold connections to multiple servers. It is not common to require more than one connection, though occasionally two are useful.

CT-Library Options

You can tune certain properties of a connection. CT–Library supports the setting of the following properties before a connection is established. They are useful for system administration from the server (Who is connected?) and configuring aspects of the connection's behavior.

CS_APPNAME   Identifies the application name for use in the sysprocesses table. This is useful to track what application is running on a particular connection.

CS_HOSTNAME   Identifies the workstation name for use in the sysprocesses table. This helps the system administrator track which workstation is using a particular connection.

CS_PACKETSIZE Sets the tabular data stream packet size for communications between the client and the SQL Server. This is useful for performance optimization. It allows the packets to be larger for more efficiently passing large datasets.

These are all useful. You will need to identify which are available to you and which are important to your application.

Connection SET Options

After a connection is established there are options that you can set to fine-tune the connection's behavior. These attributes can be modified at any time. If you are programming in CT–Library, you can set some of these attributes with the CT–Library function **ct_options.** Otherwise, they can be set by submitting T-SQL statements over the established connection. These options apply only to the connection over which the option-setting statements are issued. (Only the most important options are mentioned here; review product documentation for the complete list.) Many of these options should be standardized in the application development process so that connections will behave consistently.

arithabort	Cancels a query if an overflow or divide-by-zero error occurs. There are several options; see the documentation.
arithignore	Returns null if an overflow or divide-by-zero error occurs. If neither *arithabort* or *arithignore* is set, SQL Server returns NULL and prints a message.
no count	Eliminates the "number of rows affected" message at the end of each statement.
datefirst	Sets the first weekday (number 1–7). Standard default is 7 for Saturday.
dateformat	Sets the order of the day, month, and year for submitting dates.
language	Sets the official language for messages and errors. The default is **us_english.**
rowcount	Returns only the number of rows indicated. (This feature should be used sparingly, as SQL Server may have to do an inordinate amount of work. For example, if you want the first 10 rows of an ordered set of 5,000, it would have to sort the 5,000 rows before it found the first 10. Do not use this to control program loops.)
transaction isolation level	Sets the isolation level for the connection. Options are 0 (READ UNCOMMITTED), 1 (READ COMMITTED, the default), and 3 (SERIALIZABLE).

The following properties of a connection are available to manage the development process. They affect the kinds of result information returned by the connection and the stages of work that the server will use to process a statement.

noexec	Compiles but does not execute a query. It is often used with SHOWPLAN to examine the query plan of a statement without executing it.
parseonly	Checks the syntax of a statement and returns error information. The statement is not compiled or executed.
showplan	Returns the query plan that the optimizer generates for the execution of the query.
statistics to	Returns information about the work required to execute the query (logical reads, physical reads, pages written).
statistics time	Returns parse, compile, and execution time for the statements submitted.

Resource Use

A connection uses resources at the client and at the server. At the server each connection established by a user uses 50 to 60 KB of memory. There is a server-wide configuration value for the number of connections (users) that will be allowed. Additionally, the number of connections possible is governed by the amount of memory that the server is allowed to use. If memory is limited at the server, it is important to limit the number of connections that an application holds open. More memory will be available for caching data pages which can improve server performance.

It is common for an application to establish a connection at the opening of an application and keep it open for the duration of the application's execution. This is a good design if the sizing of the server can be large enough to generously accommodate the required number of connections, and when the users are using those connections at regular intervals.

Some large systems can do better by not holding the connections. This is true when the number of total users is great and the style of usage is occasional. That is, the users will make a request or send an update and then leave their computers or do extended work on the client machine. This application style is predominant in many service applications (e.g., hospitals). There might be a thousand total users, but only a hundred working users at any given time. Sizing a system for a hundred concurrent users is very different from sizing a system for a thousand users. (In all cases you must allow enough connections to ensure that you will never run out of connections.)

Performance and Response time

Connections take time to establish. Once established, using the connection is much faster. It is important to understand the nature of the required behavior and response time in the client application. This will help you know whether you can afford the delay caused by repeated connections.

♦ If the user application needs to access SQL Server in a continuous fashion, the delay will likely be too costly and the application should hold the connection.

♦ If the usage is occasional (every 10–15 minutes), it may be possible to release the connection and re-establish it each time, reducing the number of total connections held.

If you are constructing a large system with a large number of users, careful planning with respect to when a connection is established and how long connections are held is an opportunity to more accurately size the system requirements. In systems that need to do this, protocols for using long-running connections and short-running connections should be established.

When using SQL Server with an average application load, the most likely preference will be to hold connections.

Error Handling

There are several sources of errors and messages when you are communicating over a connection with a SQL Server. The server itself can send messages and errors. Open Client can send error messages. It is also possible to build special errors and messages into your server code.

It is necessary to handle these messages and errors in the client application.

+ If you are building a client using Open Client C interface, you will build error-handling functions yourself.
+ If you are using a client development tool, it may encapsulate some of the error handling or message passing in objects or structures provided by the environment.

In all cases, you should isolate error analysis and information in a single place in your application architecture in a reusable function or object. All error processing is reusable. This simplifies error and message management and standardizes the methods used to manage errors.

Once established, the use of these standard mechanisms should be clearly documented and enforced. Error handling mechanisms should be established very early in the development cycle to prevent the implementation of nonstandard methods and to catch developer's errors while they are writing code. SQL Server messages and errors are identified in the table sysmessages. Open Client errors are identified in the documentation. When programming with CT-Library you will program and install callback error-handling routines. If you are building with an application development environment, the error-capturing functionality may be provided. In any case, you must architect a set of responses to error information.

@@ERROR

SQL Server provides a global variable for tracking error conditions in T-SQL batches, stored procedures, and triggers. Called @@ERROR, it stores the most recent error status (0 for success, an error number for failure) and is overwritten by the next command.

For example, if you enter a database name incorrectly, you get an error message. You can use @@ERROR to get more information:

```
1> USE pbus2
Msg 911, Level 11, State 2:
Line 1:
Attempt to locate entry in sysdatabases for database 'pbus2' by name
failed - no entry found under that name. Make sure that name is entered
properly.
1> SELECT ERROR, severity, description FROM sysmessages
2> WHERE error=@@error
error severity description
----- -------- ------------------------------------------------------
  911      16 Attempt to locate entry in sysdatabases for database
              '%.*s' by name failed - no entry found under that name.
              Make sure that name is entered properly.
```

The global variable @@ERROR can be used to do control-of-flow logic in T-SQL based on the error return of statements. In transactions, for example, you may not want to continue to process a transaction if a statement in the transaction produces an error.

RAISERROR

RAISERROR is a T-SQL statement that places an error message on the standard error structure. It will then get passed directly to the calling program. The RAISERROR statement has two primary options:

♦ Displaying ad hoc, user-defined messages

```
RAISERROR 44444 'Either the name or address is invalid.'
```

♦ Displaying user-defined messages previously stored in sysusermessages with **sp_addmessage**

```
sp_addmessage 44444 'Either the name or address is invalid.'
go
RAISERROR 44444
go
Either the name or address is invalid.
```

Either includes a message string which can have optionally defined substitution parameters using a C **print()**-like syntax. If substitution parameters are used, the arguments for substitution are enumerated after the error number and message. It can be sent with the following command:

```
RAISERROR 44444 'Either the %1! or %2! is invalid.', name, address
go
Either the name or address is invalid.
```

RAISERROR syntax looks like this:

```
RAISERROR error_number [{ format_string | @local_variable } ]
       [, arg_list] [with errordata restricted_select_list]
```

Both ad hoc and predefined **RAISERROR** messages enable the construction of specific error messages. When **RAISERROR** is used with an error number and no format string, the server will look in the table sysusermessages to find the predefined error message. These messages can be fixed (no variable substitution) or will support parameter substitution. This style of error definition should be used when you wish to identify the error specifically in the client application—that is, when the application needs to interpret the error or message to determine control-of-flow for the application.

The following example illustrates the use of a user-defined message to indicate the number of rows modified by an update statement. This is a message that the server component of the application will send to the client component. User-defined error numbers must be over 20,000.

```
sp_addmessage 20010, 'The update modified %1! rows.'
go
UPDATE authors SET name = "Wong"
RAISERROR 20010, @@rowcount
go
The update modified 23 rows.
```

(@@ROWCOUNT is the number of rows affected by the most recently executed T-SQL statement.)

It is important not to obscure SQL Server errors and messages. Make sure the information generated by the server arrives in your application.

If you require a complex definition and delineation of user-defined errors and messages, it is possible to dynamically construct messages that incorporate various situational information into the message for parsing in the client application. You might send procedure name, batch identifier, table, action, column, and so on. If you standardize the messages, you can build a single function to parse them in the client application architecture.

Errors and messages are most often generated in triggers and stored procedures. There is more information in Chapter 9.

Error-handling Techniques

There are many useful techniques for managing errors. Review some of these ideas and incorporate the ones that make the most sense for your architecture. Put these behaviors into a standard reusable architecture and all of your applications can have sophisticated error-handling behavior.

♦ Establish an application-wide (global) variable that indicates whether the application is in DEBUG mode (development and BETA) or in PRODUCTION. Use this variable to turn on more in-depth error handling or a different style of error handling.

♦ Write all (or certain classes) of errors to a local or centralized file. These files can be collected and reviewed by developers.

♦ Write all (or certain classes) of errors to a centralized table. This central storage of all errors and messages provides developers and maintenance personnel easy access to monitoring the application.

♦ In PRODUCTION mode, provide a user-friendly and minimal message. In DEBUG mode, provide a robust error-handling message that will help steer developers to a quick resolution.

♦ When creating your own error messages with RAISERROR, be careful not to obscure the actual server error message which is key to understanding the source of the error.

♦ When sending a RAISERROR, consider incorporating the name of the stored procedure or a batch identifier in the message to assist in tracking the source of the error. Also include the access type and the name of a table if applicable. Some server errors already include table and column information.

Data Access

Data access refers to bringing data from the database into an application. There are very basic issues that must be understood in this environment. The primary issue is to move as little data across the network as possible. It is important to utilize the power of the SQL Server engine to reduce, manage, and structure data as it is being retrieved. This reduces the amount of work done by the network and the client. To build scalability into a system, it is very important to be as efficient as possible in using available resources.

The two primary questions are: When do we move the required information, and how? Data in a client application has a latency period. Latency is the time since it was read from the database. This has potential bearing on the current accuracy of the data. Someone else could be modifying the data in the database. You have to understand how volatile the data is and how often information is read into the application. You must read it only often enough to ensure that the user has adequately accurate information to accomplish the task.

Moving data into a client application has at least two primary aspects:

♦ Which technology to use (embedded SQL, Open Client calls, stored procedures, etc.)

♦ Whether to use a set operation or a cursor (row-at-a-time access to the data)

Performance, programming costs, and program maintenance costs all come to bear on the decision. In addition, development environments or languages may come with built-in facilities for moving data. You must understand exactly how they work and how to manage them for efficiency.

Stored Procedures

SQL Server has a strong architecture based around stored procedures, programs written in T-SQL and stored in the server. They are parsed when they are created, they are optimized and compiled the first time they are executed, and they remain in memory (cache) for subsequent users. They are the preferred way to manage much work done in the server for the following reasons:

♦ Increased performance can result because the parse, compile, and optimization work is done. This is especially important for online transaction processing systems (OLTP) that use small, discrete transactions in high volumes.

♦ Security can be controlled through procedures by granting execute permission on them and revoking any permissions on underlying objects allowing access only through the stored procedures.

♦ You can isolate the client application from any changes to the underlying database structure by accessing data only through the stored procedure.

♦ Stored procedures provide centralized, reusable software components that can be called from any application. Program the solution once.

A POPULAR QUERY

When I was in product line marketing, I used the corporate databases a lot to find out how my products were selling, to track particular customers, and so on. I had a couple of queries I ran every morning. They seemed kind of slow but they got me the info I needed, so I never really did anything to optimize them. After a while, the other marketing managers asked for copies of my queries to modify for their own products and customers.

Over time, response got poorer and poorer for my queries. I wasn't really surprised when the System Administrator called and begged me to stop using those queries and never, NEVER to give them to others. He could ignore one stupid query in the early morning, but a whole series of them running all day was too much, TOO MUCH!

I wrote a stored procedure for the department with parameters for customer and product, but my reputation was ruined as far as the MIS department went—they never really trusted me after that.

There is a caveat regarding stored procedures: Once a stored procedure is executed it is stored in cache (memory) for subsequent users. Stored procedures executed from cache have been precompiled with an execution plan optimized for the first executor. If the procedure takes parameters that are used in the stored procedure as values in a WHERE clause, it is important to understand the selectivity of the query where they are used. Selectivity is the measure of the percentage of the rows to be returned. Selectivity affects the index selection made by the optimizer when analyzing for best performance.

You must decide whether the procedure optimization can be appropriately reused. The rule of thumb goes like this:

> If the volume of data resulting from a query varies from below 5 to 10 percent of the data to above 5 to 10 percent of the data, the stored procedure should be created WITH RECOMPILE.

This will force the server to optimize each submission of the query. You will lose some of the performance advantage of preoptimization, but for large queries or for queries of varying selectivity the savings isn't much. In fact, the wrong query plan for the submitted parameters can give very poor performance results.

The optimizer can often find a useful nonclustered index to help in queries that read less than 5 to 10 percent of the data, but that same nonclustered index will be a serious detriment (more pages to read) for results sets larger than that. In many cases, a table scan is better than a nonclustered index if you are reading a lot of the data. The 5 to 10 percent is purposely vague because it depends on a calculation that relates the size of the data row to the size of the index row and how many index rows fit on a page. If you are varying in the 5 to 10 percent range, you should test how the optimizer does index selection across the entire range. If it is consistent, then you do not need the recompile option. If the optimizer changes its mind somewhere in the range, you do need to create the procedure with the recompile option.

Embedded SQL and DB-Library Calls

Many development environments allow you to submit embedded SQL to the server from the client application. These can be calls to existing stored procedures or actual SQL statements created in the client application. To provide logical isolation between the database and the client application, it is often better to not embed data retrieval logic in a client application. But sometimes the tools and the costs of efficiency lead us to do this. For simple statements (SELECT columns FROM table) or when working with tools that automatically generate the SQL for you, this is adequate. Do not embed complex data manipulation that could be reused into the client application. Try to build a stored procedure.

The exception to this is a dynamically generated statement. This is a data query or manipulation that cannot be defined at compile time, but is dependent on the state of the application at runtime. In these cases it is necessary to develop the statements from the client application and submit all the statements as a single batch (any set of Transact-SQL statements sub-mitted to the server at one time) and allow the server to execute them. To optimally use SQL Server, a development environment must provide an efficient way to submit batches.

The alternative is to submit individual statements one at a time to the server. It is important to weigh the performance degradation imposed by making multiple transmissions across the network. It is critical not to do this inside a transaction because it will decrease concurrency and performance.

Set Operations and Cursors

SQL Server is a relational database and therefore optimizes the use of data sets. Whenever possible programs should manipulate sets of data. A set may be one row or millions of rows. For performance reasons it is important not to process millions of rows one row at a time. Sometimes it is absolutely necessary, but not as often as we think.

SQL Server provides server-based cursors. These cursors enable the program to request a set of data and access it one row at a time. There are some processes that require this. There are two ways to access the cursors:

♦ From within a Transact-SQL batch, trigger, or stored procedure
♦ From a client development language or tool (C, C++, Visual Basic, etc.)

In both cases the actual cursor manipulation is done by SQL Server. There is a big difference in how the system processes the data.

When you use a cursor in Transact-SQL and do all of the cursor usage from within a single batch or stored procedure, the cursor loops through the data at the server and the data never moves onto the network or into the client application.

If you access the cursor from a client application, the server sends a buffer of rows to the client (the buffer size is tunable) and the client application works through the individual rows. Manipulating a cursor from a client is necessarily much slower than manipulating it within the server. Never move data across the network unless you need to.

Many client applications use a browsing metaphor for searching through rows of data. The user is allowed to select a relatively large data set and browse through it. There are two distinct ways to implement this:

♦ You can bring all of the data into the client application at once, a "snapshot."
♦ You can open a cursor and bring more data over as the user scrolls through the information.

The second method may give the user quicker response and may require less memory, but the first method is preferred because it frees up SQL Server resources and any locks that may be held. Of course, there are limits to how big the snapshot can be. It must fit in memory. In fact, there are very distinct size limits to how much data it is reasonable to bring into a graphical application expecting a user to browse through it in a reasonable time. The application should be designed to aid and require the user to limit the size of any snapshot set that he selects.

Cursors reading data may use a shared lock to manage the pages that they are reading. If HOLDLOCK is not used, the pages are freed as they are read, but at least one page is potentially locked while you are still processing a cursor. If this application or any other application tries to modify the locked page, the application must wait until the cursor is moved forward. What if the user went to lunch? You could set the isolation level to 0 (or use the NO LOCK keyword in a SELECT statement) to prevent the use of any lock, but that causes other locks to be ignored and introduces the possibility of inconsistency in the data you are reading.

As you can see, how to get data into the client application is not a trivial problem. Emphasize the following solutions:

- Use stored procedures for complex data manipulations and transactions and whenever else you can justify the extra coding cost.
- Use code-generating tools and embedded SQL for simple single statements.
- Bring sets of data into the client application all at once and then allow browsing.
- Program set operations instead of row-by-row operations whenever possible.
- Use cursors only inside of stored procedures or batches whenever possible.
- Send dynamic SQL to the server to be processed in a single batch.

Data Validation

Validating data is a major component of any application. It is critical to assure that each data value meets domain constraints defined by the business activity. These constraints can be:

- Fixed (value is always between 2 and 10)
- Self-referential (value A must not be greater than value B in the same table, or new value A must not be more that 1.1 times old value A)
- Referential (value A must match a value or constraint coming from another data element or table).

One advantage of SQL Server is its programmability. You can program intelligence and behavior into the server and thereby construct a server that itself controls the quality of the data. When a server is programmed properly, it is not possible to get incorrect data into the database. This is a great advantage in this age of open systems where it is possible for end users to get at data with inexpensive, over-the-counter tools, which know nothing about our data constraints. As long as SQL Server enforces its constraints, users cannot violate the data quality.

In addition, you need to validate data in the client application (field-by-field validation). Why is this? It is important to build client applications that meet high standards for usability, control, and performance. Client-side validation is a key factor in meeting these standards. For a data manipulation application to be usable, it needs to give the user constant feedback about his actions and the quality of the data. It is not sufficient to send the data to the server at the end of an editing sequence and then tell the user that the information he entered 5 to 10 minutes ago was not correct.

- ♦ It wastes time, and it irritates the user.
- ♦ It requires that the transaction is sent across the network multiple times, causing more work for the network, the application, and the server.
- ♦ In addition, the error handling that needs to be constructed in an application will need to be much more robust to deal with failures of complex transactions.

Of course, validation can never be 100 percent accurate in the client, since some reference tables may be changing at any time. The goal is to make an error condition from the server a rare instance. This improves usability, control, and performance.

This implies that each field (or in cases of self-reference validations, each set of fields) is validated as the user provides the information. In many development tools, such a mechanism is a service of the product. It is necessary to design the most efficient use of the provided mechanisms. Standards on the use of validation techniques is another critical design issue that will increase the strength of an application architecture.

SQL Server Validation Techniques

The SQL Server provides several tools for creating validation mechanisms in the server: rules, defaults, user-defined datatypes, column constraints, table constraints, triggers, and stored procedures.

Each of these tools is applicable in different situations. Rules and defaults are relatively fixed and apply to single columns or user-defined datatypes. User-defined datatypes encapsulate particular rules and defaults into datatypes that can be reused throughout a database, enforcing the defaults and rules for every column that uses it. Defaults, rules, and user-defined datatypes are used for atomic value constraints that do not reference other data objects.

Column constraints are an ANSI-compliant mechanism for providing data validation. They have the advantage of not requiring a binding step as do rules and defaults, but they are not reusable. They need to be defined on each column.

Table constraints are also an ANSI-compliant mechanism applied at the table level. They are used for internal reference validations (table.A must be greater than table.B) and for referential integrity based on primary/ foreign key relationships.

In general, apply these validation technologies as follows:

- For application-wide and reusable domains, use user-defined datatypes with defaults and rules. (Domains such as phone numbers, zip codes, states, and application-specific domains.)
- For column-specific constraints use column constraints. (For example, the age for a kindergarten applicant must be between 3 and 7.)
- For table-specific constraints (inter-column, referential, primary key, uniqueness) use the table level constraints. (For example, the school entrance date must be after the birth date or the state must be one of the states in the states table.)
- For any validations that cannot be covered with the previous technologies, use triggers. (For example, an order amount cannot exceed the sum of the stock-on-hand and the stock to be constructed in the next seven days.)
- If a trigger can't be used, use a stored procedure.

Use the most reusable and automated process to get the most utility for your effort. Remember that primary and unique constants construct indexes. As you rearrange indexes for performance, if you have used constraints to build the unique indexes, you will need to drop the constraints and recreate them using the ALTER TABLE statement. It will, at first, seem more awkward than standard index manipulation. Remember to specify CLUSTERED or NONCLUSTERED as they are relevant to your tuning process, and be aware of the device on which you build the index.

Some of the choices will depend on the tools you're using and what they support. Some database design products are generating trigger logic and constraints. It will be advantageous to use the features in the tool set that you have adopted and to use them consistently.

Client Validation Techniques

There are many tools available for validating data in the client application. The development environment used to build applications will provide some of them automatically. Use the most reusable and automated tools available.

Many graphic editing controls naturally validate data. They should be automatically populated with valid values, perhaps from the database. When available and natural to the application use check boxes, list boxes, drop-down list boxes (combo boxes), radio buttons, and edit controls with constraints.

For validations that go beyond what you can accomplish with the graphical controls, use post processing when the user leaves the data field and, only in an extreme circumstance, go to the server at that moment to see if the data is valid. It is often appropriate to make an extra transmission (round-trip communication) to the server to immediately validate a field, but it has to be measured against system load and performance. You could always wait until the user is ready to write the change to the database and notify him them. The total impact of either solution must be weighed against usability, performance, and control over the application.

Transaction Management

The most critical issue in the successful deployment and scalability of a client/server application is the proper implementation of transactions. Transactions, or permanent data modifications, are the most concise representation of the business meaning of an application. It is critical to understand the implications of managing data modifications with respect to the business being represented and with respect to the technology being used to implement the business behavior.

A transaction should be purposely defined to contain the smallest unit of work (database modifications) that has meaning to the business. Each single modification statement (INSERT, UPDATE, or DELETE) is, by default, treated as a complete unit of work, sometimes called an implicit transaction. When modifications must be grouped together to form an explicit transaction, the programmer must explicitly do this with transaction delineation statements (BEGIN TRAN and COMMIT/ROLLBACK TRAN).

In the SQL Server a transaction is guaranteed to continue to completion and be permanent or it will not have happened at all. This is regardless of the amount of work contained in the transaction. The SQL Server manages this through the use of the log and locking mechanisms. Data that is being modified by a transaction is locked from other users. When a process wants to read or write to a page that another process has locked, the process must wait. The waiting process is said to be blocked.

It is necessary that a transaction have the shortest duration possible. This is accomplished both by limiting the contents of the transaction to the smallest logical unit of work that has meaning to the business and by ensuring that the transaction executes as quickly as possible. When transactions run over a long period of time, they hold locks over a long period of time, and therefore extend the probability of blocking another user. What is a long period of time? It depends. In a high transaction rate OLTP system 200 milliseconds may be too long. In a low transaction rate system, seconds may not matter. In reality, efficiency in transaction management is a key reason why client/server applications fail to scale properly to the required volumes. They generate acceptable transaction rates at low volumes, but are too time-consuming for large volumes. The system is slowly crippled by the addition of users. It is difficult to re-architect the system's transaction management model after a system has been deployed.

To ensure that a transaction runs in the shortest possible time it is necessary to remove certain actions from within the scope of the transaction. In a programmable server like SQL Server the transaction should start and end inside the server. There are many casual styles of transaction implementation that violate this rule.

Application development environments encourage the execution of transaction controls from the client application. They do this by allowing the issuance of transaction control statements in the development environment language. In addition, they often produce multiple data modification statements and send them individually across the network. This involves activity in the client and multiple network transmissions during the scope of the transaction. This makes the transaction many times longer than necessary. The most egregious error is asking the user whether he wants to commit the transaction. He could go to lunch. Most of us succeed in avoiding this error.

To properly implement the most efficient transactions with the SQL Server, there are three basic techniques:

- ♦ The first is for single statement, implicit transactions. They need no transaction management statements. Since the server handles them implicitly as a transaction, the server will do adequate management unless you want to do a logical check to determine whether to roll back the transaction.
- ♦ The second is to embed the transaction inside a stored procedure. This stored procedure will be passed all of the data required to manage the transaction. It will validate the data, begin the transaction, execute the data modifications, do logic and error checking, and, if all is well, it will commit the transaction. It can alternately roll back the transaction if appropriate.

◆ The third is to construct the complete transaction logic in the client application and send it to the server at one time in a batch. These dynamic transactions cannot be defined during development. Their scope is determined by the state of the application at runtime (variable tables, variable numbers of rows, etc.). The batch constructed by the application will contain the beginning of the transaction, all of the data modifications, error checking, and the commit or rollback logic.

All of these transaction models exhibit optimal performance because no extraneous work is being done within the scope of the transaction. If you have also tuned the database properly to ensure optimal access paths to the data, they will be blazingly quick—well, optimally quick. This ensures minimal locking and blocking in the production system, enabling the system to support many more users effectively.

NETWORK INTERACTION IN A TRANSACTION

One of our customers called to tell us an application was becoming unusable (not one we had written fortunately). The application was fine first thing in the morning. But mid-morning performance started becoming a problem. Then it got better around noon.

It turns out that the application was processing a master-detail relationship and the standard transaction inserted the master and many detail records as a transaction. This was being done over a WAN from the warehouse to corporate headquarters. Unfortunately, each INSERT was being submitted as a separate batch to the server. Included in the transaction processing time were 10 to 15 network communication cycles. Since this was all a single transaction, the locks for the first INSERT were held for a very long time.

The reason that the users saw a performance degradation as the morning went on is that more and more users came on the system and they were blocking each other. About noon, enough users had gone to lunch so that blocking was reduced.

The solution was to submit all of the INSERTs in a single batch. This removed all of the network's delays from the transaction, and blocking effectively disappeared.

Error Checking in a Transaction

It is necessary to check for the error return of each data modification statement used in a transaction. If the error is very severe, the server will roll back the transaction. If the server error is less severe (for example, duplicate row, null values, and constraint violations), the server will not automatically roll back the transaction. You must check the global variable @@ERROR; if it is not 0, you can roll back the transaction as appropriate. Stored procedures should generally be built with very tight logical constructs so that there is generally not any processing logically following any error except to leave the procedure.

Trigger logic will be executed in the midst of a transaction. Triggers should be issuing a rollback whenever data fails trigger validation. It should also raise an appropriate error. This will terminate the transaction with appropriate information returning to the client application. The ROLL-BACK issued will roll back the transaction to the original start of the transaction whether it is implicit or explicit.

It is important that transaction control be issued as an all or nothing proposition. *Do not* decompose the definition of a transaction in the middle of a trigger. Do not, for example allow three rows of a five-row insert to be inserted and delete the other two. The application must be able to assume that the transaction is being treated as a complete logical unit of work and trust that the server implementation will honor that.

Concurrency Control

Concurrency is the measure of freedom among users in a multiuser system and the ability of the server to efficiently service multiple users. SQL Server manages concurrent multiple users by issuing locks that prevent interference at the database and ensure data consistency. Applications affect how these locks are deployed and therefore the level of concurrent access available to all users of the system.

Locks are usually managed at the page level (2,048 bytes, and some number of rows.) When multiple users want to read the same page, write the same page, or read and write to the same page, by default the server protects those operations and provides isolation and data consistency. This consistency enforcement does degrade the ability of users to freely get at data. Locking and blocking degrade concurrency and performance. No locking for concurrent users would be faster and provide higher concurrency, but would not provide adequate data consistency. These issues require software developers to manage the level of concurrency acquired. All management that manipulates the use of locks must be measured against the problems of data consistency, concurrency levels, and performance. All concurrency problems require the same question: to lock or not to lock. It depends. (See Chapter 2 for more information on locks.)

Preemptive Locking

Occasionally an application requires that a set of values (or a single value) be read before an action and that no other process read the data. This is true if you have an application that must generate a primary key for each row that depends on the last previous value. (Not needed if an IDENTITY column will do. But maybe the key is more complex and requires calculation or generation.) This style of data manipulation should be embedded in a stored procedure if possible. The data to be read must be locked as the data is read and the lock must be held until the transaction is complete. No other user must be allowed to read the data while the first user is processing it.

SELECT with HOLDLOCK will not suffice, because though HOLD-LOCK makes a shared read lock more permanent by holding it until the end of the transaction—it's still a read lock. Setting the lock promotion threshold lower for that particular table will change page locks to table locks, but it won't make shared locks exclusive. The only way to acquire an exclusive lock is by starting the transaction with a dummy update or updating the key first, then doing the read.

Browsing

It is common for applications to allow users to peruse data in their application and decide at some future point to update the data. Any time data is moved from the database and is not locked, there is the possibility of another user changing the data. The easiest solution is to lock the data. You can do this with a preemptive lock mechanism. This is not a good solution, however.

Optimistic concurrency control is a method used to manage this problem without locking records for an extended period of time. A collision is caused if one user reads data into his application and another user updates it before he does. With optimistic concurrency control you are assuming that any update you do will very likely succeed without a collision. Therefore, you do not lock the data. If you proceed with any update and write over another's update, this causes a lost update. This is a standard concurrency problem. The optimistic solution proceeds with the update conditioned with a test to see that the information being updated in the database is the same information that the application read.

There are many different mechanisms used to confirm that the row is the same. *Timestamp* is a feature of SQL Server that marks each row with a unique timestamp. When an application reads data, it reads the timestamp; when it issues the UPDATE (or DELETE), it compares the previously read timestamp with the current one. You can use the new system function **tsequal()** to compare timestamps.

```
tsequal(timestamp1, timestamp2)
```

If they are not the same, there has been a collision and the UPDATE will be rolled back. The timestamp solution requires you to carry a timestamp column on each table where you require this control. Other mechanisms can be used as well: comparing all of the columns, comparing the primary key and all of the modified columns, comparing your own datetime column, and so on. Different solutions provide differing levels of concurrency. Timestamps and all columns provide less concurrency because they will flag more collisions; using only the keys and modified columns will increase concurrency because updates of other columns will not cause a collision.

The trickiest part is deciding what to do when there is a collision. A common solution is to abort the transaction, reselect the row getting the new copy, and let the user re-edit the data. This is the simplest solution. A more complex solution will require a bigger investment in programming. It will be particularly complex if you submitted several rows and some number of them fail. In reality, this should be a rare occurrence and notification of the user that there was a problem may be enough for this rare occurrence.

Repeatable Reads

Sometimes in a transaction you require that the information you are working with is stable. That is, no one should be allowed to modify it. Repeatable reads refers to this stability enabling multiple reads of the data to be consistent. (You don't need to actually read the data multiple times.) You need a lock to ensure that other modifiers can't change the data. This is traditionally done with a HOLDLOCK on a SELECT statement. The HOLD-LOCK causes SQL Server to maintain all read locks that it obtains as it reads through the data.

```
SELECT *
FROM titles HOLDLOCK
```

You can do the same thing with the AT keyword and transaction isolation level SERIALIZABLE.

```
SELECT *
FROM titles
AT ISOLATION SERIALIZABLE
```

You can make SERIALIZABLE the default isolation level for your session with

```
SET TRANSACTION ISOLATION LEVEL 3
```

See Chapter 2 for a discussion of isolation levels.

Remember these options are locking entire tables from writers. It is necessary to completely understand the requirements, the scope, and the length of time that these locks are being held. If they are being held for any length of time, the statement should be run at a time that will minimize interference with other users.

Distributed Processing

The concept of distributed processing is the core of client/server architecture. To construct any given client/server application you will deploy application functionality on at least two processors. These processes must process cooperatively and efficiently. In deciding how to parse an application for client/server deployment there are many considerations.

It is of primary importance to build database independence.

♦ The database should be programmed to be self-defending. That is, all data consistency and data validation should be embedded in the database definition.
♦ Users should be able to use applications (well or poorly constructed) and off the shelf tools to access data without fear of damaging the database.

This implies a strong division of labor. Elements necessary to the integrity of the business are programmed as a part of the production database server: security, data validation, referential integrity, transaction control, and complex data manipulation (sorting, restriction, etc.).

In addition, SQL Server provides data storage, data access, and data administration facilities.

Client software is responsible for data presentation and manipulation, driving external processing (e.g., printing), user interface presentation and interpretation, and screen management.

Some processing is cooperative, where server and client each handle some aspect. In data validation, for example, the client can check user entries before sending them to the server, to cut down on network traffic and user work. This is also true for connection management, error handling, and security. Other tasks can be accomplished anywhere in the client/server architecture: data manipulation, calculations, ordering, presentation restrictions, analysis, and so on.

Deciding where to accomplish a given task is not always a simple decision. Many principles need to be taken into account:

♦ Do the work where the data resides.
♦ Move as little data as possible across the network.
♦ Make as few transmissions (client to server and back) across the network as possible.
♦ Off-load work to the least utilized processor.
♦ Use the processor or operating system best suited to the task.
♦ If the function is reusable, run it where it provides best access to all systems.

Many of these principles are at odds with each other. Which are critical to your system? Consider throughput, response time, network congestion, system architecture, and system load. A few sample questions to ask are:

♦ Does the task (analysis, calculation, ordering) seriously impede the throughput on the server?
♦ Can I get this information to the user's screen faster if I accomplish this task on the server? At the client?
♦ Can I reduce network degradation by minimizing what is transmitted?
♦ Does this processor or operating system lend itself to this process efficiently?
♦ Where is the system overloaded? Can I make decisions that will help balance the system utilization?

Security

Implementation of security in a client/server system is complex and often neglected. One of the first tasks in the implementation of a system should be the design of the security requirements and systems. Security can be addressed at different levels of complexity.

Primary Database Security

SQL Server enables basic security for database access to commands and database objects (tables, columns, stored procedures and views) with the GRANT and REVOKE commands. Each application designer must create a map of objects in the database, users accessing the database, and the access relationships between them. With the advent of flexible end user tools for ad hoc database access, it is necessary to properly implement database security that will always be in effect. Except in very small systems, security access should be defined by groups and then users are applied to groups.

Security for Ad Hoc Tools

If users are going to be using query tools, they should be assigned two logins in the database:

♦ Their primary login (which could be mapped to their operating system logins) should be given the most restrictive access. Any query tool that they use would inherit this level of security. This login should provide for limited access (for example, READ ONLY).
♦ Another login should be created that can be accessed only through custom-built applications that are designed to modify data. This login

can be based on (or calculated from) their primary login and password. When accessing a custom application, the user provides his primary login and password (or the operating system passes it to the server). When the application starts up, it generates the secondary password and creates a working connection to the server. Under this secondary login, the user has data modification and extended read capabilities in the custom application. The user does not know about the secondary login (or the password), but the application must be enabled to generate the secondary login and password and connect to the database.

Client Application Security and Control

It is often necessary to reflect security requirements in application presentation and behavior. The easiest way to define security for a user is to present only available actions and information. This requires that the application be programmed to be security conscious and able to configure itself based on the user's identification and the user's mapping to groups.

Large application objects (windows, menus, etc.) do not always track one-for-one to database security or database objects. In this case, define application topics that map to security usages. This will break application security into smaller units than windows or menus. For example, a billing subsystem would require a certain pattern of security for the database and for the application. If you design the security around topics and create a table that maps topics to users, the application can discover what this user is allowed to do and configure itself appropriately.

The application objects, windows, and menus must be constructed to automatically check the security status of the user and configure themselves appropriately. Windows and menus can alter their appearance and behavior based on the user. Menus can automatically enable/disable menu options. Windows can enable/disable controls on the window.

Integrated Security for Application Components

More complex extensions of user or topic-based security involve constructing objects (discrete application controls) that are security aware. Your application may require that individual controls (e.g., buttons, list boxes, etc.) alter their appearance or behavior based on the user. Every control on a window might have multiple configurations depending on user security and, by checking the user's security, configure itself appropriately. Such a security implementation prevents an application from duplicating objects that are similar, but have differing security status (for example, read-only views vs. modifiable views).

In an object-oriented environment, it is possible to build security awareness into base system objects that are used throughout a system. Integrated security approaches require the definition of security topics and the mapping of these security topics to users, database objects, and to application components. Reusable base components are programmed to check the security information against attributes that are initialized in the final implementation. To prevent excessive access to the database, maps of the security information can be moved into the application at the application opening from the database tables as required.

The more extensive your security requirements, the more effort you will need to invest during design and development. Use an architecture that gives you the level of security you require at the minimum of expense. Developing a complete reusable architecture that supports component-level security awareness will be a major developmental undertaking. If it is designed into a reusable architecture, you only have to do it once.

The sybsecurity Database

Sybase provides the optional sybsecurity database for auditing. It does not prevent or allow access, but allows you to track users and their actions on a number of levels (see Table 6.1). You start out by:

1. Installing sybsecurity with the Sybase installation utility sybinit. This creates the sybsecurity database. It holds the usual system tables and two special auditing tables: sysaudits and sysauditoptions. Sysaudits holds the audit trail.

2. Enable auditing with the sybsecurity system procedure **sp_auditoption.**

3. Set up the kind of auditing you want with special sybsecurity stored procedures listed in Table 6.1.

TABLE 6.1 Auditing Levels and Commands

Level	Auditing	Stored procedure
SQL Server	logins, logouts, reboots, remote procedure calls, fatal errors, privileged commands	sp_auditoption
Database	GRANT, REVOKE, TRUNCATE TABLE, DROP commands, USE	sp_auditdatabase
Object	tables, views stored procedures, triggers	sp_auditobject sp_auditsproc
User	SQL Server logins (not database user accounts)	sp_auditlogin

You'll probably want to start by identifying activities or objects that are critical to your application and the users who have access to them. For example:

- Changes to tables that hold sensitive information, such as employee salaries or company sales data
- Access to code or product specifications, if the information is not generally available
- Certain activities of employees in the finance, sales, or human resources department
- Removing any database or truncating any table

Once you set up the auditing, SQL Server sends records to the audit queue in shared memory. After the audit task is processed, the data is stored in the sysaudits table in sybsecurity. You can query the table and look for patterns and security problems or violations. A query to look at what a particular user has been up to might look like this:

```
SELECT *
FROM sysaudits
WHERE loginname = 'pretzel'
```

SELECT and TRUNCATE TABLE are the only legitimate commands. INSERT, UPDATE, and DELETE are not allowed.

Auditing takes planning and management.

- You need to set (and monitor) the size of the audit queue. A short queue means high recoverability: Little data is lost during a failure. However, a short queue can decrease overall system performance. If the audit queue is full, no user process that would create an audit record can complete until queue space is available. You set the audit queue size with the **audit queue size** option of the system procedure **sp_configure**.
- Because the sybsecurity database grows continually, it's important to put it on a separate physical device and create procedures for checking its size and deleting or archiving rows you no longer need. If sysaudits fills up, auditing stops and no activity that would produce an audit record can complete. You can set up a threshold to automatically fire a stored procedure when some size is reached. The stored procedure can truncate the table, removing out of date rows, or archive some of the data.
- Collecting the records doesn't do much good unless someone reviews them against a set of standards. This represents a substantial corporate investment.

C H A P T E R

7

Replication Server

Overview

Sybase introduced Replication Server in 1993 as a solution to the data distribution problem. As corporations grow, the amount of data they need to manage becomes larger and larger and it is often shared among a number of sites:

- ◆ Branch offices may need access to central headquarters data.
- ◆ Headquarters may receive and consolidate data from branch offices.
- ◆ New client/server systems may go into effect while legacy systems are still in use and the data needs to be integrated and available to all.

In many cases, there are both DSS and OLTP applications, with conflicting needs. The OLTP applications are update-intensive, with high throughput needs. DSS applications are query-intensive, and use many joins and complex computations, with resulting heavy use of system resources. If OLTP and DSS applications exist in the same database, the DSS may slow the OLTP. Since both update and query are critical to business success, you need a way to balance them. Replication Server allows you to separate the functions and give each its due.

All distributed data systems are tradeoffs. Some of the more important conflicts to balance are:

♦ Data availability/data synchronization. Making data available to every site at the same time (synchronous updates) imposes a high overhead on the primary site, causing poor response time at the primary site. On the other hand, delayed updates to secondary sites (slow asynchronous updates) means out-of-date (and possibly inaccurate) data at the secondary sites.

♦ Complexity/simplicity. Management of the components that go into distributing data—multiple sites (often with heterogeneous hardware and data management systems), complex network setups, and local versus centralized needs—is not a simple task. Here you have to weigh the risk of component failure against the level of accuracy of updates and design recovery procedures for each kind of possible component failure. As the system becomes larger, the cost of managing it may outweigh the value of up-to-the-minute data.

A distributed data system has to protect data integrity throughout the system at the transaction level. In addition, it needs to be able to

♦ Transfer data in all directions in heterogeneous environments
♦ Provide high performance for primary sites (replication procedures should not degrade it) and reliable data distribution to secondary (remote) sites
♦ Use network resources effectively
♦ Allow distributed sites to do updates without interfering with primary site data integrity
♦ Be manageable from a single central site
♦ Assure local autonomy, allowing sites to decide what data they want, how it will look, and how they will modify it

Distributed Systems

The question of how to share data among different sites is not new. If you've been in data processing 10 years or more, you've probably worked for a company that used the "sneaker-net" method: Do some work, copy it onto a tape or diskette, and trot briskly to another office, where you hand it to a colleague who loads it on another system. This is fine if you don't need absolutely current information; it usually leads to good gossip channels among departments (might as well stop and chat while you're in the other office). However, it is a manual (pedal?) system and tends to get irregular. Of course, the copy of the data you passed on is read-only.

A synchronous method is the two-phase commit Sybase has offered almost from the start. For every update, all involved sites need to concur: The update happens on all sites simultaneously. If it fails on any one site, the update is rolled back everywhere. The problem here is with the time and resources consumed by the initial agreement and the possibility of failure if one link is weak. On the other hand, actions can be bidirectional. Users can update data from any site, as well as read it.

An automated version of sneaker-net distribution is taking regular snapshots of tables and forwarding them to sites on an automated schedule. This eliminates some of the roughness of the earlier method, but it is still read-only.

Finally, some users take advantage of database triggers (changes to data that cause some database action) to distribute data to another location, such as a remote (secondary) SQL Server. This method can be fast and accurate, compared to others, but it has some shortcomings.

♦ You may get a data change, but not the whole transaction of which it is a part.
♦ The OLTP site bears the overhead burden of the distribution, since triggers originate there.
♦ Rollbacks can be complex.

Table 7.1 compares these solutions.

How It Works

Replication Server tries to meet most needs for distributed systems. An asynchronous system, it reads the primary site transaction log, detects data changes on primary site tables marked as available for replication, and transfers the changes across the network to secondary sites that have subscriptions to the primary site replication tables.

Overhead at the primary site is low, since there is no interference during the original transaction.

Replication Server maintains a *replication definition* for every table available to secondary sites. Secondary sites set up *subscriptions* to describe the columns and rows they want to receive. Once the secondary sites get the data, they can store and query it any way they like: renaming columns, creating views, imposing protections. If a component fails, in-transit data goes into stable disk queues, where it waits until it can be sent again. Table 7.2 shows how Replication Server handles the items noted for other distribution systems.

TABLE 7.1   Distribution Strategies

	Dump & load	2-phase commit	Table snapshots	Triggers
Timeliness	Asynchronous	Synchronous	Asynchronous	Asynchronous
Method	Dump data, reload at secondary site	Sites agree on each action: It takes place everywhere or not at all	Take scheduled snapshots of tables, automatically forward to secondary sites	Users set up triggers to write local data changes to secondary sites
Data age	May be old	Up-to-date	Depends on schedule	Fairly up-to-date
Read/write Transactions	Read-only Not protected	Read/write Protected, but transaction footprint extended	Read-only Not protected	Read-only Not protected
Error handling	At primary site only	Rollback for failure at any one site	At primary site only	Complex, requires coordination for rollbacks
Management	Not burdensome	Mostly for programmer	Relatively simple	Considerable planning and monitoring required
Issues	Clumsy	Complex, requires coordination of many sites, nonautonomous operations	Can be incomplete, out-of-date	Performance overhead; rollback difficult

TABLE 7.2   Replication Server Characteristics Summarized

	Replication Server
Timeliness	Asynchronous
Method	Detect changes by reading primary site transaction log and forward changes to subscribing secondary sites
Data age	Relatively up-to-date
Read/write	Read-only at secondary sites: can update data by using replication stored procedures or logging in to primary site. Changes are then replicated to secondary sites in the usual way
Transactions	Fully protected
Error handling	Incomplete transmissions are stored in queues for future action
Management	GUI Replication Server Manager works with individual components

The Components

Replication Server includes these components:

- Client applications at primary and secondary sites
- Data servers (a general term for Sybase SQL Servers and "foreign" database servers) for primary and secondary sites
- Log Transfer Managers (LTM) for every primary site
- Replication Servers
- Replication Server Manager (RSM)

Figure 7.1 shows how clients, data servers, LTMs, and Replication Servers work together. This particular configuration includes a primary site, a read-only secondary site, and a read-and-update secondary site.

- The primary site needs an LTM and a Replication Server. The SQL Server and LTM are located on one machine, with Replication Server on another.
- The read-only secondary site does not need an LTM, but has a Replication Server, since it is at a different location than the primary site. (If the read-only secondary site were co-located with the primary site, it would not require a separate Replication Server—it could use the primary site Replication Server. See Figure 7.2 for an illustration.)

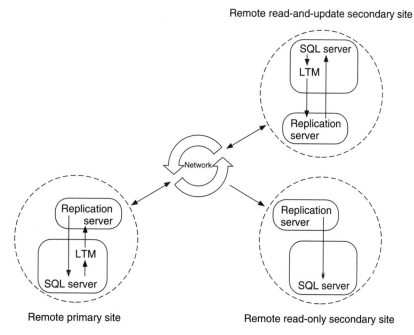

FIGURE 7.1 Skeletal Replication Server system.

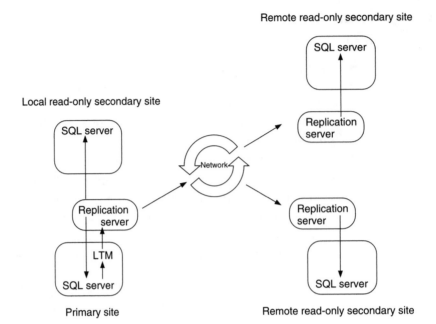

FIGURE 7.2 One primary site, multiple secondary sites.

♦ A secondary site that also performs some updates on the primary site data (with replication procedure calls) or acts as a primary site itself, needs both an LTM and a Replication Server.
♦ The Replication Server Manager resides on one site, usually at a central location.
♦ Stable queues for in-transit data (inbound or outbound) are located on disk assigned to Replication Server.

In abbreviated form, this is what happens:

1. The primary site creates and populates tables, and enables replication with a stored procedure.
2. The primary site Replication Server handles replication definitions (including column descriptions and table location).
3. Secondary sites create tables to receive replicated data.
4. Secondary sites specify the rows they want with replication subscriptions (like WHERE clauses).
5. Clients at the primary site change data as they do their work.
6. The primary site LTM detects changes in the primary site by reading the transaction log and passes the changes to the primary Replication Server.

7. Replication Servers work together to send data changes to target secondary sites on routes already set up by the administrator.

The Replication Server Manager uses a graphical user interface (GUI) to monitor activities among the components.

Client Applications

These applications are user programs that talk to a Sybase SQL Server or some other data server (see the section following on "Data Servers" for an explanation of the term). If they are primary site clients, they update the primary site data. Replication Server handles distribution of these changes to secondary sites. The primary site clients need have no knowledge of who will get the data or how.

Secondary site client applications also talk to a Sybase SQL Server or some other data server. If they are read-only sites, they don't need to know where the primary data comes from. To update the primary data, they need to have either replication stored procedures that can connect with the primary database or logins (perhaps through an application) that allow them to work in the primary database.

However the secondary site clients connect, the updates they make to the primary site data are propagated through the system by the primary database LTM and Replication Server. Secondary site clients do not make changes to primary site data on secondary site copies—they always go back to the source.

Data Servers

Data servers is a general term for Sybase SQL Server and other servers that manage data.

- ♦ Sybase SQL Servers work seamlessly with Replication Server.
- ♦ Data servers that support Sybase Client/Server Interfaces (C/SI) can easily set up a connection to Replication Server.
- ♦ Data servers that do not support Sybase C/SI can use Open Server to create a gateway and connect through it.

Check with Sybase for information on which data servers support C/SI and what prebuilt tools are available.

Log Transfer Manager

The LTM is an Open Client/Open Server application running on the same system as the primary database. You need an LTM for:

◆ Each primary site (to read the transaction log and detect when users make changes to "replicatable" data)

◆ Each secondary site using replication stored procedures (to read the transaction log and detect when users execute replication stored procedures)

A data server with only replicated data does not need an LTM. An LTM connects to a Replication Server but is often located on a separate system to cut down on overhead.

An LTM detects and captures transactions that need to be replicated on its source data server by reading the transaction logs. Its activity does not interfere with disk writes; its interaction with the primary data server is minimal. An LTM also translates captured changes into a special replication language (log transfer language or LTL) and passes these commands to Replication Server for delivery to replication sites.

If you can capture a transaction from a data source, you can map it to the Replication Server environment using Open Server/Open Client to build LTMs for data sources that have no supplied package. This means you can use Replication Server with legacy systems and "foreign" RDBMSs. You can also use Sybase products like OmniSQL Gateway.

Replication Server

Replication Server is an Open Server/Open Client application. In a local system, you may need only one Replication Server. If there are remote sites, you propagate data from the primary Replication Server to secondary Replication Servers. Routes between Replication Servers may be direct or indirect: The system administrator sets them up.

Replication Server:

◆ Receives updates from its primary data server via the LTM and distributes them to replication subscribers.

◆ Receives updates from other Replication Servers and applies these updates to local subscriber databases.

◆ Establishes a connection to other Replication Servers using subscription information stored in the Replication Server System Database (RSSD) for each replication site. The RSSD holds descriptions of replication data, user security information, routing paths for other sites, access methods for the local data server, and so on.

◆ Stores in-transit data when some component fails in inbound or outbound stable queues for later retransmission. You can change the size of the queue dynamically.

Clients use Replication Command Language (RCL) to manage information. RCL is like SQL—you can execute it with isql. LTL is a subset of RCL. After receiving replicated data, replication sites can customize replicate data just as they would any other.

Replication Server Manager

Replication Server Manager is a GUI front end for managing a Replication Server system that

- ♦ Works with collections of Replication Server components as well as individual pieces
- ♦ Provides a template for setting up subscriptions
- ♦ Handles login and permission systems
- ♦ Allows you to monitor connections and routes for delivery time
- ♦ Displays disk queue information such as used queue space and queue contents

Replication Server Configurations

Replication Server systems can have many different configurations. Some typical ones are:

1. A single OLTP primary site (perhaps headquarters) replicating read-only data to secondary DSS sites (such as branch offices).
2. Multiple remote OLTP primary sites (operations branches, say) replicating read-only data to a single secondary DSS site (central headquarters) where it is consolidated and used by management in queries.
3. Peer-to-peer hybrid sites with both primary and replicated data (separate finance, operations, and order entry sites, for example) receiving replicated data from other sites and acting as primary site for other data.
4. A single primary site replicating data to a single secondary site, which acts as a standby for the primary site in case of emergency.

One Primary Site, Multiple Replication Sites

In this configuration (see Figure 7.2) all changes happen at the primary site, then are distributed to the secondary sites. The secondary sites need the information for queries, but the primary site must be protected from resource-intensive DSS activities. Each secondary site subscribes to the information it needs. The three branch offices actually receive different subsets of the data. Notice that one site does not have a Replication Server. This is because it is located in the same office as the primary site and shares its Replication Server. The system sports only one LTM, because the primary site is the sole source of updates.

Multiple Primary Sites, One Replication Site

This Replication Server system (Figure 7.3) brings together information from remote primary locations and consolidates it in a central read-only secondary site. The primary sites do not need to talk to each other directly: They feed all information to the secondary site. Each primary site has a Replication Server and an LTM. The central secondary site has a Replication Server but no LTM.

Peer-to-Peer Hybrid Sites

The environment gets more complex as you move into two-way data distribution. For example, if each of three sites maintains sales records for its

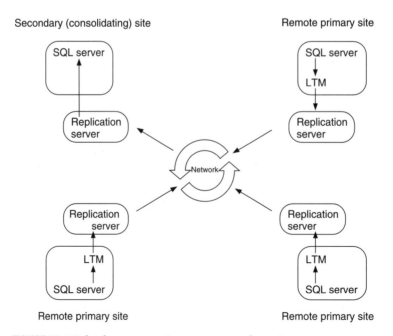

FIGURE 7.3 Multiple primary sites, one secondary site.

own areas and makes them available to other sites, all sites are both primary and secondary (see Figure 7.4 for a sketch of this configuration). As primary sites, they update their own local data. As secondary sites, they receive read-only copies of data from other sites. Each site needs an LTM to detect and capture changes to local data.

Every piece of data has a home site; it can be modified only at the home site. For example, imagine that there are three regional sales offices, each acting as a primary site. Sales data for the northwest belongs to one primary site, sales data from the southeast to another, and sales data from the west to a third. You can organize the data as either

◆ Three different tables (sales_ne, sales_se, and sales_w), each owned and updated by a particular site.
◆ One table (**sales_all**) divided into three distinct pieces (three primary *fragments*) each owned and updated by a particular site. In this case, one column or group of columns in the table is the fragmentation key. Each site checks the fragmentation key to determine if sales_all data is local or belongs to some other site.

If secondary sites need to update information from a primary site, they go back to the primary data source, rather than updating local replications and risking data inconsistency. There are two methods for doing this: asyn-

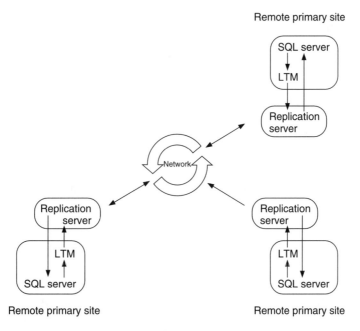

FIGURE 7.4 Peer-to-peer hybrid sites.

chronously, by transferring replication procedure calls among sites, and synchronously, by using a remote login to connect directly to the system that owns the item.

After the update from the secondary site is processed by the primary site, it is sent to the replication sites (including the one that originated it) in the usual way.

Single Primary Site, Single Replication Site

A final configuration is the warm standby, when you need an off-site copy of the system, ready to take over in an emergency. You could have copies of critical records in your San Francisco main office replicated to your underground building in Omaha. When the earthquake strikes in San Francisco, you'd know that your information was secure (up to the last successful transmission) and you had a fully-configured system ready to take over.

How much information you would lose depends on the lag time between the primary and secondary site.

Technical Issues

Replication Server is a part of a complete data management system, so the usual issues come up: relational model, transaction management, error handling, security, and data integrity.

Relational Model

Replication Server uses the relational database model. It deals with tables having a primary key, one or more columns, and a varying number of rows. Secondary sites do not have to sign up for complete table copies. They request the columns they want (and they always want the primary key) in their replication definition, which includes columns and datatypes, primary key, columns to use in a subscription WHERE clause, and location of the primary table.

Secondary sites describe the rows they want in their subscriptions. Secondary sites can rename columns, create views, and manipulate the data any way they want, except update it. The subscription includes:

- ◆ A subscription WHERE clause to spell out the rows the site wants. If there is no WHERE clause, the site gets all rows.
- ◆ An order to start transmitting data as changes are detected at the primary site.

The same primary table can be replicated at any number of sites. All replicated tables are read-only to protect data integrity: The local administrator sets up appropriate permissions. If a table holds rows belonging to the local site as well as rows replicated from a primary site, the administrator may need to designate a column or group of columns as a key to indicate whether local users can update the row. (See the previous section on peer-to-peer hybrid sites for more information.)

Transactions

All data servers in a Replication Server system follow the usual transaction rules:

- ◆ A transaction is atomic.
- ◆ A transaction is permanent.
- ◆ A transaction can be recovered.

Each data server provides transaction protection for the data it owns. If a transaction fails at the primary site, it is not distributed to secondary sites.

The LTM reads the transaction log and passes information to Replication Server for forwarding to secondary sites, where each event is handled as a single logical unit of work. For a DELETE, the LTM sends the before image of the row. For an INSERT, the LTM passes the after image. For an UPDATE, it sends both the before and after images.

Replication Server assumes that transactions successful at the primary site will complete at secondary sites. If transactions fail at a secondary site, they are recorded in a local *exception log.* Each site is responsible for reviewing its own log and deciding how to handle specific exceptions. Transactions may fail due to

- ◆ Lack of space at the secondary database
- ◆ Problems following a system recovery
- ◆ Constraints on the secondary table different than those on the primary table

Replication Server transactions are not controlled by locks.

Errors

Transaction replication failures are recorded in the local exception log. Transactions that do not reach the replication site due to network or component failure are held in a stable disk queue for later re-transmission.

Errors generated by data servers are up to you, since each vendor's error system is different. You can use RCL commands to set up error classes and tie error actions (abort, warning) to specific data server errors.

Security

Users at a replication site have access to data through their local data server permission system. System administrators should not grant UPDATE, INSERT, or DELETE permission on replicated tables.

Replication Server maintains a set of logins, separate from SQL Server logins. Most users do not need Replication Server logins: They work through applications. There are some special Replication Server permissions, conveyed with GRANT and removed with REVOKE.

- ♦ SA gives you rights to any Replication Server command.
- ♦ CREATE OBJECT allows you to CREATE, ALTER, or DROP Replication Server objects, including definitions and subscriptions.
- ♦ PRIMARY SUBSCRIBE lets you create subscriptions in a primary database (to create subscriptions from a secondary site, you need CREATE OBJECT permission on the secondary site plus CREATE OBJECT or PRIMARY SUBSCRIBE permission on the primary site).
- ♦ CONNECT SOURCE permits you to run the LTM RCL commands.

Each secondary database has a *maintenance user* account set up by the local system administrator for Replication Server use. This account needs appropriate permissions to update secondary database tables containing data replicated from other sites. Replication Server uses the account to access the tables.

Data Integrity

Local sites control their own data and use replicated data any way they like. Each piece of data belongs to one and only one data server and all updates are directed through the "owner" data server and propagated through Replication Server. Secondary site users can change data in primary sites two ways:

- ♦ Through replication stored procedures
- ♦ By logging in to the primary data server (perhaps through an application)

Replication stored procedures are Sybase stored procedures marked specifically for replication and associated with a user-defined replication function. The user-defined function is created in a primary site and connected to a primary site replication definition: Subscribing secondary sites receive copies of the function.

When a secondary site user executes a replicated stored procedure, the command and the parameters are recorded in the secondary transaction log. The secondary LTM detects the replicated stored procedure execution and passes that information and the parameters on to the local Replication Server, where it is linked to its corresponding user-defined function. The function (with parameters identical to the replication stored procedure parameters) is sent to the appropriate primary site and executed. Data changes are made, logged, and replicated back to subscribing secondary sites in the usual way.

Replication stored procedures require planning and coordination among the participating secondary and primary sites. Procedures and functions must match in name and parameter type; secondary site users need appropriate permissions for the primary site. Replication stored procedures are more efficient than standard stored procedures in the replication environment because little information (only the function call and the parameters) is passed.

System 11 Replication Server Features

Replication Server Release 11 includes some new (or improved) features.

- ◆ Internationalization: Replication Server now supports all Sybase character sets and sort orders and provides messages in three languages in addition to English: French, German, and Japanese. It can also handle replication among data servers with different character sets.
- ◆ Text and image data: Previously, Replication Server handled text and image data indirectly, with intermediate tables, triggers, and Open Server. Now you can include these columns in the replication definition and work with them directly.
- ◆ Warm standby: Replication Server provides some new commands aimed specifically at the warm standby configuration.
- ◆ Replicated functions: Previously, replicated functions were associated with replication definitions for tables and used in connection with replicated stored procedures to modify table data. Now they are constructed differently and available for broader uses.

System 11 also introduces some new commands and stored procedures.

8

Designing Databases

Overview

Building a database is usually one piece of a much larger development process (see Figure 8.1). This chapter assumes you have done the large-scale planning discussed in Chapter 3 and are ready to start putting together a specific database.

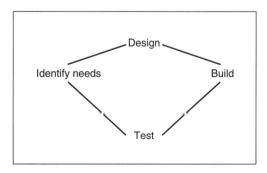

FIGURE 8.1 Database development.

In databases, as in most applications, design is where everything starts. The choices you make when you design a database influence all aspects of your work, from data integrity to performance. But don't think you can do it once: Database development is an iterative process. Be ready to test and change your design as you go along.

One common error is to work through a design and then present it triumphantly to the users. They won't be happy and it'll take a long time to get everything straightened out. Prevent this problem by surveying your users early and often. Get feedback from them at each stage of development and check your work with your peers, too.

A good database design includes:

♦ Data definition: Identify the business objects and how they relate to each other.
♦ Business functions: The database is a model of the business. It needs to support and enforce business conventions and recognize legitimate and illegitimate transactions.
♦ Performance: Review needed reports and think through how they will work with your design. Twelve joins for a common query doesn't make much sense, but it might be acceptable for something that doesn't come up frequently.

In order for you and others on your staff to support the design, strive for

♦ Flexibility: Everything changes. Keep notes and diagrams on your design. Anticipate changes and consider how they will work with your design.
♦ Readability: Make sure others can understand your design. Use meaningful names with consistent use of case and number (singular/plural).

This chapter has four main sections:

♦ Identifying needs—getting precise requirements for the application
♦ Creating a logical design—showing all the "things" in the database and how they relate to each other
♦ Building a database—translating the logical design into a physical design by creating and implementing SQL commands, resulting in a prototype
♦ Tuning—testing the database against your requirements; refining table design, indexes, and physical placement of data to improve performance

In real life, each of these steps is iterative and blurs into the others. If you understand your application and data well, you may be able to make some of the tuning decisions (denormalization, space assignment) during the logical design or physical design stages.

Identifying Needs

When designing a database, start by listing requirements. Get functional requirements in *quantifiable* terms. Press for specifics! You won't get all the information you want the first time around, but you'll get some, plus ideas on how to change your questions for the next pass. A starting checklist includes these things:

- ◆ A description of the business, with detailed information (flow charts to show how tasks relate to each other, lists of forms and reports, timing goals, notes on what works and what does not) on how data is currently handled.
- ◆ Performance and availability requirements for each functional area.
- ◆ Number and kind of users. What do they need from the application? How sophisticated are they? How stable are their requirements? Are there need conflicts between groups? Are some user groups dominant?
- ◆ Amount of data and projected growth.
- ◆ Security needs.
- ◆ Business rules (pay bills within 30 days, keep no inventory longer than 6 months, track shipments out of state for tax purposes) for each functional area.
- ◆ Reports or required output for each functional area.
- ◆ Internationalization requirements.

You also need to consider:

- ◆ General nature of application. Is it mostly online inserting, updating and deleting, primarily reporting, or a combination? Is it a new system or a conversion?
- ◆ Hardware for both client and server sides, network setup, and whether it is local or distributed.
- ◆ Interaction with other software, home grown and off-the-shelf.
- ◆ Applicable standards (ISO 9000, internal or external systems and methodologies).
- ◆ Time and staff available.
- ◆ Projected life of this application.

Creating the Logical Design

Once you've collected all the information you can get, start plotting the logical design. This involves creating an entity-relationship (E-R) model to show the "things" in the database and how they relate to each other. After you've got them all recorded, you *normalize* the things and their relationships (apply a set of rules to reduce data redundancy and protect data integrity). A good E-R diagram shows the kind of data in a database and how it relates. Anyone who understands databases and knows something about the business should be able to write intelligent queries from an E-R diagram. Make your users check the normalized E-R diagram. They'll probably be able to see errors you don't.

When you have a solid E-R diagram, examine the business rules you have coaxed from your users and consider how they will affect both the database design and the application design. Can a department exist with no employees? Can an employee exist who is in no department? Is it possible to change primary key values (e.g., an employee number or social security number)? Can your company sell more widgets than it has on hand? Are any of these principles likely to change? This information is critical to the application's behavior and determines how your "things" interrelate. Put together charts showing how the business rules apply to the database and let the users review them.

Finally, establish expectations (and requirements) for the performance of the application's various pieces as part of the logical database and application design. Among other performance statistics, it is critical to have at least:

- The volume of information and its expected rate of growth
- The initial and projected number of total users and concurrent users (those actively using the application at any one time)
- The number and nature of *interesting* transactions and reports, including target response times, data volume, and approach, if the manipulations are complex

At this point, make preliminary assessments of the performance goals. Are they reasonable and achievable? If not, why not? Performance limitations will become clearer as you create the physical design and run benchmarks, but you need to look for them during the logical design stage, too.

Entities, Attributes, and Relationships—Step 1

In designing a logical database and application, first determine what *entities* are important to the application. An entity is something you can uniquely identify. Examples are employees, departments, customers, or individual purchases.

The entities have *attributes* (also called properties). These might include the birth date of an employee, the name of a department, the address of a customer, and the date of a purchase. *Relationships* are associations among the entities—an employee is in a department, a customer makes a purchase, an employee handles a certain kind of purchase.

During the logical database design, you identify the entities, attributes, and relationships in the application. The entities will eventually translate to tables, the attributes to columns, and joins (or, occasionally, special tables called relation tables) represent the relationships. Most database designers deliberately use the terms "entity" and "attribute" during the early logical design stage, and switch to "table" and "column" as they get closer to the actual structure. Table 8.1 shows how the terms line up.

By the time you get ready to implement your design,

◆ Each table will have a name and a set number of columns: It will be square or rectangular, rather than irregular.
◆ Each column will have a name and a datatype.
◆ Each row will have a column or group of columns that uniquely identify it.

The Process

You set up entities, attributes, and relationships by going through a process like this:

1. Identify each independent entity (thing) and give it a name.
2. List the attributes (characteristics or properties) of each entity.
3. Select or create one attribute as the *primary identifier*. If a single attribute won't work, use a group of attributes. The relational model requires a primary identifier because relational data is not stored in any particular order. To retrieve, update, or delete a specific row, you must be able to describe it uniquely.
4. Classify the relationships between entities as one-to-many (departments have many employees but employees have only one department) or many-to-many (orders may include many products and products can appear on any number of orders). If the relationship is one-to-one, consider merging the two entities.
5. Change each many-to-many relationship into a connecting (*associative* or *relation*) table.

TABLE 8.1 Relational Database Terms

Database	*Relational Theory*	*Traditional*
Table	Entity	File
Row	Tuple	Record
Column	Attribute	Field

6. Make sure each one-to-many relationship includes ways to connect the entities (shared attributes you can use for joins). Typically, the primary identifier in one entity (customer identification number in a customer entity) connects with a secondary identifier in another (customer identification number in an order entity where the order number is the primary identifier). These pairs are often called *primary and secondary keys* or *primary and foreign keys*.

7. Examine the entities, attributes, and relationships again, testing them against normalization rules.

One way to get a list of entities is to work from existing paper systems, such as order forms, weekly reports, and invoice lists. You can start by listing all attributes and then grouping them into entities, or work from the other end, starting with entities and figuring out their attributes. Either way, you'll move things around more than once before you have a working system.

Entity-Relationship Diagrams

Entities are often diagrammed as named boxes, with attributes as enclosed lists and primary identifiers marked in some way (in Figure 8.2, they are underlined). Lines show the relationships between entities. The relationships are often described as verbs: A customer *issues* an order; an order *contains* products.

As you analyze the relationships between entities, you often spot problems. An order, for example, can contain more than one product, and a product can appear in more than one order. The order and product entities shown in Figure 8.2 have a many-to-many relationship. This calls for a new (associating or relating) entity and some rearranging of attributes. If you leave things as they are, it will be very difficult to design a table with a square or rectangular shape. How many product# columns will you have in the order table? What if a customer orders more products than you have

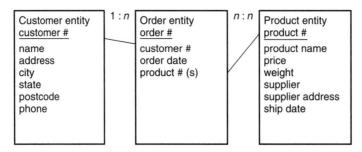

FIGURE 8.2 E-R design.

allowed for? The idea is to break the many-to-many (*n:n*) relationship down to two relationships. It usually turns into a one-to-many (1:*n*) and many-to-one (*n*:1) relationship as shown in Figure 8.3.

The primary identifier in an association entity often includes more than one attribute to ensure uniqueness.

Normalization

The purpose of normalization is to cut down on data duplication and protect data integrity. This means small tables with narrow rows, fewer null values, and less data redundancy. Normalized tables are easy to maintain and update as your design needs change.

Normalized tables also have advantages in terms of physical design:

- ♦ Accessing data and creating indexes is faster, since you have more rows per page and fewer logical and physical I/Os.
- ♦ With more small tables, you have more indexing opportunities. (Each table can have only one clustered index; it is generally your best index.) The indexes may be easier to transverse, since they are narrower and shorter.
- ♦ More tables mean more opportunities for precise data placement.

Most books describe first through fifth normal forms (and Boyce/Codd normal form, between the third and fourth forms), but database designers generally concentrate on the first three. Each normal form is a test you apply to your design. Depending on your application, you may decide to ignore some of the changes normalization suggests. Since denormalization implies prior normalization, the usual method is to normalize the database during the design stage and denormalize during the prototype phase as performance requirements indicate.

The first normal form (sometimes written as 1NF) requires every column to be atomic—it can hold only one value. A customer "name" attribute,

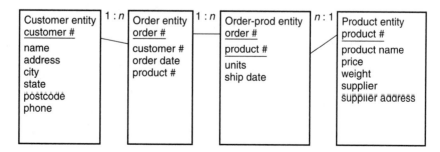

FIGURE 8.3 Refined E-R diagram.

for example, decomposes into first name, last name, and middle initial, a "phone" attribute into area code and phone number. In the same way, repeating attributes are forbidden. An order entity with "product1," "product2," "productn" doesn't pass 1NF. An E-R diagram will often help you spot these problems before you normalize. First normal form is important because the relational model does not allow a table to have varying numbers of columns or columns of uncertain size. Even ignoring theory, there are practical reasons for 1NF:

- ◆ If you have multiple columns of the same type (product1, product2, . . . product15), the table is difficult to query (how do I find all the rows with product "abc" in some product column?). This kind of table structure is also awkward to print or display on the screen—or even just to understand.
- ◆ If you have multiple pieces of information in a single column, data retrieval becomes dauntingly complex. Imagine the SQL needed to find product abc in a column that may contain up to 15 products! Sizing the column is also problematic.

The second normal form (2NF) applies to entities with compound primary identifiers and requires you to make sure that attributes apply to the whole primary identifier or key. If the primary identifier is a single attribute, the table complies with 2NF by default.

In the example sketched in Figure 8.3, "units" in the order-product entity passes the test—it applies to a particular product in a particular order not to the product or the order alone. "Ship date" may actually apply to the order as a whole, depending on the business rules. (If the company ships each line item as it is ready, ship date belongs in the order-product entity, but if the company ships only after the whole order is prepared, the ship date is an attribute of the order.) This is why database design is tough.

After you check your design against 2NF, move attributes that don't relate to the whole key to a different entity or reconsider the compound identifier. If all attributes relate to only one of the elements in the primary identifier, you may need to change the primary identifier, or create an additional entity with that column as the primary key (see Figure 8.4). Second normal form eliminates redundancy and verifies that each compound primary identifier really is the unique identifier for the entity.

The third normal form considers the tie between primary identifier and each attribute. In Figure 8.4, supplier address in the product entity applies to the supplier attribute and not to the product number primary identifier. Remove it and create a new entity to hold supplier information as shown in Figure 8.5.

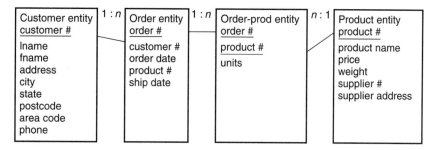

FIGURE 8.4 Second Normal Form design.

Once you've been through the normalization process, review your requirements and make sure you can create the required reports from the structure you've created. Are there paths between related pieces of data? Is all the data you need available through the entities and attributes?

A SAD STORY?

Norm was kind of a shy guy, so he was happy when Heather agreed to go to the junior prom with him. He thought the date went well, though he did spill a little punch on her dress.

When the homecoming dance came around, he invited her again. This time he even tried to dance! The little piece on the edge of her outfit that got torn when he accidentally stepped on it in his enthusiasm didn't seem critical.

He was pleased when she agreed to accompany him to the senior prom. It was a great party. He did kind of rip the cloth on the front of her dress when he pinned on the corsage (it was a delicate operation) but the flower more or less covered it up.

He was feeling so confident, he invited her to the welcome dance at college later on in the fall. Heather looked at him sadly, and said "No more parties for us. You better find another date."

Norm was astonished. "Why?" he asked.

"The first formal was nothing much. I could even forgive the second. But when you ruined my third formal, Norm, I knew there was no hope."

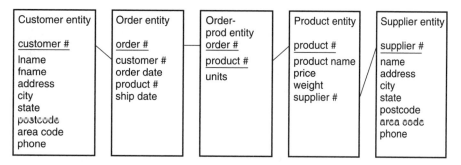

FIGURE 8.5 Third Normal Form design.

Business Functions and Rules—Step 2

The next step in logical database and application design requires the application designer (you) to apply the business functions and rules your users have provided. In SQL Server, the tools you use are datatypes (including user-defined datatypes), constraints, unique indexes, defaults, rules, stored procedures, and triggers.

♦ Columns that must be unique may need a unique index.

♦ Columns used in more than one table are candidates for user-defined datatypes.

♦ Those in which you want SQL Server to enter a particular value are possible sites for defaults.

♦ Columns with simple limits on values may take a rule.

♦ Columns with value ranges determined by cross-column comparisons should be considered for constraints or triggers.

♦ More complicated business rules are handled with stored procedures and triggers.

During the design stage, create a chart for each table, showing the requirements you know of in terms of these tools. At this point, you can start thinking of your normalized entities as tables and the attributes as columns. When you move to prototyping, use the chart to create SQL statements. (The section on building the application gives information on how to choose the appropriate SQL commands, since SQL Server provides more than one way to implement defaults, rules, and unique indexes. At this point, work on the conceptual level.)

Datatypes define the type of data you can store in a column; SQL Server provides a wide range of possibilities. For each column, consider function (the kind of data stored), range (how large or small the data can be), and storage size (how much space it takes up).

For example, a social security number can be a character datatype or a numeric datatype. The first will take nine bytes of storage. Defining it as an integer will reduce the number to four bytes. Since there is no need for alphabetic or special characters in a social security number, the integer may be a better choice.

Nulls add another wrinkle to datatypes. You can use nulls as place holders for missing information (customer declines to state age), incomplete data (middle name is illegible), or inapplicable answers (no "spouse's name" for a single person).

Specify not null for primary keys and "must enter" columns and null for columns where information is not required or is likely to be unavailable. For example, you'd always want an order date associated with each order, so you'd create that column as not null. On the other hand, you wouldn't necessarily know the ship date when you entered the order, so that column could allow nulls.

User-defined datatypes are based on system datatypes. They are one way of enforcing datatype compatibility, by specifying all aspects of a datatype, including null status and type, length, precision, and scale. You can use the same user-defined datatype for numerous columns.

A unique index is the only way to ensure uniqueness of one or more columns across a table. Not all tables need an index for performance reasons. If you know a column must be unique (such as the primary identifier) sketch in a unique index. You can decide later if it should be clustered or nonclustered.

Defaults insert values (such as today's date) when no other value is supplied. Defaults must be the same datatype as the column. A default character string ("no value") for a numerical column will not work. Some developers use explicit defaults to avoid null values.

Rules validate values. There are three types of rules:

♦ A set of values using the set operator IN
♦ A range of values with BETWEEN or comparison operators
♦ A pattern match with LIKE

Rules specified in the CREATE TABLE statement (table-level check constraints) can compare values in two columns in the same table. For example, you might want to use a check constraint rule to make sure a ship date is never earlier than its order date.

Stored procedures are named objects in the database, consisting of one or more SQL statements. They can contain procedural logic, accept input parameters and generate output parameters, and run faster than individual statements. They also prevent the user from getting bogged down in complex syntax. SQL Server system procedures offer many examples of what stored procedures can do.

Triggers enforce referential integrity or other business rules. You can have up to three triggers on each table (for INSERT, UPDATE, and DELETE actions) and the triggers can refer to other tables, call stored procedures, and execute other triggers. SQL Server fires a trigger when the specified data modification action takes place. Construct triggers to enforce business rules. For example, what happens when a customer becomes inactive? Do you keep the information on the customer as long as there is related information (a disputed sale)? Do you remove the customer information and archive it in an "inactive" table? Do you delete customer information and flag matching values in other tables (add an inactive customer column to the order table)? What the trigger does depends on how the business handles these cases.

Once you have sketched these elements for each table, revise your schema as needed. Table 8.2 is an example for one table.

Performance Requirements—Step 3

For the performance assessment, review user requirements. What are the major queries and reports? Are many joins required to get the results you need? Pin down how often reports will be run and find out if they need to happen during prime time or can be run when there is less pressure on the system.

Decision support systems (DSS) and online transaction processing systems (OLTP) address two different environments. You can clearly characterize some applications as one or the other. Others will have aspects of both, which presents difficult problems in physical design.

At this point, you can look at major activities and try to categorize them. Generally speaking, a decision support system is heavy on queries and reports but light on updates. Transactions tend to be complex and result in long locks. Speed is not usually critical—many of the reports can be run in nonpeak time. Pages are moved in and out of cache as queries run, but there are relatively few disk writes.

An OLTP system shows some opposite characteristics. The emphasis is on data modification, often with many concurrent users. Lock contention can be high, especially if there is competition with DSS activities. Referential integrity checks may involve joins with other tables. Disk writes are frequent.

TABLE 8.2 Table Design

Column	Datatype	User Datatype	Null Status	Default	1-column Rule	Other Considerations
product#	numeric	numtype	not null		btw 0000000 & 9999999	must be unique
name	varchar(20)	nametype	not null			
type	varchar		not null	appl	appl, game, edu, hardware, supply, book	
notes	varchar(200)		null			
price	smallmoney		not null			
weight	decimal		not null			
supplier#	numeric	numtype	not null		btw 0000000 & 9999999	must exist in supplier entity

Table 8.3 compares the two kinds of systems. The tuning section gives information on how to deal with the differing requirements.

Building the Application

Physical database design, like logical database design, usually requires several passes.

- Translate the logical database design (entities and relationships and business rules) into a set of tables, defaults, rules, triggers, and indexes.
- Consider physical placement issues, including database size and location, log size and location, and use of segments for individual tables. Make the best decisions you can and plan to make adjustments during the tuning phase.
- Develop a prototype.
- Run required queries and reports against the prototype and evaluate speed, accuracy, and reliability.
- Change the physical design and prototype as needed. Preliminary prototypes may use only token amounts of data, but for real results, you need a load close to what you expect in actual deployment.
- Continue to test and change the prototype until overall goals are met.
- Put the application under full load and move into the tuning phase to work on specific problems.

In many cases the progress from logical to physical design is fairly direct. Working with the SQL commands lets you create tables and indexes, set up integrity controls, review existing physical resources (disk space), and place objects on segments for maximum accessibility.

TABLE 8.3 OLTP-DSS Comparison

Topic/Action	*DSS*	*OLTP*
transactions	long-running transactions	many short transactions
locking	long locks	short locks
reports	many	few
data modifications	few	many
joins for referential checks	few	many
speed	not critical	high
user connections	not critical	many concurrent
disk input/output		significant
cache use	significant	

During this translation from logical to physical design, remember that individual tables exist in the context of the structure of the entire application. Collect information on issues and make educated choices, knowing that standardizing components in isolation won't work. When you move into the tuning phase, you'll be looking at specific queries and reports.

Creating Tables

Table creation, at its simplest, includes naming a table and its columns. For each column, you specify: name, datatype (including size or precision and scale for some datatypes), and null status.

Stripped-down create table syntax looks like this:

```
CREATE TABLE table_name
(
        column_name      datatype        [NULL | NOT NULL]
        [, column_name   datatype        [NULL | NOT NULL]]...
)
```

Full syntax involves many more options.

```
CREATE TABLE [database.[owner].] table_name
(
(col_name datatype
 [default {constraint_expression | user | null}]
 {[{identity |null | not null}]
 | [[constraint constraint_name]
        {{unique | primary key}
        [clustered | nonclustered]
        [with {fillfactor | max_rows_per_page}=x]
        [on segment_name]
        | references [[ database.]owner.]ref_table [(ref_column)]
 | check (search_condition)}]}...

 | [[constraint constraint_name]
        {{unique | primary key}
         [clustered | nonclustered]
         (column_name {{, column_name}...}])
         [with {fillfactor | max_rows_per_page}=x]
         [on segment_name]
         | foreign key (column_name [{, column_name}...])
         | references [[ database.]owner.] ref_table
         [(ref_column)[{,ref_column}...)]
 | check (search_condition)}
[{, {next_column | next_constraint}}...])
[with max_rows_per_page = x] [on segment_name]
```

It includes these elements:

♦ Name, datatype, and (optional) null and identity information for each column. The identity property generates and holds sequential numbers and is available to columns based on non-null numeric (but 0 scale) datatypes.

♦ One DEFAULT constraint per column. It can be a value, a function, the identity of the user who does the insert, or null.

♦ Column and table CHECK constraints. You can have multiple column CHECK constraints per column.

♦ One PRIMARY KEY constraint (unique index on a column that does not permit nulls) per table.

♦ Multiple UNIQUE constraints (unique indexes on columns that may permit nulls) per table.

♦ No more than one REFERENCES clause per column, pointing to one column (defined as unique) in another table. For table-level references, use FOREIGN KEY and REFERENCES together.

You can create unique indexes, defaults, rules, and referential integrity checks in the CREATE TABLE statement or separately. Table 8.4 shows how the commands relate.

There are some advantages in defining constraints in the CREATE TABLE statement.

♦ Having all the code located in one place may be convenient to maintain and easy for others to find and read.

♦ Creating defaults and rules as separate objects is a SQL Server extension and may not be as portable as using the CREATE TABLE syntax.

♦ Implementing REFERENCES is easy and direct.

♦ The table-level CHECK constraint provides features not available in rules and is less complex than a trigger.

Using separate SQL statements also has benefits.

TABLE 8.4 Table Definition Components

Category	In CREATE TABLE command	In other SQL commands
Unique index	UNIQUE constraint	CREATE UNIQUE INDEX (on null column)
	PRIMARY KEY constraint	CREATE UNIQUE INDEX (on non-null column)
Referential integrity	REFERENCES constraint	CREATE TRIGGER
1-table cross-column comparison	CHECK constraint (table level)	CREATE TRIGGER
Column value limit	CHECK constraint (column level)	CREATE RULE & sp_bindrule
Column default	DEFAULT	CREATE DEFAULT & sp_bindefault

♦ You can create libraries of defaults and rules to use with user-defined datatypes and multiple columns and prevent errors by changing defaults and rules in one place rather than in many.

♦ You can change defaults, rules, indexes, stored procedures, and triggers without touching the table structure.

♦ Triggers and stored procedures are more flexible and powerful than constraints: They can cascade changes, reference multiple tables and objects, use complex logic, and rollback illegal transactions.

♦ The syntax for the separate commands is less complex and easily tested in isolation.

In this section, we'll handle the elements conceptually, give some examples so you can compare the different methods. You are left to decide how to write the code.

Column Names

Set up some conventions for table and column names. Make the names meaningful and be consistent in case, number, use of abbreviations, special characters, and the like. Don't call one table "authors" and another "title-author;" or one column "*au*_fname" and another "*auth*_lname."

Null status is actually not required (the not null default goes into effect if you do not specify a status), but your intention is easier to understand if you explicitly include null status.

Datatypes

SQL Server determines the size of a column by the datatype and whether you allow NULLs in the table definition (see Table 8.5).

The first principle in datatype choice is to pick the "natural" datatype. Unless there are specific performance or space issues, assign a phone number a character datatype rather than a numeric datatype, because you're more likely to use it with character functions (**substring**) than with mathmatical operations (addition) or functions (**sqrt**). Other guidelines include:

♦ Use the smallest datatype possible (smallint rather than int)—small datatypes take up less space.

♦ Use numerics rather than strings—numerics compare faster.

♦ Use fixed-length character and binary datatypes rather than their variable-length relatives—fixed-length datatypes require less overhead. However, if the fixed-length field adds appreciably to the size of most rows, the variable-length datatype is going to be better.

TABLE 8.5 Datatype Sizes

Category	Datatype	Size
Character	char(n)	n
	varchar	data size
	text(n)	0 or multiple of 2K (4k for Stratus)
Binary	binary(n)	n
	varbinary(n)	data size
	image	0 or multiple of 2K (4k for Stratus)
Exact Numeric: Integers	int	4
	smallint	2
	tinyint	1
Exact Numeric: Decimals	numeric, decimal	2-17, depending on precision & scale
Approximate Numeric	double precision	8
	float (precision)	4 or 8, depending on precision
	real	4
Money	money	8
	smallmoney	4
Datetime	datetime	8
	smalldatetime	4
Bit	bit	1
	text/image	>=16 +2K (minimum)
Timestamp	timestamp	8

♦ Choose matching datatypes (down to null not-null status) for join partners—if SQL Server has to convert datatypes on one side in a join, it can't use an index on that join.

All columns that allow null values are handled as variable-length columns.

♦ For character and binary columns, SQL Server translates them internally into varchar and varbinary columns. Joining a char not null column to a char null column requires a char-varchar conversion.
♦ For other datatypes, null does not present these problems. However, there is increased overhead in data storage. SQL Server documentation gives information on how to calculate these values.

User-defined datatypes allow you to create datatypes based on system datatypes and null status, and apply them to any number of columns. Create the datatypes before you create tables that will use them. Here are examples for name columns (authors, employees, customers, managers):

```
EXEC sp_addtype 'nametype', 'varchar(20)', 'not null'
go
EXEC sp_addtype 'initialtype', 'varchar(1)', 'null'
go
```

In a create table statement, they'd look like this:

```
CREATE TABLE employees
(
fname nametype,
lname nametype,
initial initialtype,
...
)
go
```

You can note null status, but be careful—you can override the user datatype null status by spelling out a conflicting one in the CREATE TABLE statement.

```
CREATE TABLE employees
(
fname nametype NOT NULL,
lname nametype NOT NULL,
initial initialtype NULL,
...
)
go
```

If you create defaults and rules as separate objects, you can bind them to user-defined datatypes, so that the default for order dates and ship dates is today's date.

Null Status

As you create tables, explicitly specify null or not null status for each column, both to clarify your own thinking and make your work easily understood. If you don't specify null status, SQL Server uses the default not null. However, since the default can be set, with **sp-dboption** or the SET statement, the meaning of a CREATE TABLE script that does not specify null status can change dramatically and mysteriously.

In the logical design stages, you made preliminary decisions about which columns should be null. At this point, you may want to reconsider your decisions in light of physical implications. Since character and binary columns that allow nulls are treated as varchar and varbinary, define them that way explicitly and check join partners for such columns. Wherever possible, join columns should have the same datatype, including null status. Otherwise, SQL Server will perform conversions. User-defined datatypes can help you enforce datatype consistency.

Defaults and Default Constraints

You can create a default (today's date) for order dates with the CREATE DEFAULT-**sp_bindefault** combination or in the CREATE TABLE statement. Either way, you begin by defining any user datatypes you will need in the table definition.

```
EXEC sp_addtype 'datetype', 'smalldatetime', 'not null'
go
```

For the first solution, the table definition is simple.

```
CREATE TABLE orders
(
order# numeric(6,0) IDENTITY,
customer# ssntype NOT NULL,
orderdate datetype NOT NULL
)
go
```

To put a default into effect, you create it and then bind it to a specific column or (as here) to a user-defined datatype.

```
CREATE DEFAULT datedefault AS getdate()
go
EXEC sp_bindefault 'datedefault', 'datetype'
go
```

To do the same with a constraint, include it in the create table command.

```
CREATE TABLE orders
(
order#       numeric(6,0)                          IDENTITY,
customer#    ssntype                               NOT NULL,
orderdate    datetype        default getdate()     NOT NULL
)
go
```

Rules and Check Constraints

Rule creation follows a similar process. These statements create a rule that limits acceptable input for a column and binds the rule to a particular column.

```
CREATE TABLE products
(
product#         numeric(7,0)        IDENTITY,
name             varchar(20)         NOT NULL,
type             varchar(8)          NULL,
description      varchar(50)         NULL,
weight           decimal(6,2)        NOT NULL,
price            smallmoney          NOT NULL,
supplier#        suppltype           NULL
)
go

CREATE RULE typerule
AS @type IN ('appl', 'book', 'edu', 'game', 'hardware', 'supply')
go
EXEC sp_bindrule 'typerule', 'products.type'
go
```

To include the rule in the CREATE TABLE statement, as a check constraint, try this:

```
CREATE TABLE products
(
product#      numeric(7,0)        IDENTITY,
name          varchar(20)         NOT NULL,
type          varchar(8)          NULL
       CONSTRAINT typeck CHECK (type IN ('appl', 'book', 'edu',
       'game', 'hardware', 'supply')),
description   varchar(50)         NULL,
weight        decimal(6,2)        NOT NULL,
price         smallmoney          NOT NULL,
supplier#     suppltype           NULL
)
go
```

Naming a constraint (here "typeck") is not required. However, it makes your work easier if you need to change a constraint. You could write the constraint code as:

```
CREATE TABLE products
(
product#      numeric(7,0)        IDENTITY,
name          varchar(20)         NOT NULL,
type          varchar(8)          NULL
       CHECK (type IN ('appl', 'book', 'edu',
       'game', 'hardware', 'supply')),
description   varchar(50)         NULL,
weight        decimal(6,2)        NOT NULL,
```

```
price       smallmoney          NOT NULL,
supplier#   suppltype           NULL
)
go
```

Table-level CHECK constraints can compare two columns in the same table. A rule cannot handle this situation. To make sure that the ship date is never earlier than the order date, create the orders table with a CHECK constraint like this:

```
CREATE TABLE orders
(
order#      numeric(6,0)                        IDENTITY,
customer#   ssntype                             NOT NULL,
orderdate   datetype     DEFAULT getdate()      NOT NULL,
shipdate    datetype                            NOT NULL,
CONSTRAINT datecnstr CHECK (shipdate >= orderdate)
)
go
```

Integrity Constraints

Reference constraints, foreign key constraints, triggers, and stored procedures are mechanisms to protect data integrity. Reference and foreign key constraints, like other constraints, are specified in the CREATE TABLE command. Triggers and stored procedures are created with Transact-SQL CREATE TRIGGER and CREATE PROCEDURE statements. Trigger and stored procedure code can use Transact-SQL procedural extensions that allow logic such as IF-THEN, WHILE, RETURN, and GOTO LABEL. Since you can create code in modules, you can use the same pieces over and over again with procedure calls. Integrity constraints in the create table statement are less flexible and powerful.

Foreign Key and Reference Constraints

Reference constraints ensure that a column value exists in another table. For example, the order number in the orderlines table must match a unique order number in the orders table. In this example, the uniqueness of the order number in the orders table is guaranteed by declaring it a primary key (more about this in the index section). The orderlines CREATE TABLE statement includes a references clause.

```
CREATE TABLE orders
(
order#          numeric(6,0)                        IDENTITY
        CONSTRAINT pko# PRIMARY KEY,
customer#       ssntype                    NOT NULL,
orderdate       datetype        default getdate()   NOT NULL,
shipdate        datetype                   NOT NULL,
CONSTRAINT datecnstr CHECK (shipdate >= orderdate)
)
go


CREATE TABLE orderlines
(
order#          numeric(6,0)         NOT NULL
        REFERENCES orders(order#),
product#        numeric(7,0)     NOT NULL,
unit            smallint         NOT NULL
)
go
```

For references to multicolumn keys, use the table-level references syntax. Each multicolumn key must have a unique index.

```
CREATE TABLE hiorderlines
(
order#          numeric(6,0)     NOT NULL,
product#        numeric(7,0)     NOT NULL,
unit            smallint         NOT NULL,
        CONSTRAINT hiolfk FOREIGN KEY(order#, product#)
                REFERENCES orderlines(order#, product#)
)
go
```

Stored procedures allow you to control user actions and improve performance. Generally speaking, you deny the user access to underlying tables and force queries and updates through stored procedures. The stored procedure has its own permission system, separate from underlying tables. Since stored procedures are parsed and resolved on creation, they run faster than individual statements. They also reduce network traffic.

Users must execute stored procedures to perform the tasks the stored procedures handle, but triggers fire automatically. They are activated by INSERT, DELETE, or UPDATE actions on a table and exist outside the permission structure. No one, not even the sa, can stop a trigger from firing, except by removing it. A trigger is the final defense of data integrity.

Both triggers and stored procedures offer performance advantages.

♦ They reduce network traffic. The actual code is stored on SQL Server: The client passes only the command.

- ◆ They run faster than independent statements because they are parsed on creation and compiled on first execution.

Stored Procedures

System procedures are examples of how you can use stored procedures. Stored procedures allow you to:

- ◆ Create reusable reports (**sp_depends**, **sp_helptext**)
- ◆ Steer users through multistep operations (**sp_configure**, **sp_dboption**)
- ◆ Enforce referential integrity (**sp_adduser**)
- ◆ Prevent direct changes to critical tables (**sp_addtype**, **sp_bindrule**)

A simple CREATE PROCEDURE statement looks like this:

```
CREATE PROCEDURE tally
AS
SELECT orderdate, count(order#)
FROM orders
GROUP BY orderdate
RETURN
go
```

You run a procedure with the execute statement:

```
EXECUTE tally
go
EXEC tally
go
```

If it's the first statement in a batch, you can just give the procedure name.

```
tally
go
```

Stored procedures run quickly because they are precompiled. See Chapter 9 for more information.

Stored procedures can prevent illegal entries by checking for the correct number and type of entries, and a value that exists in another table (customer# in the orders table must exist in the customer table).

Triggers

Each table can have up to three triggers, one each on insert, update, and delete. Base triggers on your business rules. How do you handle changes to primary keys, such as product number? What do you do about modifications to foreign keys? Actions include, but are not limited to, what is described in Table 8.6.

You can handle some, but not all, of these situations with constraints in the CREATE TABLE statement.

Triggers can:

♦ Check data validity (a customer number in a new order matches one in the customer table)
♦ Cascade a change through the database (discontinue one product and substitute another for it in all orders starting today)
♦ Cancel or roll back illegal changes (don't delete a customer who has outstanding orders)
♦ Enforce complex rules (sales are not allowed on holidays unless the customer is an employee and the product is on the holiday special list)
♦ Perform calculations or make comparisons and take steps based on the results (keep totals up-to-date, give a discount to customers with orders over some amount)

Triggers typically roll back a transaction if it is not appropriate. A simple trigger, forbidding all deletes to the customers table, looks like this:

```
CREATE TRIGGER deltrig
ON customer
FOR DELETE
AS
BEGIN
      PRINT "You cannot delete rows from this table."
      ROLLBACK TRANSACTION
END
go
```

TABLE 8.6 Trigger Actions

Action	Primary key	Foreign key
INSERT	Make sure it is unique (in most cases you'd use a unique index for this)	Validate it against primary key
DELETE	Keep it as long as there is related information *or* Delete it and archive related information *or* Delete it and all related information (cascade delete) *or* Delete it and flag matching values in other tables	No integrity implications
UPDATE	Change all the matching values in other tables *or* Forbid changes to primary keys *or* Change and archive old values	Validate new value against primary key

You could accomplish the same end by denying all users delete permission on the table.

Triggers use the conceptual *inserted* and *deleted* tables to perform comparisons and make decisions (see Table 8.7). The rows in the inserted and deleted tables have the same structure as the rows in the target table. Updates with triggers are handled as deletes followed by inserts, so rows are stored in both tables. (When no trigger is involved, an update is sometimes done "in place." See the sections on update mode in your system manuals for more information.) For insert, the row is added to both the target table and the *inserted* table. For deletes, the row is removed from the target table and stored in the *deleted* table. For updates, the row is changed in the target table. The original version of the row is held in *deleted* and the new version in *inserted*.

Sybase manuals give examples of code using the two tables.

Here's a trigger that cascades a delete from the master table (orders) to the detail table (orderlines) using the deleted table. Integrity constraints in the **CREATE TABLE** command cannot handle this kind of action.

```
CREATE TRIGGER orddeltrg
ON orders
FOR DELETE
AS
DELETE orderlines
FROM orderlines ol, deleted d
WHERE ol.order# =d.order#
go
```

Triggers can also move data from one table to another. This example handles deletes from the products table. It rolls back the delete if there are outstanding orders for the product and archives the rows in another table if there are no orders.

```
CREATE TRIGGER proddeltrg
ON products
FOR DELETE
AS
```

TABLE 8.7 *inserted* and *deleted* Tables

Action	*Target Table*	**inserted** *Table*	**deleted** *Table*
INSERT	New row added	New row added	
DELETE	Row removed		Pre-delete row added
UPDATE	Row changed	Post-update row added	Pre-update row added

```
IF @@rowcount =0
      RETURN
ELSE
      IF EXISTS
      (SELECT * FROM deleted d, orderlines ol
      WHERE d.product#=ol.product#
      AND shipdate IS NULL)
      BEGIN
            RAISERROR ("There are outstanding orders. Delete rolled
            back", 16, -1)
            ROLLBACK TRANSACTION
      END
ELSE
      INSERT INTO oldproduct
      SELECT * FROM deleted
go
```

When you design triggers, look at the database or application as a whole. You'll probably see some overlapping needs, where you can use the same code. You'll also get ideas of how action on one integrity constraint might affect others. Table 8.8 shows how you might analyze your needs for one table.

Since triggers are critical to data integrity, it's important to test them very thoroughly before putting them in place.

Creating Indexes

Unindexed data is stored as heaps and accessed by table scans. Indexes help locate data for retrievals. They are also useful for data modification commands in that they find the row you want to change. But indexes also need SQL Server maintenance. As you add, delete, and update rows, the index pages may change, depending on the kind of indexes you have and how full the pages are. Index upkeep can slow performance. You can create indexes as part of a CREATE TABLE statement or separately, with CREATE INDEX statements.

TABLE 8.8 Trigger Design

Table	Change	Trigger Action
orders	insert row	check customer# against customers table
		generate new order#
	delete row	cascade delete to orderlines table
	update order#	forbid: force delete + insert

Types of Indexes

There are two types of indexes: clustered and nonclustered. Either can be created as unique. Clustered and nonclustered indexes are both b-tree structures, but there are important differences between them.

The bottom level of a clustered index is the actual data. Rows are stored in index order. This means you can have only one clustered index per table, because rows can have one physical order. A clustered index does not add significantly to the size of the table. A 10-byte index on a 100-byte table adds 1 to 2 percent to the table size (see Figure 8.6).

Nonclustered indexes, on the other hand, point to the data: The physical order of the data has no particular relationship to a nonclustered index. You can have as many as 249 nonclustered indexes per table. A nonclustered index tends to be about one level deeper than a clustered index and adds a significant amount of space. A 10-byte nonclustered index on a table with 100-byte rows adds about 20 percent to the total size of a table (see Figure 8.7).

Because of their structures, clustered and nonclustered indexes have different interactions with queries and data modification statements (see Table 8.9). Properly designed indexes greatly aid data retrievals. Clustered indexes determine the physical order of data, so when rows are added or deleted, the clustered index changes too; these modifications can be expensive. Nonclustered index changes prompted by data modifications are usually less radical. In designing your indexes, you have to weigh the frequency and importance of queries against inserts, updates, and deletes. Of course, tables usually have more than one index, and you have to consider indexes in that context, too.

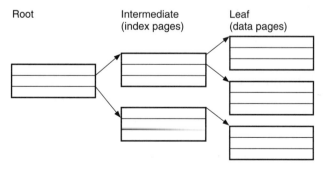

FIGURE 8.6 Clustered index.

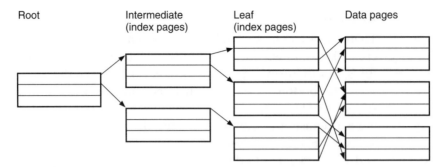

Root   Intermediate   Leaf   Data pages
          (index pages)   (index pages)

FIGURE 8.7 Nonclustered index.

What Should You Index?

Indexes are the single best tool for performance. To determine which indexes to create, you need to understand the logical design, know which queries and data modification commands users will run, and have some idea of how often these will run.

In some instances—often decision support environments—you don't know what the queries are or the mix of queries. You can still make sensible decisions in this case. Start by considering indexes on primary keys and foreign keys. If this is too many (say, more than about three per table), back off on some that are not likely to be used. You will refine these choices as you test and tune.

Strive for a level of acceptable overall database performance before you solve individual problems. Here are some more specific guidelines.

Index all primary keys.

Typically, many transactions reference primary keys. If you have a primary key that is seldom used in a query (you have a surrogate key) and its uniqueness is guaranteed by some external mechanism, consider removing the index on it. But remember: The only way to guarantee uniqueness is with a unique index.

Index all foreign keys.

Foreign keys, except for foreign keys to lookup tables, should be indexed. Foreign keys commonly appear in WHERE clauses in queries. If all foreign keys and primary keys have indexes, the query optimizer can consider executing the join in either direction, that is:

1. By first finding each row in the primary table and then using the foreign key index to find the corresponding rows in the foreign table.

TABLE 8.9 Index Access Implications

Command	Nonclustered	Clustered
SELECT	◆ Speeds search ◆ Makes no changes to index or data pages	◆ Speeds search ◆ Makes no changes to index or data pages
INSERT	◆ No help in search for data location; insert goes to last page if there is no clustered index ◆ Adds new pointer on index page ◆ Adds pointers in other nonclustered indexes pointing to new row	◆ Speeds search for data location ◆ Reorganizes data and possibly index pages to make room for new row ◆ Updates associated nonclustered indexes ◆ If page splits, adds new page and changes nonclustered indexes affected by the split
DELETE	◆ Speeds search ◆ Removes pointer from index page ◆ Removes pointers for other nonclustered indexes pointing to deleted row	◆ Speeds search ◆ Reorganizes data and possibly index pages to remove deleted row ◆ Updates associated nonclustered indexes ◆ If row is last on page, page is deallocated
UPDATE	◆ Speeds search ◆ Reorganizes index pages if row is deleted from one page and inserted in another	◆ Speeds search ◆ Requires index changes for split or removed pages

2. By first finding each row in the foreign table and then using the primary table index to find the corresponding rows in the primary table.

If there are too many indexes on a given table, consider not putting indexes on foreign keys to lookup tables. There is a good chance that the query plan will find the selected rows in the principal tables and then locate the matching rows in the lookup tables.

Index both sides of common joins.

For common joins, consider creating an index on the appropriate columns of both tables. In a given query, the optimizer will use the index on one table or the other. Having both lets the query optimizer choose the most efficient access order for the specific query. Make sure, however, you don't end up with too many indexes.

Index columns often used in range queries, sorts, and grouping.

Indexes can give you an advantage in all these areas.

Index primary keys for uniqueness.

A primary key implies that all rows must have a unique value in the primary key column or columns. With SQL Server, you can ensure this by creating a unique index on the primary key columns. A unique index is no more costly than a non-unique index.

Index for uniqueness whenever index columns are unique.

There is no penalty for using uniqueness in indexes. If the columns of an index must be unique, explicitly make the index unique. It'll ensure uniqueness and help the optimizer. For example, if a column or group of columns is labeled as unique and a query calls for an equality match with a column in another table, at most one row in this table will match. This knowledge is particularly useful when the optimizer evaluates the order to process a join.

Index columns that "cover" common queries.

If the information is in a nonclustered index and you don't need to read the data pages, access can be very fast.

At this point, note possible sites for indexes, as shown in Table 8.10. Then review them against the "Don't" rules following.

Don't have more than three to five indexes on a table.

If you have more than this many indexes on a table, the disadvantages of indexes start outweighing the advantages.

♦ The overhead of updating the indexes becomes large.
♦ The chances that a given index will be used gets diminished.

TABLE 8.10 Refined Table Example with Index Requirements

Column	Datatype	User Datatype	Null Status	Other	Index
product#	numeric	numtype	not null	must be unique	unique, primary key
name	varchar(20)	nametype	not null		sorts? single row matches
type	varchar		not null		few types
notes	varchar(200)		null		
price	smallmoney		not null		matches, range searches?
weight	decimal		not null		
supplier#	numeric	numtype	not null	must exist in supplier entity	foreign key, limited number of rows in supplier table

♦ Symmetric multiprocessor versions of SQL Server (starting with Release 4.8) provide increased throughput which exacerbates lock contention problems when updating rows in tables with multiple indexes.

Don't create compound indexes (indexes on two or more columns) with columns in any old order.

Make sure the first column of the index has high selectivity (does not have a large percentage of duplicates). Since SQL Server only keeps distribution statistics on the first column of an index, the query optimizer gets more information if that first column is highly selective. This is especially true of a nonclustered index.

Don't index tables with fewer than about five pages.

A table this size will usually remain in cache and will require fewer than five reads to find the matching rows, so the query optimizer won't use the index. Of course, you may still want to index for uniqueness.

Don't create indexes that won't be used (except for ensuring uniqueness).

Indexes require time and space. SQL Server must maintain every index each time you add rows to the table; each interesting nonclustered index may add 20 percent to the table's size.

Clustered or Nonclustered?

Now that you have an idea of what columns to index, decide if the indexes should be clustered or non-clustered.

Clustered

A clustered index is your single best index and you only have one per table. All tables except very small ones should have a clustered index! Almost any query that references the column with a clustered index will find it useful.

In addition, clustered indexes lead to more compact space use. A table with no clustered index is stored as a heap, or chain of pages, with all new rows added to the last page (or to a new page after the last page). As rows are deleted, they are removed from their locations, and you end up with a table that looks like Swiss cheese. Adding a clustered index will reorganize the table, remove the holes, and result in fewer pages. You'll do best by putting the clustered index on a column or set of columns that is updated relatively randomly. If you pick a column like order_date, where you mostly add rows for the current date and delete some older rows, you'll develop a *hotspot* (a location that many users access) and grow Swiss cheese again.

Choose a clustered index when you often:

- ◆ Use the column in queries or joins and performance is important.
- ◆ Use the column in range queries (date >= 1/1/90 and date <= 1/1/91). Clustered indexes are much faster than nonclustered indexes in range queries.
- ◆ Use the column in order-by queries. Here again, clustered indexes are much better than nonclustered ones.
- ◆ Request a single row (i.e., equality match on all columns of a unique index). A clustered index is slightly faster than a nonclustered index.
- ◆ Need to distribute data randomly.

Primary keys on most tables need indexes, but clustered indexes may not be the best choice. Weigh the frequency of queries and joins involving the primary key against those selecting a range of values or an ordered set, where nonclustered indexes are not very useful. Consider a table (such as authors) with authors' names and social security numbers. The social security number is the primary key, but you will seldom look for social security numbers between 111111111 and 111223333 or list them in ascending order. However, these range and sort queries will probably be common on the name column.

When accessing a single row, a nonclustered index is just one read worse than a clustered index. Many accesses against a primary key are in fact single row accesses (searching for a particular social security number, for example). Use the powerful clustered index where it does the most good and put a unique nonclustered index on the primary key.

Avoid creating clustered indexes on a serial field, date field, or other field that has activity clustered around certain pages of the table when there is heavy insert activity. If you have a clustered index on one of these fields or no clustered indexes, all inserts and many updates will try to access the same page. This will cause lock contention problems. It may help to create a clustered index on something else (a user-id field, a region code) that will help to spread the access across the table. On the other hand, if the column is mostly used in range or sort queries, a clustered index can be very useful. In choosing the clustered index for a table, pick the column (or group of columns) that has the physical ordering most often used.

Nonclustered

You can have up to 249 nonclustered indexes, but beware of too many! Indexes take up room, take time to maintain, and slow down update performance. Use a nonclustered index when you:

◆ Request a single row (equality match on all columns of a unique index). The clustered index is only a little faster than the nonclustered in this case. If you've used the clustered index elsewhere, a nonclustered index is useful for this kind of query.

◆ Can take advantage of index covering. If all the columns of a table required to satisfy a query are in a nonclustered index and the search argument matches the nonclustered index, then the index *covers* the query. The query may be satisfied by reading only the index pages. If there is a composite nonclustered index on product name and id and supplier # in the products table, both these queries are covered.

```
SELECT supplier#
FROM products
WHERE name = "gizmo" AND product# = 9977236
go

SELECT name, product#
FROM products
WHERE supplier# = 78
go
```

The first query is more efficient because the leading index item is in the WHERE clause, but the second also benefits. A covering nonclustered index will work with aggregate queries (if grouped or grouping columns are in the index) and order by queries. Index coverage may help you even if the first column of the nonclustered index doesn't show up in the WHERE clause. Consider:

```
SELECT count(name)
FROM products
go
```

SQL Server can do this by counting the number of leaf index entries in the name, product#, supplier# nonclustered index which have a non-null name. SELECT count(*) FROM products will also do this. To cover common queries, consider adding columns to an index, but be careful that the index doesn't get too wide.

◆ Need more than one index on a table. Since you're only allowed one clustered index, use it where it will do the most good, and put nonclustered indexes on other columns you often access. This may include the primary key.

◆ Need to ensure uniqueness, but retrieval performance is not critical or the clustered index has been used elsewhere. Use a unique nonclustered index.

Don't use a nonclustered index if more than about five percent of the rows have to be read. SQL Server will generally do a table scan rather than use a nonclustered index to satisfy the query. The same is true of range and sort queries. SQL Server will often not use a nonclustered index for these queries.

Planning Indexes

Review your index notes. After looking at the queries and reports in your requirements document, make decisions about the kind of indexes you need for each table. If you do a lot of sorts and range retrievals based on price, you might end up choosing the three indexes shown in Table 8.11.

If you usually retrieve product rows with both product number and product name in the WHERE clause, you could use a single unique composite index (name, product#) on those fields, ending up with two indexes instead of the three, as shown in Table 8.12.

Syntax

You can create indexes in the CREATE TABLE or CREATE INDEX statement. The CREATE TABLE does not allow non-unique indexes, but otherwise the methods have the same capabilities. Here's how you would build a unique nonclustered index on the product name-product number combination with a CREATE TABLE command.

TABLE 8.11 Refined Table Example with Indexes Defined

Column	Datatype	User Datatype	Null Status	Other	Index	Index Notes
product#	numeric	numtype	not null	must be unique	unique nonclustered	unique, primary key
name	varchar(20)	nametype	not null		nonclustered	sorts? single row matches
type	varchar		not null			few types
notes	varchar(200)		null			
price	smallmoney		not null		clustered	matches, range searches?
weight	decimal		not null			
supplier#	numeric	numtype	not null	must exist in supplier entity		foreign key, limited number of rows in supplier table

TABLE 8.12 Alternate Index Definition

Column	Datatype	User Datatype	Null Status	Other	Index	Index Notes
product#	numeric	numtype	not null	must be unique	unique nonclustered index on name, product#	unique, primary key
name	varchar(20)	nametype	not null		(see product#)	sorts? single row matches
price	smallmoney		not null		clustered	matches, range searches?

```
CREATE TABLE products
(
product#       numeric(7,0)        IDENTITY,
name           varchar(20)         NOT NULL,
type           varchar(8)          NULL
        CHECK (type IN ('appl', 'book', 'edu',
        'game', 'hardware', 'supply')),
description    varchar(50)         NULL,
weight         decimal (6,2)       NOT NULL,
price          smallmoney          NOT NULL,
supplier#      suppltype           NULL,
CONSTRAINT prodix UNIQUE NONCLUSTERED (name, product#)
)
go
```

You can remove unique and primary key constraints with the **ALTER TABLE** statement only. To add indexes on existing columns, use the **CREATE INDEX** command.

The **CREATE INDEX** statements for handling the indexes separately are:

```
CREATE UNIQUE NONCLUSTERED INDEX prodix
ON products (name, product#)
go


CREATE CLUSTERED INDEX priceix
ON products(price)
go
```

You can remove these indexes with the **DROP INDEX** command.

Good Index Practices

Choosing and creating indexes is just the first step. As you select indexes, record your rationale. This will save you time later when you need to revisit the indexes. Plan to test indexes. The only practical way to find out if an index is actually used is to SET SHOWPLAN ON and look at the query plans for those using the indexed columns.

A PLETHORA OF DEADLOCKS

We were out-of-town getting some technical training. We received a call from our office. A customer had a critical problem with performance and deadlocks on a system that had to go live immediately. When could we look at the problem? We were pretty busy, but thought we could get them started on research and the problem resolution and we'd be back in a couple of days to finish the problem.

We talked to the customer. They had constructed an OLTP SQL Server-based application and put it through testing. It was a customer support application that had to run with about 100 users simultaneously. Their testing had gone pretty well. How many users did they test for? Not enough, as it turns out. When they took it live, the system got very slow, generated lots of deadlocks, and then came to a virtual halt. The users gave up after two days and refused to use the application. The IS team was under pressure to get the system live.

They had been working three days on debugging the problem, but weren't making any progress. They were new to SQL Server and the development environment and, though they knew which tables were deadlocking, they couldn't track where the deadlocks were coming from.

We asked our office to request the following from the customer:

◆ The complete database design extracted from the database, not the scripts they thought they'd run
◆ A picture of the schema
◆ Data volumes for the tables involved
◆ The source code for all of the procedures that modified the tables involved

The customer did not have the capability to extract the definition of the database from the live database, but we knew another department at his company that did have that ability and we put them in touch.

The customer was anxious and managed to collect and fax this information to our offices who forwarded it to our hotel. It was there when we returned from dinner with a customer. We began to study the database definition extracted from the database. (We're nuts. We think these puzzles are fun to work on even at midnight.) We focused in on the tables involved in the deadlocks. It didn't take long to find the problem. One of the tables had 26 indexes. It turned out that the customer had not been able to look at the extracted database definition, but had depended on the scripts generated by a database development tool. The index names were strange and clearly generated by a tool. But there were two identical sets of 13 indexes. Somehow, using the database tool they had managed to generate a duplicate set of differently named indexes.

The problem was that the indexes were deadlocking themselves. It is not reasonable for 100 users to make modifications to a table that has so many indexes. It will deadlock. The update of every row has to update all 26 indexes. This traversing of so many multiple index structures will eventually cause the UPDATEs to deadlock on the indexes.

Watch what your helpful development tools do for you. You must be in control and you must be able to look at the results. In this example, the developers would have solved the problem themselves if they had been able to see what was actually in the database as opposed to what they thought was in the database.

In reality, 13 indexes is too many. Keep it to 3 to 5 unless you have a compelling reason and understand the consequences.

Planning Capacity

Once you have a preliminary physical design for your application, you can consider how much space it will require. You can project sizes for tables, indexes, databases, and transaction logs.

When you create the database, you specify the database size and log size (if you put it on a separate device, which you should) in the CREATE DATABASE command. It's important to have some idea of how large you want the database to be before you execute the command. It's relatively easy to make the database and log larger (with the ALTER DATABASE command) but more complicated to make it smaller.

To create a 100 Mb bigbiz database with a 20 Mb log on a separate database device, the command looks like this:

```
CREATE DATABASE bigbiz
ON datadev=100
LOG ON logdev=20
go
```

Estimating Table and Index Size

Sybase provides the **sp_estspace** stored procedure to estimate table and index size. It bases its guesses on information in system tables, rather than on the actual data. Since you want to know about how big a database will be before creating it,

- ♦ Create tables and indexes (but add no data) in a "spare" database
- ♦ Run **sp_estspace** once for each table, providing the table name and your estimate of the number of rows the table will have as parameters
- ♦ Total the values and analyze the results
- ♦ Drop the tables and indexes

Here's what you'd type to get the size of the products table, with two indexes and 10,000 rows:

```
EXEC sp_estspace products, 10000
go
```

name	type	idx_level	Pages	Kbytes
products	data	0	333	667
prodix	clustered	0	5	8
prodix	clustered	1	1	2

```
priceix                    nonclustered          0          56          112
priceix                    nonclustered          1           1            2


Total_Mbytes
----------------
          0.77
```

The output shows the space the data and each level of each index occupy. For a larger table (100,000 rows), you get more levels of index: two for the clustered index and three for the nonclustered.

```
        EXEC sp_estspace products, 100000
          go
name                        type         idx_level Pages        Kbytes
----------------------      ------------ --------- ------------ ----------
products                    data              0         3324         6649
prodix                      clustered         0           40           80
prodix                      clustered         1            1            2
priceix                     nonclustered      0          553         1106
priceix                     nonclustered      1            5           10
priceix                     nonclustered      2            1            2


Total_Mbytes
----------------
          7.66
```

Since a database is more than the sum of its tables, add more space for:

♦ Stored procedures, defaults, rules, and triggers you plan to create (include a factor for object text and procedure plan space in system tables)

♦ Expanding system tables (additional logins and user accounts, more rows in sysobjects, etc.)

Comparing the size of new and mature databases at your site may give you some ideas on what the non-table space fudge factor is. The figures you get in **sp_estspace** are estimates only, of course. More parameters are available. For more precise information, see the Sybase manuals. The *Performance and Tuning Guide* has a section on predicting the size of a table and its indexes.

Sizing the Transaction Log

You specify the size of the transaction log in the CREATE DATABASE command LOG ON option or (when allocating additional space for the database) in the ALTER DATABASE command LOG ON option.

Determining the transaction log's size depends on a number of things; there are no crisp guidelines on how big it should be. A good first guess is between 10 percent and 25 percent of the size of the database.

If the transaction log is not large enough, you will get an error message when the server attempts to do the next logged activity. If that happens on a regular basis, you should increase the size of the transaction log. These factors impact the log size:

♦ A transaction that makes many changes. Until SQL Server completes that transaction, all its transaction log entries must remain in the transaction log, even if the database owner does a DUMP TRANSACTION or has the TRUNC. LOG ON CHKPT. option turned on.

♦ A transaction that runs for a long time. Until SQL Server completes that transaction, all transaction log entries subsequent to the beginning of this transaction (even transaction log entries for other transactions) must remain in the transaction log, even if the database owner does a DUMP TRANSACTION or has the TRUNC. LOG ON CHKPT. option turned on.

♦ Multiple transactions.

Put the log on a separate database device to prevent competition with other objects and allow use of the Enterprise Manager and Performance Monitor to trigger dumps. A separate physical disk is a better choice yet—it improves performance and allows full recovery if there is a failure on the database disk.

Tuning the Application

The tuning phase is for zeroing in on particular problems. Once you've got the database working and have met or approached your overall goals, look for specific areas where you're not getting the performance you need. Changes you can make include:

♦ Modifying logical and physical design
♦ Examining your indexes
♦ Changing data storage and distribution

Where you start depends on your application and specific problems. The best performance comes from sound database design and appropriate indexes. Placement of objects can also have some effect.

Modifying Design: DSS versus OLTP

Decision support systems (DSS) and online transaction processing systems (OLTP) have different requirements for table structure, indexes, and physical storage. You may need to modify your database design to get the performance you need.

Decision support systems often support long-running queries that analyze some portion of the database and produce reports and summary information. This means a large number of analysis queries or reports and relatively few data modification commands. DSS applications move many pages through the data cache, which can reduce performance of OLTP transactions running on the same SQL Server.

When tuning for DSSs, it makes sense to:

♦ Add extra indexes to speed SELECT statements (but usually keep the total per table below five).

♦ Selectively denormalize tables (reduce the number of tables and increase the number of columns in each table) so that you can access commonly retrieved information without excessive joins. Use this technique with caution and only as a solution to a specific problem! Remember that normalization produces narrow rows and increases your opportunities for indexes. Careless denormalization can lead to slower performance and data integrity problems.

Characteristically, an OLTP system has many small transactions, mostly involving changes to the data. Because of this, it requires sophisticated data integrity protections, generally resulting in a large number of joins, as foreign keys are checked against primary keys. Each transaction typically must be very fast (sub-second response time). Many users need to make changes simultaneously, so there are multiple on-line connections and significant disk input/output.

For OLTP applications:

♦ Have indexes targeted precisely for the actions you want to perform (but not too many—each additional index increases the amount of work for data modification transactions).

♦ Adjust the table design so each transaction affects only a small number of tables. The application code needs to minimize how much each transaction does and how long the transaction takes.

Never Tune "In General"

Applications are seldom 100 percent DSS or OLTP. When you tune, you consider the whole application, but you make changes in particular areas. Each time you tune one activity to improve its performance, you slow something else down. If you do not understand the side effects of your actions, you can make things worse. Test after each change and assess its effect on the activity in question and the application as a whole.

Keep notes on you actions and their results. If overall performance suddenly degrades, you want to know why.

Denormalization

Denormalization implies normalization, so unless you know your application extremely well, normalize first and denormalize only with cause—and then conservatively. Create and prototype the entire application (or complete segments of it) before you measure performance of particular parts. Identify critical transactions and

- ♦ Required response time
- ♦ Frequency of execution
- ♦ Number of users
- ♦ Size of data set and physical distribution
- ♦ Particular periods of use
- ♦ Participating tables, columns, and associated integrity constraints

When denormalization is effective, it allows you to speed retrievals by cutting down on the number of some or all of relevant tables, rows, joins, indexes, and on-the-fly computations.

But beware! Even as denormalization makes retrievals faster, it may slow data modifications. It's likely to introduce data integrity issues and complicate application maintenance. You'll want to review these areas as your application grows and changes.

Denormalization techniques include:

- ♦ Splitting tables
- ♦ Merging tables
- ♦ Copying columns from one table into another (data duplication)
- ♦ Adding columns for reverse indexing
- ♦ Creating derived columns for calculated data
- ♦ Using summary columns (existence counts, aggregates)
- ♦ Adding inter-row derived data columns
- ♦ Creating new tables to short-cut paths among indirect relationships

Splitting Tables

There are two kinds of table splits, horizontal and vertical. (Supertype-subtype splits are a special type of vertical split.) Both can improve performance under certain circumstances and both make your application more complex. In either case, you trade one large table for two or more smaller ones (see Figure 8.8).

You accomplish this for horizontal splits either by segmenting the table so that one table contains the most commonly accessed rows and the other contains the rest of the rows or copying some parts of the table so that one table contains the most commonly accessed rows and the second contains *all* the rows.

For vertical splits, the technique is applied to columns instead of to rows. You either divide the table so that one table contains the most commonly accessed columns and the other contains the rest of the columns or copy some parts of the table so that one table contains the most commonly accessed columns and the second contains *all* the columns.

Use table splitting with care. Make sure you understand why you are doing it and what you want to gain.

Horizontal

Use horizontal table splitting when

- ♦ Reducing a large table will reduce the number of index pages read.
- ♦ You can make a distinction in the kind of data, such as national and international accounts.
- ♦ You need to distribute the data physically.

Horizontal splitting can improve the statistics information in an index by dividing the table based on the values in an indexed attribute.

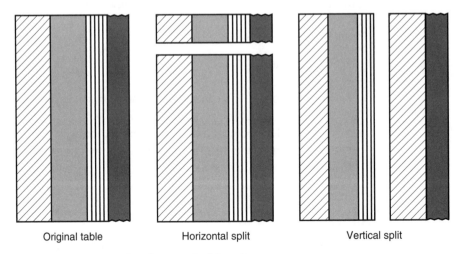

Original table   Horizontal split   Vertical split

FIGURE 8.8 Horizontal and vertical table splitting.

You might want to put authors who haven't written a book in the last five years in a separate table, since there will be few queries about them. Indexes on author names and id numbers will be more useful, and access to current authors will be faster. You'll still be able to get hold of information about inactive authors by querying the oldauthors table.

Administrators often use horizontal splitting to archive historical data when it is seldom queried. Maintaining two separate tables can be a headache; data that should be in one can show up in another, unless there are clear business rules (no new edition in the last three years; no new title in the last five) that dictate which table a row belongs in. If one of the segments contains a small proportion of the rows, and these rows are the active ones, horizontal splitting is a huge win. You may even find that the relevant rows stay in cache.

Vertical

Use vertical splitting when

- ◆ Common transactions frequently access a particular subset of table columns.
- ◆ The table has a very broad row, making it difficult to fit on data pages.
- ◆ A large number of optional fields exist in many rows.

Placing frequently-used columns in a separate table can make access much faster. For example, if most queries about books include title, price, and sales, move those columns into a separate table (add title_id) for joins). Keep the less-used information (type, publisher, advance, notes, etc.) in a *background* table. Finding critical information will be much faster, particularly because one of the background columns is notes, a varchar(250) column. The data pages for the new titles table are much narrower, so you will get many more rows per page.

Notice that two tables (titles and titles_bkgr) now have the same primary key (title_id). You'll have to introduce new integrity constraints to make sure that every row in one table has a matching row in the other, and that foreign keys are valid against both tables.

The subtype-supertype problem is a special case of vertical table splitting. Sometimes an individual thing has characteristics different from other things in a table. Consider city employees. Some are firefighters; these firefighters have attributes (badge numbers) you want to maintain—but other employees don't have badges. In this case, employee is a supertype, and firefighter is a subtype. You might represent this two ways:

- ◆ Make one table for the supertype and all its subtypes (all employees). The firefighter-specific **badge_no** is NULL for any employee who is not a fireman.

```
CREATE TABLE employee (
        lname           char(15) NOT NULL,
        fname           char(15) NOT NULL,
        emp_id          char(5) NOT NULL,
        badge_no        char(5) NULL)
go
```

♦ Make two tables: one for the supertype (employees) and one for the special features of the subtype (firefighter_badges). The nulls for **badge_no** are avoided, but you need an extra join to get information about firefighters. You'll also need to put logic in queries to check whether employees are firefighters.

```
CREATE TABLE employee (
        lname           char(15) NOT NULL,
        fname           char(15) NOT NULL,
        emp_id          char(5) NOT NULL)
go
CREATE TABLE firefighter_badges (
        emp_id          char(5) NOT NULL,
        badge_no        char(5) NOT NULL)
go
```

If you have many subtypes (firefighters with badges, police with guns, social workers with specialties, etc.) what do you do?

♦ Make one table for each subtype (n tables: firefighters, police, social workers, etc.) and eliminate the supertype.

```
CREATE TABLE police (
        lname           char(15) NOT NULL,
        fname           char(15) NOT NULL,
        emp_id          char(5) NOT NULL
        gun_id          int not null)
go
CREATE TABLE firefighters(
        lname           char(15) NOT NULL,
        fname           char(15) NOT NULL,
        emp_id          char(5) NOT NULL,
        badge_no        char(5) NOT NULL)
go
```

♦ Make one table for each subtype and one for the supertype ($n + 1$ tables).

The number of attributes in the supertypes and subtypes, the distribution of rows between the subtypes, and access to the tables influence your choice of strategy. You need to balance the danger of duplicate columns against improved performance.

The supertype-only solution, at best, has a few rows with nulls in one column. At worst, it results in long rows with many null columns, leading to large data and index pages. You may end up with many indexes (badge_no, gun_no, specialty) on the table. Both of these conditions can lead to poor performance.

The subtype-only solution works well when most of the attributes are subtype characteristics. You can keep the rows narrow and create good indexes. However, to get information on all employees, you'll need to look at many separate tables. It may be difficult to maintain consistent supertype characteristics.

The subtype-supertype combination is worth considering when attributes are divided evenly between subtype and supertype characteristics. Getting full information on employees will require joining the supertype and subtype tables (see Table 8.13).

It is possible to implement hybrid solutions; that is, you may put a number of subtypes into separate tables and combine others in a single table.

Merging Tables

When problem queries usually call for data from two tables, it may make sense to merge them into one. For example, if the most common report on book titles is on financial data—advances and royalties—you could collapse

TABLE 8.13 Subtypes and Supertypes

	Supertype table only	*Subtype tables only (one for each)*	*Supertype table & subtype tables*
# of Tables # of Attributes	1 table If most attributes belong to the supertype, keep one supertype table.	*n* tables If few attributes belong to the supertype, and many to the subtypes, create subtype tables only.	*n* + 1 tables If attributes are divided roughly equally between the supertype and the subtypes, create a supertype table and supporting subtype tables.
Distribution of Rows		If rows are unevenly distributed with many NULLs, use subtype tables or the supertype-subtype combination.	
Access to Tables	If access to the data is commonly from a mixture of subtypes, keep the data together.	If access to subtype data is independent, use separate subtype tables.	If access to subtype data is independent, or from more than one subtype, use the combination.

the titles and roysched tables into one table. The obvious problem here is the possibility of a very wide row. You may be able to accomplish your aims by duplicating one or two columns instead of merging tables.

Adding Columns for Duplicated Data

Joins can slow performance, particularly in commonly run reports. You can reduce the number of joins by duplicating attributes. (But test to make sure it is really more efficient to run queries against a lot of duplicated data than to do the joins.) Consider adding columns when the duplicated columns will benefit common transactions and

- ♦ The joins require access to many rows and the table with the join column has a very broad row or is clustered on an unrelated attribute.
- ♦ The data is duplicated from the master to the detail tables.
- ♦ The duplicated attribute's table is rarely updated but is accessed often.

Consider three tables representing divisions, departments, and employees. Employees are in one department, and departments are in one division.

```
CREATE TABLE div(
name          char(15),
div_num       char(5))
go


CREATE TABLE dept(
div_num       char(5),
dept_name     char(15),
dept_num      char(5))
go


CREATE TABLE emp(
dept_num      char(5),
emp_name      char(15),
emp_num       char(5))
go
```

You need a three-way join to find everyone in the Western division. If you copy one column from the div table (div_name) into the emp table, you can get the information you need by querying just the emp table.

```
CREATE TABLE emp(
dept_num      char(5),
emp_name      char(15),
emp_num       char(5)
div_name      char(15))
go
```

There are some problems with this technique.

♦ You now have the div_name in two tables, and you need to create ways to make sure the data remains consistent.
♦ Having the same data in two places requires more storage space.

Adding Columns for Reverse Sorting

SQL Server will not use an index to satisfy descending sorts (ORDER BY . . . DESC). If you regularly need data in descending order, consider adding a special reverse order column. In the example below, values in the num column range from 00001 to 10,000.

```
name        num
----------  -----------
Jones                99
Wong                613
Aziz                  6
Tarragon           2000
```

To use an index to get num in descending order, add a column (desc-num, equal to 10,000 – num) to hold the relative values of num in reverse order., and index the new column. Sorting by ascending descnum has the same effect as sorting by descending num, but SQL Server will consider using the descnum index because the sort is ascending.

```
SELECT *
FROM names
ORDER by descnum ASC
```

```
name        num          descnum
----------  -----------  -----------
Tarragon           2000         8000
Wong                613         9387
Jones                99         9901
Aziz                  6         9994
```

SQL Server will not use the descnum index for this query:

```
SELECT num
FROM names
ORDER by num DESC
```

Adding Columns for Calculated Data

When queries require calculations, you can save time by adding a column to store results. If year-to-date sales and book prices are stored in the titles

table, and many queries perform math to figure total sales (price *
ytd_sales), you may want to add a column to hold this data, so that
retrievals are easier. This is particularly useful when:

- ♦ Calculations are complex
- ♦ Calculations involve many rows
- ♦ Results are ordered by the calculated result
- ♦ You use the expression to identify which rows to select and might want
  to index it
- ♦ Inserts and updates are less important than queries
- ♦ The row size does not increase significantly

Adding Columns for Aggregate Values

Many transactions call for existence checks to validate master rows associated with detail rows. For example, to determine whether a given publisher
has published books, you might do a count.

```
SELECT count(*)
FROM titles
WHERE pub_id= '1234'
go
```

If this kind of transaction is common, you can improve performance
by establishing a count column in the master table (publishers in this case),
although the technique is even more useful if the detail table is not a direct
child of the master table. Use triggers to update the count in the master
table whenever you INSERT or DELETE a detail row, and whenever you
UPDATE its foreign key. Consider using counts when

- ♦ The transactions only request existence checking.
- ♦ The master table is related to many detail tables and they all require
  checking for associated rows.
- ♦ The existence checks cover many entities or must read many tables.
- ♦ The overhead of maintaining the counts is low; that is, the data does
  not often change.

You can use the same method for other aggregates (SUM, AVG, MAX,
or MIN). This method has the limitations associated with any calculated
column. You need a mechanism to update the aggregate column each time
its data changes (usually implemented in triggers) and data modification
performance slows.

Adding Columns for Inter-Row Derived Data

Some transactions often use data derived from the comparison of two or more rows of the same table. These comparisons show up as self-joins or aggregates in SQL. You can create an inter-row column to hold that information directly. Consider a start-up company, where employees often change departments. The employee table holds the employee's number, department, and the date the employee joined the department.

```
CREATE TABLE empl
  (id char(9),
   dept char(3),
   joindate datetime)
go
```

To find current departments for all employees, you need to search all the rows on the employee and find the one with the latest join date, like this:

```
SELECT id, dept
FROM empl e
WHERE joindate =
      (SELECT max(joindate) FROM empl WHERE id = e.id)
go
```

On the other hand, you can add an *active* column where "Y" indicates the current department. When the employee leaves a department, and you enter a new row, a trigger can change the active status of the earlier row (based on joindate) to "N" and assign "Y" to the new one.

```
CREATE TABLE empl
  (id char(9),
   dept char(3),
   joindate datetime
   active char(1))
go
```

With the new table definition, the query to find the employee's current department is less complex.

```
SELECT id, dept
FROM empl
WHERE active = 'Y'
go
```

Inter-row derived data rows can reduce performance for INSERTs, UPDATEs, and DELETEs, since you have to calculate the new value for each data modification.

Creating Tables to Speed Indirect Relationship Queries

Sometimes you can identify a common query requiring a large number of tables in a join, reducing performance. Frequent culprits are queries on indirectly related tables and the associative tables that connect them.

For example, in the pubs database there are six tables that report on authors, titles, and sales of books: titles, titleauthor, authors, sales, salesdetails, and stores. If you want to determine which authors have had their books sold by a given store, you need a six-way join. To improve the performance of this query, you might create a table (author_stores) with two columns, author_id and a store_id. When a store sells a book, you add a row to that table for each author of the book. In this way, SQL Server can display the names of authors and stores with just a three-way join (authors, author_stores, stores).

Indirect relationship tables usually have many rows with complex many-to-many relationships that are hard to maintain. A single sale already calls for inserts to sales and salesdetails. With the new table, it also requires look-ups against titleauthor (to find the author_id for the title) and inserts into the author_sales table. However, for particular queries, adding a table for an important indirect relationship may significantly improve performance.

Tuning Indexes

For slow performance on particular queries or updates, one of the most useful things you can do is review them carefully, in light of how the query optimizer handles them. Good indexes can be invalidated by queries that don't take advantage of how the optimizer works. Some areas to check when you review indexes include hotspots, index widths, use of segments, query coverage, and FILLFACTOR AND MAX_ROWS_PER_PAGE. You should also get familiar with the UPDATE STATISTICS command.

Are There Hotspots?

Avoid creating clustered indexes on a serial field, date field, or other field that has activity clustered around certain pages of the table. If you have a clustered index on one of these fields or no clustered indexes, all inserts and (perhaps) many updates will try to access the same page. This will cause lock contention problems. It may help to create a clustered index on something else (e.g., a user-id field, or a region code—something that will help to spread the access across the table).

Are Indexes Too Wide?

The narrower the index, the more index entries will fit on an index page and the fewer levels you'll need. The fewer levels in the index, the better it is. Avoid indexes on many columns.

Should the Nonclustered Index Be on a Separate Segment?

There is some value to placing a commonly used nonclustered index on a separate segment from the data. This may help to spread the disk accesses across multiple devices. If you have disk striping, this is not important. Remember: A clustered index and its data are always on the same segment.

Is the Query Covered?

If all the columns of a table required to satisfy a query are in a nonclustered index and, if there is a search argument that matches the nonclustered index, then the index covers the query. The query may be satisfied by reading only the index pages. The optimizer will consider this in evaluating the cost of the index. So it can cover common queries, consider adding additional columns to an index. Be careful that the index doesn't get too wide.

Is There Enough Free Space?

For tables that are seldom updated, keep the free space to a minimum for fast-running queries. Two index options allow you to control the amount of free space on index and data pages.

- ♦ The FILLFACTOR parameter in the CREATE TABLE, ALTER TABLE, and CREATE INDEX commands lets you specify what percentage fullness initial index pages (for clustered and nonclustered indexes) and data pages (for columns with clustered indexes only) should have. The default FILLFACTOR of 0 creates indexes that are full at the leaf level and have room for about two rows in the intermediate pages. This is a reasonable compromise between too full and too empty, since it reduces the space required while leaving some room for the next inserts. SQL Server does not maintain the FILLFACTOR after index creation. With random UPDATE and DELETE, expect the pages to become about 75 percent full. Legal values (percentages) range from 1 to 100.
- ♦ The MAX_ROWS_PER_PAGE parameter in the CREATE TABLE, ALTER TABLE, CREATE INDEX, and **sp_chgattribute** commands is similar, but SQL Server maintains the value over time.

FILLFACTOR is a short-term solution, useful when you expect a flurry of inserts or updates after you create an index and you want to

- Reduce lock contention (in effect, simulating row level locking)
- Prevent page splits as data is added to full pages
- Spread initial rows across multiple pages

If you need to reestablish the FILLFACTOR (for another temporary boost) drop and recreate the index, specifying FILLFACTOR.

MAX_ROWS_PER_PAGE is more long-term. Use it to set the number of rows per page to reduce lock contention.

Nothing is free—FILLFACTOR and MAX_ROWS_PER_PAGE extract a price, requiring

- More memory
- More disk space
- More pages to read in queries and in dbcc commands
- More pages in dump database
- More locks

Placing Objects

When you create a database, you automatically get three segments:

- The system segment holds all system tables (sysobjects, sysusers, etc.).
- The default segment contains all user tables.
- The logsegment is for the database log (syslogs table).

You can create additional segments and put objects on those segments. But be careful! A complicated segment structure can make managing space very difficult. Generally speaking, make sure the logsegment is on a separate device from the data. This will give improved performance because reads and writes to the log and data do not compete. At the same time, it makes for better recoverability.

You can also place heavily-used tables on separate segments in order to allow reads and writes to multiple tables at the same time. Splitting a table and its nonclustered (not clustered!) index has the same effect. However, dividing activity evenly between two disks seems to give about a 20 percent improvement, instead of the 50 percent improvement you might expect.

SEGMENTS FILLING

We arrived at a customer site to work on some performance tuning. When we walked in the door, we were shuttled to the morning production change-over meeting where they had a serious problem. Overnight, one of their databases had experienced an 1105:

```
Can't allocate space for object 'abc' in database 'xyz' because the 'pqr'
segment is full.
```

This had terminated the entire overnight batch loading for one of their applications.

They wanted to know what they should do. We analyzed the segments that they had established. They had about eight segments and had done a good job of distributing their data across the various segments. Unfortunately, they had encountered this same error message in the past and had modified some of their segments onto devices that already held other segments. This meant that a given disk fragment participated in multiple segments and it was no longer possible to figure out which segment was causing a device to fill up.

Our advice was to abandon all segments. They protested that (1) they were in production, and (2) performance would get worse. I responded: (1) that makes me nervous, but it is still the right thing, and (2) because their segments already overlap, I bet there would be no performance degradation.

We removed all segments (required judicious use of **sp_placeobject, sp_dropsegment,** a little bit of direct access of the sysindexes table to resolve text and image datatypes, and some undocumented magic. (If you really want to know—see sp_placeobject. There is an undocumented DBCC command issued near the end. We had to use that after modifying the sysobjects table directly). As it turned out, performance was not impacted at all.

By the way—before we started, we did indeed get coffee, and asked to "borrow" one of the customer's administrators. We told him everything we were going to do as we did it. We made him look at the screen and we described the commands. Some things he understood and some he didn't, but by explaining it, we made sure that we had thought through the steps. Several times, while explaining what we were going to do we remembered "just one more thing" that was required.

See Chapter 12 for information on partitioning tables.

9

Coding

Overview

There are a large number of special SQL language features in SQL Server. One of the difficulties in developing applications with SQL Server is figuring out how to put the various features together. This chapter presents an overview of various SQL Server features and gives examples of how to code those features.

- ♦ The chapter starts with a discussion of simple SQL techniques. We provide simple examples of familiar statements (SELECT, INSERT, UPDATE, and DELETE statements).
- ♦ Next, a number of "Neat" SQL tricks are covered. These are more sophisticated techniques that can be useful to solve specific problems.
- ♦ The following two sections provide examples for using stored procedures and triggers. These each start with the basic syntax of procedures or triggers and then give specific examples for solving specific problems.
- ♦ The final section provides an explanation of how you can add your own messages to the sysmessages table and reference those messages in a RAISERROR statement.

SQL Techniques

This section contains some examples of SQL statements. It starts with absolutely trivial examples, then presents more complicated examples. All of the examples in the section can be used in the sample database, pubs2, shipped with SQL Server.

SELECT

The simplest form of a SELECT statement includes a SELECT list (identifying which columns to return), FROM clause (identifying which table to access), and a WHERE clause (identifying which rows are desired).

```
SELECT title
FROM titles
WHERE title_id = 'BU1032'
go


title
--------------------------------------------
The Busy Executive's Database Guide
```

This query selects the title column from the titles table for all rows (in this case at most one row, because there is a unique index on the **title_id** column) that have a **title_id** of BU1032.

Correlated SELECT

SQL Server allows you to specify a SELECT statement almost any place that you can put an expression in another SELECT statement. In the following example, the fourth column is actually another SELECT statement. But notice in the embedded SELECT statement, there is a reference to the table in the containing SELECT statement.

This query allows you to compare the price of an individual book to the average price for books of that type. The first three columns in the SELECT list are the title identification number, type, and price of each book. The fourth item (the embedded SELECT) finds the average price of books of that type.

```
SELECT title, type, price,
        (SELECT avg(price) FROM titles t2 WHERE t2.type = t1.type)
FROM titles t1
go
```

title_id	type	price	
BU1032	business	19.99	13.73
BU1111	business	11.95	13.73
BU2075	business	2.99	13.73
BU7832	business	19.99	13.73
MC2222	mod_cook	19.99	11.49
MC3021	mod_cook	2.99	11.49
MC3026	UNDECIDED	NULL	NULL
PC1035	popular_comp	22.95	21.48
PC8888	popular_comp	20.00	21.48
PC9999	popular_comp	NULL	21.48
PS1372	psychology	21.59	13.50
PS2091	psychology	10.95	13.50
PS2106	psychology	7.00	13.50
PS3333	psychology	19.99	13.50
PS7777	psychology	7.99	13.50
TC3218	trad_cook	20.95	15.96
TC4203	trad_cook	11.95	15.96
TC7777	trad_cook	14.99	15.96

It might be more efficient in this case to break the query into two pieces:

♦ Create a temporary table (#titles) to hold summary data (each type and its average price).

```
SELECT type, average_price=avg(price)
INTO #titles
FROM titles GROUP BY type
go
SELECT type, average_price
FROM #titles
go
type          average_price
------------  ------------------------
UNDECIDED                         NULL
business                         13.73
mod_cook                         11.49
popular_comp                     21.48
psychology                       13.50
trad_cook                        15.96
```

♦ Join the summary data from # titles and the detail data from titles.

```
SELECT t1.title_id, t1.type, t1.price, t2.average_price
FROM titles t1, #titles t2
WHERE t1.type = t2.type
go
```

```
title_id type          price               average_price
-------- ------------  ------------------  -----------------------
MC3026   UNDECIDED                   NULL                     NULL
BU1032   business                   19.99                    13.73
BU1111   business                   11.95                    13.73
BU2075   business                    2.99                    13.73
BU7832   business                   19.99                    13.73
MC2222   mod_cook                   19.99                    11.49
MC3021   mod_cook                    2.99                    11.49
PC1035   popular_comp               22.95                    21.48
PC8888   popular_comp               20.00                    21.48
PC9999   popular_comp                NULL                    21.48
PS1372   psychology                 21.59                    13.50
PS2091   psychology                 10.95                    13.50
PS2106   psychology                  7.00                    13.50
PS3333   psychology                 19.99                    13.50
PS7777   psychology                  7.99                    13.50
TC3218   trad_cook                  20.95                    15.96
TC4203   trad_cook                  11.95                    15.96
TC7777   trad_cook                  14.99                    15.96
```

This approach finds the types and calculates their average prices once, rather than many times.

Nested SELECT

A nested select is a SELECT statement in which another SELECT statement appears. The following is a simple example of this construct.

List the names of all publishers who publish books of type "psychology."

```
SELECT pub_name
FROM publishers
WHERE pub_id IN
       (SELECT pub_id FROM titles WHERE type = 'psychology')
go


pub_name
----------------------------------------
New Age Books
Binnet & Hardley
```

Select the list of publisher ids for all books of type "psychology." For each publisher id, select the name of the publisher.

INSERT

The simplest form of an INSERT statement adds a single row to a table. The values for the columns are specified. It is also possible to include a list of which columns you are inserting (and the order that the columns will appear in the VALUES clause). The values in this case must be constants or variables. The original publishers table looks like this:

```
pub_id  pub_name                            city              state
------  ----------------------------------  ----------------  -----
0736    New Age Books                       Boston            MA
0877    Binnet & Hardley                    Washington        DC
1389    Algodata Infosystems                Berkeley          CA
```

Here's how you insert a new publisher, with **pub_id** equal to 9910, **pub_name** of SQL Publishing, city of Healdsburg, and state of CA.

```
INSERT INTO publishers
      VALUES ('9910','SQL Publishing', 'Healdsburg', 'CA')
go
```

If you look at the table again, you'll see the additional row.

```
pub_id  pub_name                            city                  state
------  ----------------------------------  --------------------  -----
0736    New Age Books                       Boston                MA
0877    Binnet & Hardley                    Washington            DC
1389    Algodata Infosystems                Berkeley              CA
9910    SQL Publishing                      Healdsburg            CA
```

INSERT . . . SELECT

It is also possible to insert zero, one, or many rows into a table with an INSERT statement using a SELECT clause. The SELECT clause is evaluated, returns zero, one, or many rows; all of these rows are inserted into the table specified in the INSERT statement.

```
USE pubs
go
CREATE TABLE ca_publishers
(pub_id char(4),
pub_name varchar(40),
city varchar(20),
state char(2)
go
INSERT INTO ca_publishers
      SELECT * FROM publishers WHERE state = 'CA'
go
```

The previous statement inserts into the **ca_publishers** table all of the rows in the publishers table where the state is equal to CA. If there are no matching rows, then no rows are inserted. If one row has a state equal to CA, then that one row is inserted into **ca_publishers.** If many rows have a state of CA, they are all inserted into the **ca_publishers** table.

The new **ca_publishers** table contains only California publishers (two rows):

```
pub_id pub_name                        city                  state
------ ------------------------------- --------------------- -----
1389 Algodata Infosystems             Berkeley              CA
9910 SQL Publishing                   Healdsburg            CA
```

DELETE

The DELETE statement deletes zero, one, or many rows from a table. It deletes all rows that match the WHERE clause. The following statement deletes all rows from the publishers table where the **pub_id** is 1756. This may be one row or zero rows (it cannot be many rows in this case, because there is a unique index on the publishers table **pub_id**).

```
DELETE publishers
WHERE pub_id = '1756'
go
```

In the pubs2 database, this DELETE statement will produce the following message:

```
(0 rows affected)
```

No such row exists in the publishers table.

Referencing Another Table with DELETE

It is possible to reference additional tables in the DELETE statement. These other tables would then be referenced in the WHERE clause to identify which rows are to be deleted from the original table.

This example deletes all publishers who publish psychology books. If there are no rows in the titles table with a psychology type, or no rows in the publishers table for publishers that publish books with a psychology type, then no publishers will be deleted.

```
DELETE publishers
FROM publishers, titles
WHERE publishers.pub_id = titles.pub_id
AND titles.type = 'psychology'
go
```

If you run the command, then look at the publishers table, you'll see only two rows (instead of the four you had originally):

```
pub_id pub_name                                   city                 state
------ ----------------------------------- -------------------- -----
1389   Algodata Infosystems                       Berkeley             CA
9910   SQL Publishing                             Healdsburg           CA
```

This is probably not what you had in mind.

♦ It deletes from the publishers table any publisher who publishes psychology books, even though the publisher may also publish other types of books.
♦ It does not affect the titles table—books published by the now-defunct publisher are still listed.

Declarative referential integrity (foreign key constraints) or triggers could prevent this from happening. Both enforce business rules you have defined. In this case, you don't want to remove publishers with current titles, because you can't have titles published by a publisher who does not exist.

UPDATE

An UPDATE statement modifies zero, one, or many rows, setting the columns specified in the SET clause. All rows that match the WHERE clause are modified. The following UPDATE statement changes the publisher identification number of title BU1032 to 0736.

```
UPDATE titles
SET pub_id = '0736'
WHERE title_id = 'BU1032'
go
```

If there is no row with a **title_id** equal to BU1032, then no rows are affected. There can be at most one row matching this **title_id** since there is a unique index on the **title_id** column of the titles table.

Referencing Another Table with UPDATE

In an UPDATE statement, you can specify additional tables in the FROM clause in order to identify which rows of the table you want to update. The following UPDATE statement updates all rows in the titles table published by **pub_id** 1389 (Algodata Infosystems) to specify that they are now published by New Age Books. The publishers table is included in the FROM list and a clause is added to the WHERE clause to specify that that the new

pub_id should be the **pub_id** of the row in the publishers table with a **pub_name** equal to New Age Books.

```
UPDATE titles
SET titles.pub_id = publishers.pub_id
FROM titles, publishers
WHERE publishers.pub_name = 'New Age Books' /* Which row to read */
AND titles.pub_id = '1389'                  /* Which row to update */
go
```

Checking for Duplicates

After using bulk copy to load many rows into the titles table, you may want to find which books have the same title.

```
SELECT DISTINCT t1.title_id
FROM titles t1, titles t2
WHERE t1.title = t2.title
  AND t1.title_id != t2.title_id
go
```

The AND clause makes sure that we don't include all **title_ids** (since all titles are equal to themselves). We only include those cases where two titles are the same and the corresponding **title_ids** are different.

The results from this query show there are no rows with duplicate titles:

```
title_id
-----------
(0 rows affected)
```

THE DIFFERENCE A PARENTHESIS OR TWO CAN MAKE

The client was running a query—after 20 minutes with no results run, he gave up. The consultant didn't even sort out exactly whether ANDs happen before ORs, or try to understand the problem. First thing he did was introduce parentheses exactly where they needed to be logically. Bingo—not only did it work quickly, but we got the right answer.

Numbers of rows in the tables:
v: 20,000
y: 132,000

The query looked like this. Notice the two sets of parentheses.

```
SELECT DISTINCT v.customer_number, v.vehicle_nu
INTO #t1
FROM ytd_charges_detail ycd, vehicles v
```

```
WHERE (ycd.customer_number = v.customer_number
AND ycd.vehicle_number = v.vehicle_number)
AND (v.sub = "00001"
OR v.sub = "00002"
OR v.sub = "00003"
OR v.sub = "00004"
OR v.sub = "00005")
SELECT @@rowcount
go
```

GROUP BY

The GROUP BY clause in a SELECT statement allows you to develop summary information, grouping the results by one or more of the columns in the result set. A GROUP BY clause is usually used with an aggregate (SUM, COUNT, etc.), and the aggregate is then calculated for various values. For example, the following query (without a GROUP BY) calculates the average price of all of the books.

```
SELECT avg(price)
FROM titles
go
```

```
--------------------------
14.77
```

The following query (with a GROUP BY) calculates the average price for each type of book.

```
SELECT type, avg(price)
FROM titles
GROUP BY type
go
```

```
type
------------ -------------------------
UNDECIDED                        NULL
business                        13.73
mod_cook                        11.49
popular_comp                    21.48
psychology                      13.50
trad_cook                       15.96
```

GROUP BY can also be used in a query that involves a join. The following example lists each author id, last name, and first name, with a count of how many books that author has written.

```
SELECT a.au_id, a.au_lname, a.au_fname, count(*)
FROM authors a, titleauthor ta
WHERE a.au_id = ta.au_id
GROUP BY a.au_id, a.au_lname, a.au_fname
go
au_id          au_lname                 au_fname
-----------    --------------------     -----------------
172-32-1176 White                       Johnson            1
213-46-8915 Green                       Marjorie           2
238-95-7766 Carson                      Cheryl             1
267-41-2394 O'Leary                     Michael            2
274-80-9391 Straight                    Dick               1
409-56-7008 Bennet                      Abraham            1
427-17-2319 Dull                        Ann                1
472-27-2349 Gringlesby                  Burt               1
486-29-1786 Locksley                    Chastity           2
648-92-1872 Blotchet-Halls              Reginald           1
672-71-3249 Yokomoto                    Akiko              1
712-45-1867 del Castillo                Innes              1
722-51-5454 DeFrance                    Michel             1
724-80-9391 MacFeather                  Stearns            2
756-30-7391 Karsen                      Livia              1
807-91-6654 Panteley                    Sylvia             1
846-92-7186 Hunter                      Sheryl             1
899-46-2035 Ringer                      Anne               2
998-72-3567 Ringer                      Albert             2
```

Note that the ANSI standard requires that all of the columns in the select list appear either as an argument to an aggregate function or in the GROUP BY clause.

Sybase allows you to execute a non-ANSI command like this, where only some of the select list columns appears in the GROUP BY clause:

```
SELECT a.au_id, a.au_lname, a.au_fname, count(*)
FROM authors a, titleauthor ta
WHERE a.au_id = ta.au_id
GROUP BY a.au_id
```

If ANSI compliance is important, you can use the SET command to turn the FIPSFLAGGER option on, and you'll get a warning when you execute commands that do not conform to 1992 ANSI SQL entry-level standards.

```
SET FIPSFLAGGER ON
go
SELECT a.au_id, a.au_lname, a.au_fname, count(*)
FROM authors a, titleauthor ta
WHERE a.au_id = ta.au_id
GROUP BY a.au_id
go
```

```
Line number 1 contains Non-ANSI text. The error is caused due to the
use of column name(s) in a select list with aggregates but column
name(s) not in group by list.
```

With or without the FIPSFLAGGER option, SQL Server displays the results. Use the Transact-SQL extension to GROUP BY with caution. For more information, see the section on "Dangerous GROUP BY" in this chapter.

GROUP BY and HAVING

In a SELECT statement with a GROUP BY clause, the HAVING clause determines which groups should be returned. Logically, SQL Server

- ♦ Evaluates all of the rows of the table,
- ♦ Develops the appropriate aggregates, and then
- ♦ Uses the HAVING clause to determine which rows should be returned to the user.

In the following example, SQL Server determines how many books were written by each author. It then uses the HAVING clause to determine which rows should be returned. Only those authors who have written more than one book (HAVING count(*) > 1) will be returned.

```
SELECT a.au_id, a.au_lname, a.au_fname, count(*)
FROM authors a, titleauthor ta
WHERE a.au_id = ta.au_id
GROUP BY a.au_id, a.au_lname, a.au_fname
HAVING count(*) > 1
go
```

au_id	au_lname	au_fname	
213-46-8915	Green	Marjorie	2
267-41-2394	O'Leary	Michael	2
486-29-1786	Locksley	Chastity	2
724-80-9391	MacFeather	Stearns	2
899-46-2035	Ringer	Anne	2
998-72-3567	Ringer	Albert	2

Execution of GROUP BY

The following describes the logical order of activities that the SQL Server does when processing a SELECT statement with a GROUP BY clause (the second and third item can, in fact, be combined).

1. Build a work table with the columns in the GROUP BY lists, plus one additional column for each aggregate to be calculated. This table has a unique clustered index with the option **ignore_dup_key** turned on.

2. Load the groups into this work table, taking advantage of the **ignore_dup_key** option to discard any duplicates.
3. Calculate the aggregates for the each of the groups.
4. Get the values for any column in the select list that is neither grouped nor aggregated. This is done by joining to the original table on the grouping columns.

Dangerous GROUP BY

SQL Server allows you to include columns in the SELECT list that are not in the GROUP BY clause and that were not aggregated. However, it's best to avoid this Transact-SQL extension: You may get unexpected answers. Sometimes you notice you are getting the wrong answer, and sometimes you do not.

Consider the example of GROUP BY previously shown:

```
SELECT a.au_id, a.au_lname, a.au_fname, count(*)
FROM authors a, titleauthor ta
WHERE a.au_id = ta.au_id
GROUP BY a.au_id
go
```

It makes sense to remove the **au_lname** and **au_fname** from the GROUP BY, since the **au_id** is the primary key of the authors table and grouping by that should be sufficient. This will give the correct answer. Nineteen rows are returned.

Next, modify this slightly by changing which table you select **au_id** from in the SELECT list:

```
SELECT ta.au_id, a.au_lname, a.au_fname, count(*)
FROM authors a, titleauthor ta
WHERE a.au_id = ta.au_id
GROUP BY a.au_id
go
```

You expect to get the same result, since your change is only which table you take the **au_id** from; right in the WHERE clause you say that **a.au_id = ta.au_id.** Unfortunately, your result includes 475 rows. The reason is captured in the fourth step (previously given):

4. Get the values for any column in the select list that is neither grouped nor aggregated. This is done by joining to the original table on the grouping columns.

SQL Server joins on the grouping columns to get the value of **ta.au_id**. Unfortunately, none of the grouping columns are in the titleauthor table. The result set includes the 19 rows expected, but each one is joined to every row in the titleauthor table. There are 25 rows in the titleauthor table, so you get 25 × 19 = 475 rows in the result set.

Here is another example:

```
SET FIPSFLAGGER ON
go
SELECT title_id, avg(qty)
FROM salesdetail
WHERE title_id = 'PS2091'
go
```

FIPS WARNING: Select list contains aggregate function(s) but GROUP BY clause not specified.

```
title_id
-------- -----------
BU1032           681
BU1032           681
BU1032           681
BU1032           681
BU1032           681
BU1032           681
BU1032           681
BU1032           681
BU1032           681
BU1111           681
. . . . .
```

The average quantity is correct for salesdetail rows with PS2091 as the **title_id**, but why are other **title_ids** returned, and why are there 116 rows in all? After generating the average, SQL Server had to "join" back to the salesdetail table (with 116 rows) to get the **title_id** column; again it generated one result row for every row in the salesdetail table.

Sometimes, the extension yields reasonable results, but it often yields strange results. On previous releases, this feature was described as a *black hole*. You can now avoid the black hole by turning on the FIPSFLAGGER option.

GROUP BY

Many SQL users forget about GROUP BY: Perhaps they confuse it with ORDER BY when they first learn the language. At any rate, the database news groups (such as comp.databases.sybase) seem to have a lot of questions about how to get summary values for categories.

One example of attempting to find a count for each group included variables, loops, and more, where something along these lines would have solved the problem:

```
select type, count(*)
from titles
group by type
go
```

Cursors

Support for cursors was introduced in System 10. Cursors allow you to step through the rows of a query, and take some additional action with each row. They are an important new feature in the SQL Server, but it is important that you only use them when they are needed. In particular, you can often replace a cursor with set level processing. See Chapter 5 for a discussion of the importance of relational thinking.

Sometimes, a cursor will be exactly the right solution to a problem. It will allow you to use Transact-SQL to solve a problem, allowing the entire solution to be executed on SQL Server. That is one of the advantages of the use of cursors; the individual rows do not have to be returned across the network.

Cursor Processing

There are five primary steps to using a cursor:

- ♦ Declare the cursor
- ♦ Open the cursor
- ♦ Fetch the next (or first) row
- ♦ Close the cursor
- ♦ Deallocate the cursor

Each of these steps will be looked at, including a description of the syntax and a discussion of how to use the syntax.

Declare the Cursor

The DECLARE cursor statement defines the SELECT statement that will be associated with the cursor. It also identifies whether updates are allowed to the selected rows. An example of a DECLARE statement is the following:

```
DECLARE getdbs CURSOR
     FOR SELECT name
     FROM master..sysdatabases
FOR READ ONLY
```

This declares a cursor for the SELECT statement "SELECT name FROM master..sysdatabases." This cursor will be read-only, so only shared locks will be held. The DECLARE CURSOR statement must be in a batch by itself unless it is part of a stored procedure (see the example in "Using Cursors to Create Serial Numbers" in this chapter). The SELECT statement is not executed at this point.

Open the Cursor

The OPEN statement opens the cursor. The SELECT statement is executed and the results are ready to be accessed. The following example opens the cursor getdbs.

```
OPEN getdbs
```

Fetch the Next (or first) Row

The FETCH statement allows you to select the next row in the result set and put the column values in variables. The following two statements declare a variable (@a) and select the next row into the variable.

```
DECLARE @a varchar(30)
FETCH getdbs INTO @a
```

After executing this statement, you should always check the value of the global variable @@sqlstatus. This variable will have one of the following values:

0—Row successfully accessed

1—Error

2—No more data in the result set

FETCH is an alternative to the FETCH INTO statement. It returns one or more rows to the client application, rather than holding values in variables.

Close the Cursor

The CLOSE statement closes the cursor. After the execution of the CLOSE statement, you could open it again with the OPEN statement. The following statement closes the cursor getdbs.

```
CLOSE getdbs
```

Deallocate the Cursor

The DEALLOCATE statement deallocates the cursor. After the execution of the DEALLOCATE statement, you could declare the cursor again with a DECLARE cursor statement. The following statement deallocates the cursor getdbs:

```
DEALLOCATE CURSOR getdbs
```

Cursors Example

The following example demonstrates how cursors work. The cursor steps through all of the database names listed in the sysdatabases table. For each database, the WHILE loop executes a PRINT statement. (For an example where a row needs to be updated, see "Using Cursors to Create Serial Numbers" in this chapter.)

```
DECLARE getdbs CURSOR
      FOR SELECT name
      FROM master..sysdatabases
      FOR READ ONLY
go
OPEN getdbs
DECLARE @a varchar(30)
FETCH getdbs INTO @a
WHILE @@sqlstatus <> 2
BEGIN
      PRINT @a
      FETCH getdbs INTO @a
END
CLOSE getdbs
DEALLOCATE CURSOR getdbs
go


master
(1 row affected)
model
(1 row affected)
msdpco
(1 row affected)
pubs2
(1 row affected)
sybsystemprocs
(1 row affected)
tempdb
(0 rows affected)
```

A more meaningful use substitutes a series of DBCC statements instead of the PRINT statement. For each database, it runs DBCC CHECKDB, CHECKALLOC, and CHECKCATALOG.

```
DECLARE getdbs CURSOR
      FOR SELECT name
      FROM master..sysdatabases
      FOR READ ONLY
go
OPEN getdbs
```

```
DECLARE @a varchar(30)
FETCH getdbs INTO @a
WHILE @@sqlstatus <> 2
BEGIN
      DBCC CHECKDB(@a)
      DBCC CHECKALLOC(@a)
      DBCC CHECKCATALOG(@a)
      FETCH getdbs INTO @a
END
CLOSE getdbs
DEALLOCATE CURSOR getdbs
go
```

The cursor steps through the databases one by one, running the commands on each. Fragments of the output look like this:

```
Checking master
Checking 1
The total number of data pages in this table is 4.
Table has 55 data rows.
Checking 2
....
Checking model
Checking 1
The total number of data pages in this table is 1.
Table has 21 data rows.
Checking 2
....
```

Neat SQL Tricks

We spend much of our time developing relational database applications, reviewing applications for others, or consulting on application development. One of the things that we have noticed is that using SQL as a development language requires a different set of tricks than we use in other application development languages that we do. This section includes a set of techniques that we have found useful in developing relational database applications.

Difference Operations and Outer Joins

Applications often have to identify all of the rows in one table that don't have a match in another table. This is often called a subtraction, or difference, operation. Consider the following two tables:

```
a
id
-----------
          1
          2
          3
          4
b
id
-----------
          3
          4
          5
```

Then a-b (The ids in "a" that don't have a match in "b") would be:

```
id
-----------
          1
          2
```

And b-a (The ids in "b" that don't have a match in "a") would be:

```
id
-----------
          5
```

The common (and perhaps most obvious) way to phrase a-b would be:

```
SELECT a.id
FROM a
WHERE NOT EXISTS
       (SELECT b.id FROM b WHERE a.id = b.id)
go

id
-----------
          1
          2
```

An alternative would be to do this using an outer join and a temporary table. In an outer join, the table whose column appears in the WHERE clause on the side of the * is called the *preserved* table. That is, all rows that have a match in the nonpreserved table appear in the result. In addition, one row appears in the result set for each row of the preserved table that does not have a match.

```
SELECT a.id aid, b.id bid
INTO #dif
FROM a,b
WHERE a.id *= b.id¹
go

SELECT *
FROM #dif
go
aid bid
----------- -----------
          1        NULL
          2        NULL
          3           3
          4           4
```

Then, to identify those that are in a but not in b:

```
SELECT aid
FROM #dif
WHERE bid IS NULL
go


aid
-----------
          1
          2
```

The second approach using an outer join was faster on previous releases, but new optimizations in system 11 make the WHERE NOT EXISTS approach faster for this example.

Outer joins are a useful technique in certain instances. You should consider adding them to your tool box.

Cross Tabulations

A cross tabulation allows you to summarize data in a two-dimensional grid. Cross tabulations are commonly required for viewing data summaries by month or by quarter. Table 9.1 shows order information from the pubs2 database, with a line for each book, including the book title identification number, the publisher identification number, the type of book, and the number of sales for each book.

What you'd like to see is an analysis, with each publisher in one row, and columns showing the number of sales by type, as in Table 9.2.

Preparing this output is not trivial using SQL. Three different ways to develop this output will be shown. All are making one critical simplifying assumption: You know ahead of time how many columns you want and how

TABLE 9.1 Publisher, Type, and Sales by Title

Title	Publisher	Type	# Sales
BU1032	1389	business	4095
BU1111	1389	business	3876
BU2075	0736	business	18722
BU7832	1389	business	4095
MC2222	0877	mod_cook	2032
MC3021	0877	mod_cook	22246
PC1035	1389	popular_comp	8780
PC8888	1389	popular_comp	4095
PC9999	1389	popular_comp	NULL
PS1372	0877	psychology	375
PS2091	0736	psychology	2045
PS2106	0736	psychology	111
PS3333	0736	psychology	4072
PS7777	0736	psychology	3336
TC3218	0877	trad_cook	375
TC4203	0877	trad_cook	15096
TC7777	0877	trad_cook	4095

TABLE 9.2 Publisher Sales by Type

Publisher	Business	Psychology	Cooking	Computer
0736	10722	9564		
0877		375	43844	
1389	12066			12075

the columns are identified (in this case, "Business," "Psychology," "Cooking," and "Computer"). The problem is much more difficult if you don't know this ahead of time.

The first approach is to use a sequence of outer joins—where each one develops another column of the result. The first SELECT creates a temporary table **temp_pub** which contains a list of the publishers. This is done to ensure that every publisher appears in the result.

```
SELECT DISTINCT pub_id
INTO temp_pub
FROM titles
go
```

The **temp_pub** table now contains these rows:

```
pub_id
------
0736
0877
1389
```

The second SELECT creates a table **temp_biz** table which contains a row for each publisher, with one column identifying the publisher and a second column giving the quantity of business books bought. Publishers with no business books have a quantity of NULL in that column.

The table is created with an outer join on the **temp_pub** table and the titles table. Outer joins are used to ensure that all publishers will be listed in the final set. Without outer joins, we would only see rows for those publishers who sell all of the book types.

```
SELECT      temp_pub.pub_id, Business = sum(total_sales)
INTO        temp_biz
FROM        temp_pub,titles
WHERE       temp_pub.pub_id* itles.pub_id
AND         type = 'business'
GROUP BY    temp_pub.pub_id
go
```

The new **temp_biz** table contains these rows:

```
pub_id Business
------ -----------
0736        18722
0877         NULL
1389        12066
```

The third SELECT creates another temporary table, **temp_psych**. This table contains the two columns created in **temp_biz** and a third column for the quantity of psychology books.

```
SELECT      temp_biz.pub_id, Business, Psychology = sum(total_sales)
INTO        temp_psych
FROM        temp_biz,titles
WHERE       temp_biz.pub_id* itles.pub_id
AND         type = 'psychology'
GROUP BY    temp_biz.pub_id, Business
go
```

The new **temp_psych** table contains these rows:

```
pub_id Business    Psychology
------ ----------- -----------
0736        18722        9564
0877         NULL         375
1389        12066        NULL
```

The next select creates a table with the three columns you already have and a new one for any kind of cooking book.

```
SELECT      temp_psych.pub_id, Business, Psychology,
     Cooking = sum(total_sales)
INTO        temp_cook
FROM        temp_psych,titles
WHERE       temp_psych.pub_id* itles.pub_id
AND         type like '%cook%'
GROUP BY    temp_psych.pub_id, Business, Psychology
go
```

The new **temp_cook** table contains these rows:

pub_id	Business	Psychology	Cooking
0736	18722	9564	NULL
0877	NULL	375	43844
1389	12066	NULL	NULL

The last table has a column for each type of book.

```
SELECT      temp_cook.pub_id, Business, Psychology,
     Cooking, Computer = sum(total_sales)
INTO        temp_comp
FROM        temp_cook,titles
WHERE       temp_cook.pub_id* itles.pub_id
AND         type = 'popular_comp'
GROUP BY    temp_cook.pub_id, Business, Psychology, Cooking
go
```

The **temp_comp** table contains these rows:

pub_id	Business	Psychology	Cooking	Computer
0736	18722	9564	NULL	NULL
0877	NULL	375	43844	NULL
1389	12066	NULL	NULL	12875

The second approach is to do a self-join of the table. It does the same operations as the previous series of SELECTs, but in only two select statements. To set this up, first create a temporary table with a list of all publishers, types, and sums. Then this table is joined to the **temp_pub** table (which holds the list of distinct publishers) and to itself once for each of the product columns.

```
SELECT pub_id, type, qty = sum(total_sales)
INTO        aggs
FROM        titles
GROUP BY    pub_id, type
go
```

```
SELECT temp_pub.pub_id, Business =b.qty, Psychology = p.qty,
       Mod_Cooking=c.qty, Trad_Cooking c.qty, Computer=cp.qty
FROM   temp_pub,aggs b, aggs p, aggs c, aggs tc, aggs cp
WHERE temp_pub.pub_id *= b.pub_id
  AND temp_pub.pub_id *= p.pub_id
  AND temp_pub.pub_id *= c.pub_id
  AND temp_pub.pub_id *= cp.pub_id
  AND temp_pub.pub_id *= tc.pub_id
  AND b.type = 'business'
  AND p.type = 'psychology'
  AND c.type = 'mod_cook'
  AND tc.type = 'trad_cook'
  AND cp.type = 'popular_comp'
go
```

pub_id	Business	Psychology	Mod_Cooking	Trad_Cooking	Computer
0736	18722	9564	NULL	NULL	NULL
0877	NULL	375	24278	19566	NULL
1389	12066	NULL	NULL	NULL	12875

(The results are slightly different here, just because of the way we set the tables up: There's a separate column for each kind of cookbook, instead of one column for all cookbooks.)

Programmers usually have an easier time visualizing the first scheme. It is also more easily extensible to large numbers of columns. The second solution usually has much better performance. Don't try to collapse the aggregation (the **sum()** and the GROUP BY) into a single step with the self-join. It doesn't work that way.

Here's a third solution:

```
SELECT pub_id,
       Business=sum(patindex('business',type)*total_sales),
       Psychology=sum(patindex('psychology',type)*total_sales),
       Mod_Cooking=sum(patindex('mod_cook',type)*total_sales),
       Trad_Cooking=sum(patindex('trad_cook',type)*total_sales),
       Computer=sum(patindex('popular_comp',type)*total_sales)
FROM titles
GROUP BY pub_id
go
```

This is more efficient, because it makes a single pass through the data.

The patindex function returns the location within the second parameter at which it found the first parameter. It returns 0 if the string is not found. In this case, it returns a 1 if the first parameter is found, and 0 if it is not. Therefore, the **total_sales** is added in to the result Business only when the type for that row is business. This is taking advantage of a technique called *characteristic functions.* For more information on characteristic functions, see *Optimizing Transact-SQL: Advanced Programming Techniques* by Dr. David Rozenshtein, Dr. Anatoly Abramovich, and Dr. Eugene Birger, SQL Forum Press, 1995.

Creating Serial Numbers in an Existing Table

There is often a need to insert a sequence number into an existing table or to generate a unique number to identify individual rows. There are a number of different approaches that can be used. This section will demonstrate a way to insert a unique sequence number into a column in an existing table, as well as show how to use cursors and the identity property to facilitate creating serial numbers.

Crude Serial Number Creation

Let's start with a two-column table with a unique index on the primary-key table.

```
create table table_name
 (seq_num_field int null,
primary_key char(6))
go
CREATE UNIQUE CLUSTERED INDEX abc
ON table_name(primary_key)
go
```

To have some data to work with, insert distinct **title_ids** from the titles table.

```
INSERT table_name (primary_key)
SELECT DISTINCT title_id
FROM titles
go
```

The table now looks like this:

```
seq_num_field primary_key
------------- -----------
         NULL BU1032
         NULL BU1111
         NULL BU2075
         NULL BU7832
         NULL MC2222
         NULL MC3021
         NULL MC3026
         NULL PC1035
         NULL PC8888
```

```
NULL PC9999
NULL PS1372
NULL PS2091
NULL PS2106
NULL PS3333
NULL PS7777
NULL TC3218
NULL TC4203
NULL TC7777
```

The following statement updates the table setting a column called **seq_num_field** to a unique integer. This example assumes that there is an existing column (**primary_key**) which uniquely identifies each row. This column must not be null.

```
UPDATE table_name
  SET t1.seq_num_field =
  (SELECT count (*) FROM table_name t2
   WHERE t1.primary_key >= t2.primary_key)
 FROM table_name t1
go
```

The table contents now look like this:

```
seq_num_field primary_key
------------- -----------
            1 BU1032
            2 BU1111
            3 BU2075
            4 BU7832
            5 MC2222
            6 MC3021
            7 MC3026
            8 PC1035
            9 PC8888
           10 PC9999
           11 PS1372
           12 PS2091
           13 PS2106
           14 PS3333
           15 PS7777
           16 TC3218
           17 TC4203
           18 TC7777
```

This correlated UPDATE statement sets the **seq_num_field** for each row to be the number of rows that have a primary key value less than or equal to this column's key value. This scheme will not work if the existing primary key has more than one column.

This will execute quite slowly for a large table. For each row, it makes another pass through the table, checking to see how many rows have a primary key value less than this row. We have found this useful in a number of instances where the existing primary key was a long variable-length character string, and we wanted to create a serial number.

Using Cursors to Create Serial Numbers

With System 10 and System 11, you can do something similar using cursors. The approach is to read each row of the table, and update the "sequence" column to the next integer value. Prior to System 10, a similar approach could be taken using DB-Library programming.

The following example has been written as a stored procedure, but it could have been done as batches instead.

```
CREATE PROCEDURE update_keys
AS
DECLARE @primary_key char(1), @seq int
DECLARE @count int
SELECT @count=0
DECLARE addseq cursor FOR
        SELECT primary_key, seq_num_field
        FROM table_name
        FOR UPDATE OF seq_num_field
OPEN addseq
FETCH addseq INTO @primary_key, @seq
WHILE (@@sqlstatus=0)
BEGIN
        SELECT @count=@count+1
        UPDATE table_name
          SET seq_num_field=@count
          WHERE CURRENT OF addseq
        FETCH addseq INTO @primary_key, @seq
END
CLOSE addseq
DEALLOCATE CURSOR addseq
go
```

Note that there must be a unique index on the table in order to have an updateable cursor.

First the procedure declares the cursor. Note that it uses the FOR UPDATE OF clause. This indicates that the procedure expects to update the table, setting the specified column. If that row is updated, SQL Server will hold an exclusive lock on that page.

The procedure then SELECTs each row, updating the sequence number to the next integer value. It continues until the global variable @@sqlstatus is not 0. This indicates that there are no more rows in the result set.

Creating Serial Numbers Using the IDENTITY Property

Numeric columns can be given the IDENTITY property starting with System 10. This specifies that every time a new row is inserted into the table, the specified column will be given a unique value (unique across that table). Each table may have at most one identity column; the column must be of type numeric with a scale of 0. Compare two tables, one with a column with the identity property and one without:

```
CREATE TABLE y
(primary_key int)
go
CREATE TABLE x
(primary_key int,
sequence numeric(6,0) IDENTITY)
go
```

If you populate the table y with distinct **title_ids** from the titles table, it will have 18 rows. The following example inserts rows into the table x by selecting all of the rows of table y. Since table x has a column with the identity property, each row of the table x will have a unique value in that identity column.

```
INSERT INTO x (primary_key)
      SELECT primary_key FROM y
go
```

The output from a query of table x will show 18 rows, each with a unique identifier.

After the INSERT statement, the global variable @@identity contains the last identity value inserted. It is possible for the table owner, the database owner, or the system administrator to explicitly insert values into this column.

Managing Serial Numbers

If you don't want to use the IDENTITY property (and in most cases we recommend using IDENTITY) to maintain unique serial numbers in a table, you can create a surrogate key field using a column of type "int" and control the inserts into the table to increment the serial column values. This serial field column in a table guarantees each row in a table will be different. We will work through four refinements of an approach to managing serial numbers.

One approach uses the **table_name** table. This particular approach is safe; that is, you will never get two rows with the same value of id. As long as you have a unique clustered index on the id column of **primary_key**, access using INSERT, UPDATE, DELETE, or SELECT will be efficient. However, it may lead to performance problems in the application. Assuming there is a clustered index on **primary_key**, any INSERT statement inserts all new rows at the end of the table. This last page may become a hotspot in your application.

```
INSERT into table_name (seq_num_field, primary_key)
      SELECT max(seq_num_field)+1, 'BU9999'
      FROM table_name
go
```

Here's a fragment of the table. Notice that the new row has a **seq_num_field** value of 19 (the next sequential number).

```
seq_num_field primary_key
------------- -----------
            1 BU1032
            2 BU1111
            3 BU2075
            4 BU7832
           19 BU9999
            5 MC2222
            6 MC3021
            ....
           16 TC3218
           17 TC4203
           18 TC7777
```

One of the problems with this approach is that you don't know what value was assigned for id. But consider the following approach:

```
DECLARE @var int
SELECT @var  ax(seq_num_field)+1
FROM table_name
INSERT INTO table_name (seq_num_field, primary_key)
VALUES (@var, 'TC9999')
go
```

It is possible that some other process will add a new row to the table between the execution of the SELECT and the INSERT statements. You can improve on this approach by doing the SELECT and INSERT in a transaction.

```
BEGIN  TRAN
      DECLARE @var int
      SELECT @var  ax(seq_num_field)+1
      FROM table_name HOLDLOCK
```

```
        INSERT INTO table_name (seq_num_field, primary_key)
        VALUES (@var, 'TC9999')
COMMIT TRAN
```

Now the operation is safe (no user can insert a new row after you have done your SELECT—assuming that there is a unique index on the id column), but you can now deadlock if another user executes this same transaction while you are executing it. If you both do the SELECT, and then attempt the INSERT, the result is a deadlock, since you each hold a lock that conflicts with a request of the other user.

The following refinement is safe and will avoid a deadlock. Create a second table (**id_table**) containing a single row, single column, holding the largest id value. When you need a new value, execute the following transaction. At the end of the transaction, @varnam contains the next available id number.

```
CREATE TABLE id_table
(id int)
go
INSERT id_table
VALUES (25)
go
BEGIN TRAN
DECLARE @varnam int
      UPDATE id_table
      SET id = id+1
      SELECT @varnam=id FROM id_table
COMMIT TRAN
INSERT INTO table_name (seq_num_field, primary_key)
VALUES (@varnam, 'PS9999')
go
```

This approach still has one problem. It is possible that after executing the transaction (updating the table holding the highest value used) the application will fail before it has successfully inserted the new row into the table **table_name**. This will result in some id numbers not being used. For most applications, this is acceptable.

Code Generation Techniques

Several years ago, we were using another relational database product and had a significant revelation. We realized that we could use the SQL language to help generate code. We could create a series of tables with information about our application, and then use SQL statements to write SQL code that we could submit to the database engine or even C code. These techniques are great practice for your SQL skills and are often very productive ways to get a job done.

Using SQL to Create SQL

The first technique is to use SQL to generate SQL statements. SQL Server provides a very powerful database engine; you can harness that power. This is particularly useful for system administrators, writing queries against the SQL Server system tables. It can also be extended beyond that.

```
SELECT 'UPDATE STATISTICS ' + name
FROM sysobjects WHERE type = 'U'
```

This will generate the following results:

```
--------------------------------------------
UPDATE STATISTICS authors
UPDATE STATISTICS publishers
UPDATE STATISTICS roysched
UPDATE STATISTICS sales
UPDATE STATISTICS salesdetail
UPDATE STATISTICS titleauthor
UPDATE STATISTICS titles
UPDATE STATISTICS stores
.....
```

This gives you a script that you can use to update statistics on all of the user tables in your database.

Here is a refinement to the previous technique. The following **SELECT** will write a script to do an **UPDATE STATISTICS** on those tables that don't have any index statistics (indicated by the distribution column in sysindexes being 0 for at least one of the indexes on the table).

```
SELECT DISTINCT "UPDATE STATISTICS " + o.name
FROM sysobjects o, sysindexes i
WHERE o.id = i.id
AND i.indid BETWEEN 1 AND 250
AND i.distribution = 0
AND o.type = "U"
go
```

With a little thought you could write a procedure that would generate code for the following:

◆ A trigger for INSERT that would validate presence of foreign keys in other tables.

♦ A stored procedure that takes as parameters all of the columns for a table and does an INSERT into the table. You might use SQL to generate this starting point, then modify each one to add specific validations that are required for that table.

You may find that you can get close with just the SQL code, but that you need to use C or a GUI scripting language to complete the activity.

Using SQL to Create C

We inherited a large application that did statistical analysis of large volumes of insurance claim data. The application was given a table with a large number of columns and calculated various ratios. In this example, we are summing three columns and dividing by the sum of two others:

```
(c1+c2+c3)/(c4+c7)
```

We were asked to make some modifications to the code. We were able (with quite a bit of effort) to model the problem into a set of relations. The relations captured the sums that would be formed into numerators and denominators, and ratios of those numerators and denominators. We were able to work with the customer to adjust parts of the definition of the problem so that our model would apply.

Initially, we did the code directly using SQL from the tables. SQL was too slow for the volume of calculations that we had to do on each row, so we used SQL to generate C code to do the calculations. The tables looked roughly like Tables 9.3 and 9.4.

TABLE 9.3 Sample Data from the Aggregate Table

aggregate_name	bucket_name
c1_2_3sComps	g_p2330
c1_2_3sComps	g_p2331
c1_2_3sComps	g_p2332

TABLE 9.4 Sample Data from the Ratio Table

dividend_agg	divisor_agg	factor
c1_2_3sComps	c2_amalgams	1
c2_amalgams	c2_4xrays	1.19
c2_amalgams	total_procedures	1

The first table indicates that the sum called "c1_2_3sComps" is the sum of buckets g_p2330, g_p2331, and g_p2332. This is then used as the dividend in a ratio (where the divisor is c2_amalgams).

Sample generated code looks something like the following:

```
c1_2_3sComps    =
(g_p2330 ) +
(g_p2331 ) +
(g_p2332 ) +
(g_p2333 ) +
0 ;
c1sAmal_Perm    =
(g_p2140 ) +
0 ;
c1sAmal_Pri    =
(g_p2110 ) +
0 ;
```

The rest of the C program reads a row, does the calculation, and then accumulates results or does inserts into the SQL Server.

There were a number of advantages to this scheme. The first is the use of the relational model—which allowed a better understanding of the problem. The second is that the customer can change the formulas that he is using and automatically recreate the code. Although this is not a daily occurrence, the customer does find that about once a year there is reason to make some modifications. Finally, while still having control over the process, we were able to get optimal performance. This particular activity needed to be coded in C. We were able to do it without writing hundreds of lines of C code. Instead, we generated hundreds of lines of C code.

Handling a Hierarchy (Bill of Materials)

A database will commonly require you to use the bill of materials technique for a parts explosion problem, where parts may be made of other parts. The following is an example of building a bill of materials based on the table PCGdp that is built by a database analysis tool in order to display a call tree. This technique is commonly required for a parts explosion problem, where parts may be made of other parts.

The table PCGdp has the following description:

```
CREATE TABLE PCGdp
        (
    fromdb        varchar(30)      NOT NULL,
    fromown       varchar(30)      NOT NULL,
```

```
fromobject     varchar(30)     NOT NULL,
toserver       varchar(30)     NULL,
todb           varchar(30)     NULL,
toown          varchar(30)     NULL,
toobject       varchar(30)     NOT NULL,
    )
```

This table maintains a list of which procedures reference which object within the SQL Server. If procedure A called (using EXEC) procedure B, there would be a row in PCGdp something like

```
DBNAME, dbo, A, SERVERNAME, DBNAME, dbo, B
```

Using this table, the following procedure (**display_tree**) will produce a call tree showing all the objects that A references directly, as well as indirectly: If A calls B and C, and both B and C call D, the output would look as follows:

```
A
      B
                 D
      C
                 D
```

The procedure makes the temporary table **#stack** to develop intermediate results and remember your place. The procedure makes the temporary table **#lines** to build up the results, including spacing.

```
CREATE PROCEDURE display_tree (@cursrvr varchar(30),@curdb varchar(30),
      @curown varchar(30),@curobj varchar(30)) AS
DECLARE @level int, @line1 varchar(80),@line2 varchar(80)
/* The table #stack will contain all of the objects referenced by @curobj */
/* srvr - srvr name
   db -    database name
   own -   owner
   obj -   object name
   level - reference level. If A is the parameter,
   its rows in #stack will
   have a 'level' of 1. Any object that A calls, will have a level of 2
*/
CREATE TABLE #stack (srvr varchar(30),db varchar(30),
      own varchar(30),obj varchar(30), level_num int)
/* The table #lines contains the lines that will be output - with spaces
inserted at the beginning of each line to create the indenting in the
output. */
CREATE TABLE #lines (srvr_db varchar(61),own_obj varchar(61))
```

```
/* Insert the parameters as the first row in #stack */
INSERT INTO #stack VALUES (@cursrvr,@curdb,@curown,@curobj,1)
SELECT @level = 1
/* @level starts at 1, and proceeds up and down, as rows are
processed. If there are any calls at the current level, those are processed -
and any calls at that level are processed. Given the example above, the rows
encountered would be A, C, D, B, D. This is a depth first search - and
inserts
the rows in the correct order into #lines */
WHILE @level>0 AND @level < 8
BEGIN
/* If there are any more rows at this level, process the next one */
      IF EXISTS (SELECT * FROM #stack WHERE level_num = @level)
      BEGIN
/* Set the variables as the values from #stack (note this will get the last
row in #stack with this level number */
            SELECT @cursrvr=srvr,@curdb=db,@curown=own,
                  @curobj=obj FROM #stack WHERE level_num = @level
/* Insert this row into #lines */
            SELECT @line1=SPACE(2*(@level-1)) + @curown + '.' + @curobj
            SELECT @line2=SPACE(2*(@level)) + 'ON ' + @cursrvr + '.' + @curdb
            INSERT INTO #lines VALUES(@line1,@line2)
/* Remove the row from #stack - since it has now been processed */
            DELETE FROM #stack WHERE level_num=@level AND srvr=@cursrvr
                  AND db=@curdb AND own=@curown AND obj=@curobj
/* Insert into #stack any row from PCGdp that represents a call from this
current row*/
            INSERT #stack
                  SELECT toserver,todb,toown,toobject,@level+1
                  FROM PCGdp
                  WHERE fromdb=@curdb AND fromown=@curown
                    AND fromobject=@curobj
/* If any rows were found, increment level, and process those rows */
                  IF @@ROWCOUNT>0
                  BEGIN
                        SELECT @level=@level+1
                  END
            END
/* We are done processing at the current level, go back up one level */
            ELSE
            BEGIN
                        SELECT @level=@level-1
            END
END
/* Display the results */
SELECT * FROM #lines
/* Drop the temporary tables */
DROP TABLE #lines
DROP TABLE #stack
RETURN
```

Stored Procedures

Stored procedures provide a number of advantages over using a series of Transact-SQL statements.

♦ They provide improved performance because SQL Server only parses them when created and, once optimized, the query plan stays in cache (until forced out because it is least recently used). Having the query plan stay in cache is typically only a significant advantage if the stored procedure completes in under one or two seconds. Otherwise, the relative gain is small.

♦ They provide improved performance because of reduced network traffic.

♦ They allow you to create reusable code that resides on the server, making it easy to find and reuse.

♦ They provide an extra level of security and control. You can GRANT access to the procedure, and deny (REVOKE) direct access to the tables or views.

Stored Procedure Syntax

```
CREATE PROCEDURE [owner.]procedure_name[;number]
[[(]@parameter_name
      datatype [(length) | (precision [, scale])]
        [=default][OUTPUT]
        [,@parameter_name
         datatype [(length) | (precision [, scale])]
         [=default][OUTPUT]]...[)]]
[WITH RECOMPILE]
AS sql_statements
```

Output Parameters

Output parameters allow you to return values to a calling procedure from a stored procedure. The calling procedure can then reference the returned values. As an example, see the following pair of procedures.

```
CREATE PROCEDURE callee (@parm int OUTPUT) AS
      SELECT @parm = 7
      RETURN
go
CREATE PROCEDURE caller AS
      DECLARE @var int
      EXEC callee @var OUTPUT
      SELECT @var
go
EXEC caller
```

```
go


-----------
    7
```

Giving Help for Stored Procedures

By using a default value for parameters, you can provide users with help on how to use a stored procedure. Inside the procedure you test the parameter value. If it is still the default, the procedure can display a help message. Create this logic as follows:

```
CREATE PROCEDURE test (@a int = NULL)
AS
        IF @a IS NULL
        BEGIN
                PRINT "To run this procedure enter EXEC test value"
                PRINT "where the value is an integer between 1 and 10"
                RETURN
        END
        /* The real part of the procedure... */
        RETURN
```

SP_GOFIGURE

I was teaching an advanced SQL class at a customer's site. I had been teaching classes at this site for a couple of years—some of the students had been using SQL Server for three or four years.

As two of the students were leaving class one afternoon, one turned to the other and said, "I forgot to tell you, Henry asked you to give him a call," and the other replied, "Oh, you mean sp_gofigure?"

And I thought to myself—yea—I've known several people like that.

Using Stored Procedures as Parameters

You can use stored procedures to run other stored procedures, dynamically deciding what procedure to run. This can be a useful system administration tool. Here's an example:

```
CREATE PROCEDURE callproc @a varchar(30), @b varchar(30)
AS
EXEC @a @b
go
```

Here are some of the ways you can use the procedure.

```
EXEC callproc 'sp_help', 'callproc'
go
```

```
Name                             Owner   Type
-------------------------------  ------  -------------------------
callproc                         dbo       stored procedure
Data_located_on_segment          When_created
-------------------------------  -------------------------
not applicable                             Dec 26 1995 9:32AM
Parameter_name  Type             Length Prec Scale Param_order
--------------  ---------------  ------ ---- ----- -----------
@a              varchar          30     NULL NULL             1
@b              varchar          30     NULL NULL
EXEC callproc 'sp_helpindex', 'sysobjects'
go
index_name           index_description
       index_keys    index_max_rows_per_page
-------------------  -----------------------------------------------
       ------------- -----------------------------------------------
sysobjects           clustered, unique located on system
        id                   0
ncsysobjects         nonclustered, unique located on system
 name, uid                   0
```

Note: This is an undocumented feature, which may or may not appear in subsequent releases.

Using Temporary Tables in Stored Procedures

If you create a temporary table in a stored procedure and then try to reference it, the query optimizer will not have accurate information about table size and data distribution when it compiles the stored procedure. It assumes the table has 10 data pages and 100 rows.

In the following example, the query optimizer will not consider using the index on the table #temp to process the stored procedure:

```
CREATE PROCEDURE summarize_prices
AS
SELECT type,avg_price=avg(price)
       INTO #temp
       FROM titles
       GROUP BY type
CREATE UNIQUE CLUSTERED INDEX #tt ON #temp(type)
SELECT titles.title_id, titles.type, titles.price/#temp.avg_price
FROM #temp, titles
WHERE #temp.type = titles.type
go
```

In order to allow the query optimizer to consider using this index, one technique is to split the work:

- Create the table and index in one stored procedure and insert rows into it
- Execute a second stored procedure that will do the select with the join

However, be aware that Sybase warns that this technique can be dangerous. Using it in release 4.9.2 and System 10 caused some problems, which were cleaned up for System 11. The fix may result in extra compilations for this kind of stored procedure, with performance implications. Be sure to test your code thoroughly before you go into production.

But let's go back to the trick: Note that the order of creation is important.

1. Create the temporary table first or the CREATE PROCEDURE statement for **summarize_prices_inner** will fail.

2. Create the inner procedure (**summarize_prices_inner**) which references the temporary table.

3. Drop the temporary table (it was only needed to allow CREATE PROCEDURE **summarize_prices_inner** to succeed).

4. Create the outer procedure. We had to create the inner procedure first or we would have gotten an error message when we created the outer procedure.

Create the **summarize_prices_inner** using the WITH RECOMPILE option to ensure that it will be recompiled each time the procedure is run. This will ensure that the execution plan for this procedure created by the query optimizer takes into account the current number of rows and distribution of values in the table #temp1 every time the procedure is executed.

```
CREATE TABLE #temp1
(type char(12) not null,
avg_price money null)
go
CREATE PROCEDURE summarize_prices_inner
WITH RECOMPILE
AS
SELECT titles.title_id, titles.type, titles.price/#temp1.avg_price
FROM #temp1, titles
WHERE #temp1.type = titles.type
go
DROP TABLE #temp1
go
CREATE PROCEDURE summarize_prices_outer
AS
SELECT type,avg_price=avg(price)
        INTO #temp1
        FROM titles
        GROUP BY type
```

```
CREATE UNIQUE CLUSTERED INDEX #tt1 ON #temp1(type)
go
EXEC summarize_prices_inner
go
```

When you run **summarize_prices_outer,** you get results like this:

```
title_id type

-------- ------------   --------------------------
  MC3026   UNDECIDED                          NULL
  BU1032   business                           1.46
  BU1111   business                           0.87
  BU2075   business                           0.22
  BU7832   business                           1.46
  MC2222   mod_cook                           1.74
  MC3021   mod_cook                           0.26
  PC1035   popular_comp                       1.07
  PC8888   popular_comp                       0.93
  PC9999   popular_comp                       NULL
  PS1372   psychology                         1.60
  PS2091   psychology                         0.81
  PS2106   psychology                         0.52
  PS3333   psychology                         1.48
  PS7777   psychology                         0.59
  TC3218   trad_cook                          1.31
  TC4203   trad_cook                          0.75
  TC7777   trad_cook                          0.94
```

Stored Procedure Transaction Error Handling

The following example shows how to manage transaction logic and error
handling in a stored procedure. This stored procedure modifies the primary
key of the tasks table, and then cascades that change to two other tables. If
there is an error in modifying any of the three tables, the transaction is rolled
back, and an appropriate error message is returned with RAISERROR.

```
CREATE PROC rename_task (
@oldtaskid id10type,
@newtaskid id10type)
AS
DECLARE @numrows int,
        @rowsave int,
        @message varchar(50),
        @error smallint
BEGIN TRAN
UPDATE  tasks
SET     task_id = @newtaskid
WHERE   task_id = @oldtaskid
SELECT  @numrows = @@rowcount,
```

```
                @message = convert (varchar(50), @numrows),
                @error = @@error
    IF @error = 0
       BEGIN
       IF @numrows = 1
          BEGIN
             UPDATE consult_task
             SET    task_id = @newtaskid
             WHERE  task_id = @oldtaskid
             SELECT @numrows = @@rowcount + 1,
                    @message = convert (varchar(50), (@@rowcount+1)),
                    @error = @@error
             IF @error = 0
                BEGIN
                   SELECT @rowsave = @numrows
                   UPDATE works
                   SET    task_id = @newtaskid
                   WHERE  task_id = @oldtaskid
                   SELECT @numrows = @@rowcount + @rowsave,
                          @message = convert(varchar(50),(@@rowcount+@rowsave)),
                          @error = @@error
                   IF @error = 0
                      BEGIN
                      RAISERROR 30001 @message
                      COMMIT TRAN
                      END
       ELSE
                      BEGIN
                      RAISERROR 30002 'Update of works table failed.'
                      ROLLBACK TRAN
                      END
                END
             ELSE
                BEGIN
                RAISERROR 30003'Update of consult_task table failed.'
                ROLLBACK TRAN
                END
          END
       ELSE
          BEGIN
             IF @numrows = 0
                BEGIN
                   RAISERROR 30004'No rows in task table to update.'
                   ROLLBACK TRAN
                END
             ELSE
                BEGIN
                   RAISERROR 30005 'More than one row in task table to rename.'
                   ROLLBACK TRAN
                END
          END
       END
```

```
ELSE
   BEGIN
   RAISERROR 30006 'Update of tasks table failed.'
   ROLLBACK TRAN
   END
```

Triggers

Triggers are special stored procedures that are associated with a table for one or more of the following actions: INSERT, UPDATE, or DELETE. When the specified action occurs, the trigger is automatically invoked.

Some application designers use triggers to implement part of the application. We try to make a (somewhat fuzzy) distinction between application logic (which goes in the client side of the application or in stored procedures) and database design (which is implemented in triggers).

Examples of code that we view as database design and place in triggers are the following:

♦ Referential Integrity (although some of this can now be done using declarative referential integrity).

♦ Business rules internal to a table that can't be done in rules. This would include things like: The termination date must be after than the start date. It is possible to do this using constraints; the use of constraints is preferable, when possible, over the use of triggers.

♦ Cascading changes required by certain types of denormalization. For example, you have an invoice header table and an invoice detail table. The invoice detail table has one row for each invoice item. In the invoice master table you have decided to maintain a total invoice value column, which is the sum of the value of the items for this invoice. You can create a trigger for INSERT, UPDATE, and DELETE on the detail table that adjusts the total in the invoice header table every time there is a modification to the detail table.

In addition, we might use code in a trigger to watch for certain conditions in the table, and call stored procedures either within the server or (using DLLs or Open Data Services) outside the server. An example of this would be a trigger for INSERT or UPDATE for an inventory table that monitored stock on hand and placed orders as the stock reached some threshold.

Trigger Syntax

```
CREATE TRIGGER [owner.]trigger_name
  ON [owner.]table_name
```

```
    FOR {INSERT , UPDATE , DELETE}
    AS sql_statements
```

Or, using the IF UPDATE clause, the syntax would be:

```
CREATE TRIGGER [owner.]trigger_name
    ON [owner.]table_name
    FOR {INSERT , UPDATE}
    AS
      [IF UPDATE (column_name)
         [{AND | OR} UPDATE (column_name)]...
      SQL_statements]
         [IF UPDATE (column_name)
         [{AND | OR} UPDATE (column_name)]...
      SQL_statements...]
```

A single trigger may be for one action, two actions, or all three actions (INSERT, UPDATE, and DELETE). In a trigger for UPDATE or INSERT, you can use the "IF UPDATE(column_name)" test. This will be true if the column appeared in the SET clause of an UPDATE statement or if the column is assigned a values clause or select list for an INSERT statement. The "IF UPDATE(column_name)" test can be useful in a trigger if you only want to execute certain code when a given column is affected.

Trigger Guidelines

Triggers are invoked once by the server for each INSERT, UPDATE, or DELETE statement for the table. If there are multiple rows affected by the statement, the trigger is invoked once for all of the rows.

When the trigger is invoked, two special tables are created called *inserted* and *deleted*. These two tables are created when any trigger is invoked. They have exactly the same columns, column names, and datatypes as the table this trigger is associated with.

When a trigger is invoked, the changes required by the statement that caused the trigger to be invoked (an INSERT, UPDATE, or DELETE statement) have already occurred. In a trigger for INSERT, the rows are already in the associated table. In a trigger for DELETE, the rows have already been deleted from the table. In a trigger for UPDATE, the rows have already been modified. None of these changes are yet visible to other users. The pages that contain these rows or the entire table are locked.

If the statement that caused the trigger to be invoked was an INSERT, the *inserted* table has all of the rows that were just inserted into the table and the deleted table has no rows. If the statement that caused the trigger to be invoked was a DELETE, the rows that were deleted appear in the deleted table, and the inserted table has no rows. If the statement that caused the trigger to be invoked was an UPDATE, the affected rows are all in the deleted table, with the values that they had at the beginning of the statement, and the inserted table contains the rows, with the new values based on the execution of the UPDATE statement. These two tables, inserted and deleted, can be used in SQL statements in the trigger to make appropriate changes to other tables or to determine whether business rules have been violated.

The trigger is invoked regardless of how many rows were affected by the INSERT, UPDATE, or DELETE statement. In particular, even if no rows were affected (for example, executing a DELETE statement where no rows match the WHERE clause), the trigger is still invoked.

At the beginning of a trigger, the value of the global variable @@rowcount is the number of rows affected by the statement that caused the trigger to be invoked. The value of @@rowcount is changed by the next INSERT, UPDATE, DELETE, or SELECT statement that is executed. Therefore, the first thing you will want to do in most triggers is to assign the value of @@rowcount to a local variable.

Whenever you review a trigger, it is a good idea to make sure that it handles three different cases depending on how many rows were affected by the statement that caused the trigger to be invoked: zero rows, one row, or many rows.

It is a common mistake to assume that a trigger will only be invoked with a single row in inserted or deleted. Even though that may be true for the moment in your application, you should always create triggers that cope with all three cases.

The case of zero rows affected is usually not a significant problem. However, on complicated triggers, we usually check for the zero row case at the beginning and return (exit the trigger) if zero rows are affected.

Verifying the Presence of Foreign Keys

The following trigger for INSERT on sales verifies that every row inserted into the salesdetail table has a matching row in the titles table. Notice that the first thing it does is to capture the value of @@rowcount into a local variable (@rows). If there is any row in inserted that doesn't have a match in titles, then the transaction is rolled back and an error code is returned to the application (using the RAISERROR statement).

This same functionality can be done using the declarative referential integrity available in SQL Server.

```
CREATE TRIGGER salesins
ON salesdetail FOR INSERT
AS DECLARE @rows int
SELECT @rows = @@rowcount
IF @rows != (SELECT count(*)
     FROM inserted, titles
     WHERE inserted.title_id = titles.title_id)
BEGIN
     RAISERROR 20005 'Invalid title identifier.'
     ROLLBACK TRANSACTION
END
```

Cascading Delete Trigger

Use a cascading delete trigger when, for example, deleting rows from the titles table should also delete all of the corresponding salesdetail rows: You can't sell a book you no longer have.

This trigger does an "IF EXISTS" test to see if there are any rows in the salesdetail table that match the rows in the deleted table. It only does the delete from the salesdetail table if there are matching rows. The trigger could just execute the DELETE statement without doing the test. The advantage of this style of coding is that in the case where there are no matches, a DELETE statement has not been executed; therefore, no exclusive locks are held on the salesdetail table and the delete trigger on the salesdetail table is not invoked. There is some extra reading required with this approach, however, since the SELECT statement must be executed (at least until one matching row is found) and then the DELETE statement requires reading the same rows again.

```
CREATE TRIGGER titlesdel
ON titles FOR DELETE AS
IF EXISTS (SELECT *
FROM salesdetail, deleted
WHERE salesdetail.title_id =deleted.title_id)
     BEGIN
          DELETE salesdetail
          FROM salesdetail, deleted
          WHERE salesdetail.title_id = deleted.title_id
     END
```

Imposing a Business Rule on UPDATE

The following trigger compares the old and new price in the titles table on update of the titles table. It compares the two prices and disallows the change if the increase is greater than 10 percent.

The test to see if the title_id changed is common in some triggers. Note that the "IF EXISTS" test is joining inserted and deleted on **title_id**. If the user has changed a **title_id**, this join will not find matching rows. Many database designs disallow changing the primary key value, though this is not always acceptable. We have assumed this requirement in this trigger. There is a subsequent example that shows how you can use a trigger to cascade a change to a primary key.

The "IF EXISTS" test is comparing the old and new values of the price column, checking to see if there are any rows which exceed a price increase of 10 percent. The "IF EXISTS" test will work regardless of the number of rows in inserted and deleted.

```
CREATE TRIGGER titlesupd
ON titles
FOR UPDATE
AS
IF UPDATE(title_id)
      BEGIN
            RAISERROR 20006 'Cannot change title_id'
            ROLLBACK TRANSACTION
      END
IF EXISTS (SELECT * FROM inserted, deleted
      WHERE inserted.title_id = deleted.title_id AND
      inserted.price/deleted.price > 1.1)
      BEGIN
      RAISERROR 20007 'Bad Increase.'
      ROLLBACK TRANSACTION
      END
```

Changing the Primary Key Trigger

The following trigger allows changes to a primary key in the titles table. It ensures that, at most, one row is being changed (This is required to make the changes in the tables where this column appears as a foreign key). The change is propagated to the foreign key tables.

Note that the requirement of only one row being affected occurs because we have no way to match the rows in inserted and deleted if there are more than one. The UPDATE statement involves three tables (inserted, deleted, and titleauthor), but there is only one join clause (where **ta.title_id = d.title_id**). This is only reasonable when inserted and deleted each contain only one row.

Note also the test for @row equal to 0. If no rows are affected by the UPDATE statement that caused this trigger to be invoked, there is no need to do any work. The test is not necessary since the update to the titleauthor table would work correctly for no rows in the inserted and deleted tables. However, it often makes it easier to write triggers if you deal with each of the interesting cases one at a time. Here we deal with three different cases:

- No rows affected (doing nothing)
- Many rows affected (denying the change by rolling back the transaction)
- One row affected (cascading the change to the titleauthor table)

```
CREATE TRIGGER updtitles
ON titles FOR UPDATE     AS
DECLARE @rows int
SELECT @rows = @@rowcount
if(@rows = 0)
        RETURN
   IF UPDATE(title_id)
        BEGIN
        if(@rows != 1)
               BEGIN
               RAISERROR 30006 'cannot change title_id for more than one row'
               ROLLBACK TRAN
               RETURN
               END
        UPDATE titleauthor
        SET ta.title_id = i.title_id
        FROM titleauthor ta, inserted i, deleted d
        WHERE ta.title_id = d.title_id
        UPDATE salesdetail
        SET s.title_id = i.title_id
        FROM salesdetail s, inserted i, deleted d
        WHERE s.title_id = d.title_id
        END
```

RAISERROR

There are two styles of **RAISERROR** that can be used in your stored procedures, triggers or batches:

- Displaying ad hoc user-defined messages

```
RAISERROR 20005 'Cannot change the title_id.'
```

- Displaying user-defined messages previously stored in sysusermessages with **sp_addmessage**

```
sp_addmessage 20005 'Cannot change the title_id.'
go
RAISERROR 20005
```

See Chapter 6 for more information on **RAISERROR**.

After adding a message to the sysusermessages table, you can use a **RAISERROR** statement in a trigger, stored procedure, or batch. In the **RAISERROR** statement, you specify the number of the message you want to issue and optionally, substitution arguments.

This form of **RAISERROR** is very useful for errors that are identified in triggers. After the error has been raised, the trigger can issue a ROLL-BACK to rollback the transaction. The application can then check the value of @@error to determine which error had occurred. The **SELECT** list in a **SELECT** statement may contain two forms of column aliasing. These column aliases change the heading that will appear in the results and change the name that will be used for the column if you are using a SELECT INTO statement. The two forms of column aliasing are:

SELECT alias = expression

SELECT expression alias

For example: "SELECT cost=quantity*price FROM tablename" or "SELECT quantity*price cost FROM tablename." These two SELECT statements are equivalent. For both, the column heading in the result will be cost. Both styles of column aliasing have been used in the book.

10

Setting Up SQL Server

Overview

This chapter concerns installation and physical aspects of SQL Server. It includes:

- ◆ Advice on installation
- ◆ A review of Sybase system databases
- ◆ Information on database devices and mirroring
- ◆ A summary of threshold management techniques

Installation

SQL Server Installation is getting easier. If you're new to this business, take the defaults the installation program offers and see how they work for you.

- ◆ Pay attention to permissions.

WHEN "SA" IS NOT "SYBASE"

I got caught by this many years ago, and then again several years ago; then earlier this year (you get the idea).

I changed some configuration settings, (or I had a connection that I couldn't kill) so I used the SHUTDOWN statement to shut down SQL Server. Then I tried to restart it. Whoops, I didn't have permission to run the startserver command.

You can shutdown the server if you know the Sybase "sa" password. But to start it again, you need to have the right operating system level of permission.

♦ Avoid making the master device too large. The default value is about 20 Mb; that should be plenty.

♦ If you want an area to experiment, use the Transact-SQL DISK INIT command to add some database devices after you complete the installation or increase the size of the device that holds sybsystemprocs (it is about 15 Mb).

♦ Use the default character set unless your site supports a different one—and in that case make sure you use whatever will work with other SQL Servers in your environment.

♦ Avoid the case-insensitive-with-preference sort order: It can cause poor performance. After the installation, you can get details about the installed character set and sort order with **sp_helpsort**.

```
EXEC sp_helpsort
go
Sort Order Description
-----------------------------------------------------------------
Character Set = 2, cp850
    Code Page 850 (Multilingual) character set.
Sort Order = 50, bin_cp850
    Binary Sort Order for Code Page 850 (cp850).
Characters, in Order
-----------------------------------------------------------------
  ! " # $ % & ' ( ) * + , - . / 0 1 2 3 4 5 6 7 8 9 : ; < = > ?
  @ A B C D E F G H I J K L M N O P Q R S T U V W X Y Z [ \ ] ^ _
  ` a b c d e f g h i j k l m n o p q r s t u v w x y z { | } ~ □
  □ □ , ƒ „ … † ‡ ^ ‰ Š < Œ □ □ □ □ ' ' " " • - — ˜ ‰ š > œ □ □ Ÿ
  ¡ ¢ £ ¤ ¥ ¦ § ¨ © ª « ¬ - ® ¯ ° ± ² ³ ´ µ ¶ · ¸ ¹ º » ¼ ½ ¾ ¿
  À Á Â Ã Ä Å Æ Ç È É Ê Ë Ì Í Î Ï Ð Ñ Ò Ó Ô Õ Ö × Ø Ù Ú Û Ü Ý Þ ß
  à á â ã ä å æ ç è é ê ë ì í î ï ð ñ ò ó ô õ ö ÷ ø ù ú û ü ý þ ÿ
```

Sybase Databases

Sybase SQL Server includes three kinds of databases: required system databases, optional system databases, and user databases. SQL Server has the following required system databases:

- master is the administrative database.
- model is a template SQL Server copies and uses as a base for all new databases.
- tempdb is a work area (for sorting, grouping, and joining) and the home of any objects you define as temporary.
- sybsystemprocs is the location of all system stored procedures.

SQL Server automatically creates these databases when you run the installation program.

In addition, optional system databases are available, depending on your needs.

- pubs2 is a practice database, used in many Sybase examples. You install it with a script in $SYBASE/scripts. It is useful for learning SQL and simple tests. However, the data set is not large enough for system testing.
- sybsyntax allows you to use the system stored procedure **sp_syntax** to display SQL syntax. You install sybsyntax with a script in $SYBASE/scripts. If you don't install the database, the stored procedure is not available.
- sybsecurity is the auditing database. You install sybsecurity from the installation program. (See Chapter 6 for a discussion of auditing.)

Most important are the user databases, the ones you create yourself to hold your data. They will tend to be much larger than the system databases.

You can get information on databases with the system procedure **sp_helpdb.**

```
        EXEC sp_helpdb
        go
name            db_size    owner    dbid created       status
------------    ---------- -------- ---- ------------  -----------------
master             5.0 MB  sa          1 Jan 01, 1900 no options set
model              2.0 MB  sa          3 Jan 01, 1900 no options set
msdpco             2.0 MB  bowman      5 Nov 13, 1995 no options set
pubs2              3.0 MB  bowman      6 Dec 27, 1995 select into/bulkcopy
sybsystemprocs    16.0 MB  sa          4 Nov 11, 1995 trunc log on chkpt
tempdb             2.0 MB  sa          2 Dec 27, 1995 select into/bulkcopy


name            attribute_class attribute      int_value  char_value  comments
------------    --------------- -------------  ---------- ----------- ---------
tempdb          buffer manager  cache binding 0           temp_cache  NULL
```

The status column shows any **sp_dboption** values you have set; the second result set shows attributes (such as cache binding, covered in Chapter 12).

If you run **sp_helpdb** giving a specific database name as a parameter, the information is slightly different.

◆ It includes a section for device fragments, where you see a list of each database device used in this database. The pubs2 database used in this example has two megabytes of space on the **pubs_dev** database device for system and user tables. It has a one megabyte **pubs_log** device for its log.

◆ It includes a section for segments. When you create a database, SQL Server assigns three standard segments. *Default* represents the database user tables, *system* the database system tables, and *logsegment* the transaction log (syslogs). In this example, default and system segments share the **pubs_dev** device, while the logsegment segment is on the **pubs_log** device. When more than one database device is assigned to a database or log, you can label each device as a segment (with **sp_addsegment**) and create tables and indexes on specific segments. The examples in this chapter involve only the default segments.

```
name            db_size owner    dbid created      status
-------------- ------- -------- ---- ------------ -----------------
pubs2           3.0 MB bowman      6 Dec 29, 1995 select into/bulkcopy


device_fragments                 size          usage                   free kbytes
------------------------------- ------------- --------------------- -----------
pubs_dev                         2.0 MB        data only               784
pubs_log                         1.0 MB        log only                688


device              segment
------------------- ----------
pubs_dev            default
pubs_dev            system
pubs_log            logsegment
```

Disk Resources

When you install SQL Server, it creates a number of database devices (disk areas dedicated to database use) for you. The specific names and sizes are platform-dependent, but the device list usually looks something like this just after installation:

◆ One device for the master database (holding the master, model, and tempdb databases)

♦ One device for sybsystemprocs (holding only sysbsystemprocs)
♦ Two devices for tape dumps
♦ A device for auditing, if you installed sybsecurity

You can find out what devices you have with a query of **sysdevices:**

```
SELECT name
FROM sysdevices
go


name
-----------------------
master
pubs_dev
pubs_log
sysprocsdev
tapedump1
tapedump2
```

In this particular case, there are two non-default devices, **pubs_dev** and **pubs_log.** In a default installation, pubs2 and its logs would be on the master device.

To get more detailed information, run **sp_helpdevice.** It shows the device name, the physical name, a description, and other information.

```
      sp_helpdevice
      go
device_name        physical_name        description
        status cntrltype device_number low              high
--------------------------- -----------------------------------------------
        ----------------------------------------------------------------------
master          master.dat              special,default disk, physical disk, 30.00 MB
                3       0         0          0      15359
pubs_dev        D:\sybase\data\pubs.dat   special, physical disk, 2.00 MB
                2       0         2      33554432    33555455
pubs_log        D:\SYBASE\data\pubs_log   special, physical disk, 1.00 MB
                2       0         5      83886080    83886591
sysprocsdev     D:\SYBASE\DATA\SYSPROCS.DAT special, physical disk, 18.00 MB
                2       0         1      16777216    16786431
tapedump1       \\.\TAPE0               tape, 625 MB, dump device
                16      3         0          0      20000
tapedump2       \\.\TAPE1               tape, 625 MB, dump device
                16      3         0          0      20000
```

DISKDUMP

This isn't true for System 10 or System 11, but it once was; it illustrates why it's a good idea to know your database devices.

A customer called up, says he has a problem. They have just had a database failure, and are trying to load from a dump. But they can't find the dump. They have been doing DUMP DATABASE religiously for months, but they can't find the dumps. I asked, "Have you been dumping to the device called *diskdump?*" They said "Yes—that was it."

That device was mapped to the null device: write-only storage.

Planning Device Use

A database device is physical disk space you initialize for database use. It can be either a raw disk partition or an operating system file. On all UNIX platforms, the raw disk partitions are a better choice. They have higher reliability in recovery, because SQL Server (not the operating system) handles the disk I/O. (One exception is tempdb, where a file device works fine and may boost performance.) Consult your Sybase installation documents for specifics on your platform.

Using DISK INIT

To initialize a two-megabyte database device called **test_dev** on the disk/dev/rxy3, use a command like this:

```
DISK INIT
NAME = 'test_dev',
PHYSNAME = '/dev/rxy3',
VDEVNO = 3,
SIZE = 1024
go
```

The VDEVNO must be unique. Check the **sp_helpdevice device_number** column to find out what numbers are available. The size is in 2K pages. After initializing the database device, you can use it in CREATE DATABASE and ALTER DATABASE commands.

Changing the Initial Setup

In most cases, you want to change the initial distribution of databases on devices by:

◆ Protecting the master database by ensuring its database device is not labeled as the default storage area. After installation, the default database device (where SQL Server creates user databases and their logs if you don't give a specific location in your CREATE DATABASE commands) is the master device, home of the master database. To change the master device to a non-default device, use a command like this:

```
EXEC sp_diskdefault 'master', 'defaultoff'
go
```

- ◆ Labeling other devices as default (perhaps the device you use for sybsystemprocs or other devices you initialize with DISK INIT). You can have more than one default device. SQL Server uses them in alphabetical order.
- ◆ Adjusting the size and location of system databases (tempdb, sybsecurity) depending on how you use them.

Considering Application Needs

How you distribute system databases, user databases, and logs depends on the kinds of applications you are running.

For example, in some development environments, speed and convenience are the paramount values. It may make sense to create databases on file systems while you develop, using scripts to create and drop objects, including databases. If the data is mostly "junk," recovery may not be important and logs don't need to be on different devices. Your code is archived with separate software tools.

In a test environment, your setup changes, depending on the current assignment. You may want to store test results in a fully recoverable database, but the data you use in the tests may not be important.

A production database is different. You need to get the best performance you can, while allowing for logging, regular dumps, backups, and (in some cases) mirroring. As a minimum, you want to put the data and logs on separate devices. You may also decide to distribute the data among two or more disks.

If tempdb sees heavy use, it should be on its own device. However, consider placing tempdb on a file system device rather than a raw disk or disk partition if you get better performance on the file system devices. Recovery is not an issue for tempdb, so you should go for convenience and speed.

If you use auditing, put sybsecurity on a separate database device, preferably on a disk that does not hold frequently accessed objects. For stringent security systems with many inserts to the auditing database, put it on its own disk.

In planning database devices, consider two factors: recoverability and performance.

Recoverability

In a production environment, protecting data is the most important issue. There are three general levels in planning for recoverability.

- Putting data and logs on separate database devices
- Putting data and logs on database devices that occupy separate disks
- Mirroring

Using Separate Data and Log Devices

If recovery is important at all, put the data and logs on separate database devices as shown in Figure 10.1. This method

- Keeps the log from growing into the space on the device the data uses
- Makes DUMP TRANSACTION (incremental dumps of the transaction log) possible
- Allows you to use thresholds to manage logs (more about this later)

It does not guarantee full recovery (all is lost but your backups if the physical disk goes).

If you try to do a DUMP TRANSACTION on the master database, where data and logs are on the same device, you'll get a message like this:

```
Syslogs does not exist in its own segment in database '1' with segmap '7'
with logical start page number of '0'. You may not use DUMP TRAN in this
case, use DUMP DATABASE instead.
```

Put user databases and logs on separate devices with the LOG ON clause of the CREATE DATABASE command. Use a database device you have initialized with DISK INIT and plan to keep for logs only:

```
CREATE DATABASE pubs2
ON pubs_dev =2
LOG ON logdev =1
go
```

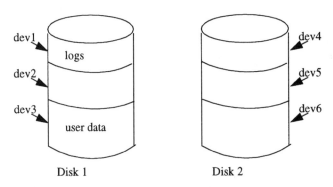

FIGURE 10.1 Database data and logs on separate database devices.

If the database already exists and you want to put the log on a separate device, use ALTER DATABASE with the LOG ON clause.

```
ALTER DATABASE pubs2
LOG ON logdev =1
go
```

Use **sp_logdevice** to move all future log activity for the database to the new log device.

```
EXEC sp_logdevice pubs2, logdev
go
```

Using Data and Log Devices on Separate Disks

For full recovery of a database, put the data and the logs on separate physical disks, not just different database devices (Figure 10.2).

♦ As in the first scheme, you can use thresholds to manage the logs.
♦ If you have a disk catastrophe, you can load a dump of the database and apply the log records. If data and log devices are on the same physical disk, you'll probably lose both. Putting them on separate disks gives you more protection.
♦ In addition, you get good performance, because writes to the database and the log use separate I/O.

Mirroring

For nonstop recovery, mirror (create duplicates of) the data and log devices on separate physical disks. All writes to the primary device are copied to the

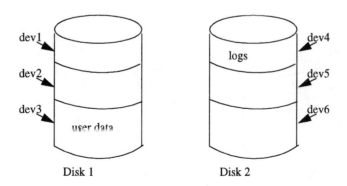

FIGURE 10.2 Data and log on separate disks for full recovery.

secondary (mirror) device. You can recover immediately by switching from the primary disks to the secondary disks. See Figure 10.3 for an illustration of this configuration.

The mirror device must be on a separate physical disk. If the primary and secondary copy are on the same disk, you are not protected in a disk failure. When deciding what devices to mirror, weigh recovery needs, storage space availability, and performance issues. Mirroring a database can slow writes (but has no effect on reads, since they always come from the primary copy).

When a read or write to either device fails, mirroring stops and you see an error message. SQL Server continues to run on the unharmed device.

This command mirrors the **pubs_dev** database device onto a file system on another disk (when mirroring, you don't initialize the mirror device with DISK INIT):

```
DISK MIRROR
NAME = pubs_dev
MIRROR = "C:\SYBASE\data\mirror_dev"
go
```

Mirroring starts as soon as you enter the command.

The mirror device must not be: already initialized with **DISK INIT** or an existing operating system file.

A database device and its mirror are one logical unit. You won't get a separate listing in sysdevices for the secondary device, but you will see information about it listed under the primary device.

```
SELECT name, phyname, mirrorname
FROM sysdevices
go
```

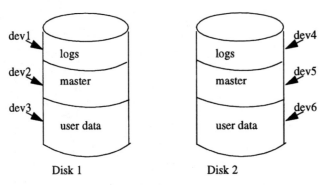

FIGURE 10.3 Device mirroring for nonstop recovery.

```
name            phyname                        mirrorname
-------------   -----------------------------  -------------------------------
master          master.dat                     NULL
pubs_dev        D:\sybase\data\pubs.dat        C:\SYBASE\data\mirror_dev
sysprocsdev     D:\SYBASE\DATA\SYSPROCS.DAT    NULL
tapedump1       \\.\TAPE0                      NULL
tapedump2       \\.\TAPE1                      NULL
```

You'll also spot a change in the description **sp_helpdevice** displays for the primary device.

```
device_name      physical_name      description
        status cntrltype device_number low       high
---------------------------  ---------------------------------------------
        ---------------------------------------------------------------------
pubs_dev        D:\sybase\data\pubs.dat     special, MIRROR ENABLED, mirror =
'C:\SYBASE\data\mirror_dev', serial writes, reads mirrored, physical disk, 2.00 MB
                        738     0        2   33554432  33555455
```

(Serial is the default for mirror writes. It means SQL Server completes a write on one device before it starts the same write on another. Serial is slower but more reliable than its alternative, noserial, since it precludes a single write failure from affecting both devices.)

You can unmirror devices with DISK UNMIRROR, temporarily or permanently. The devices can be active during any of the mirror commands. To halt writes to the primary device, continue writing to the secondary, and keep the primary device available for future use, use a command like this:

```
DISK UNMIRROR
NAME = pubs_dev,
SIDE = 'primary',
MODE = retain
go
```

(You need quotes around "primary" because it is an SQL Server keyword.) Your action shows up in **sp_helpdevice** output:

```
EXEC p_helpdevice pubs_dev
go

device_name      physical_name      description
        status cntrltype device_number low       high
---------------------------  ---------------------------------------------
        ---------------------------------------------------------------------
pubs_dev        D:\sybase\data\pubs.dat only device 'C:\SYBASE\data\mirror_dev' of
mirror is enabled -- device 'D:\sybase\data\pubs.dat' is disabled, serial writes,
reads mirrored, physical disk, 2.00 MB          482      0        2
33554432        33555455
```

Alternatively, you could halt the secondary device and keep the primary one active.

You can restart mirroring (copy the active device to the idle device) with **DISK REMIRROR**.

```
DISK REMIRROR
NAME = pubs_dev
go
```

To remove mirroring entirely, use a command like this:

```
DISK UNMIRROR
NAME = pubs_dev,
SIDE = secondary,
MODE = remove
go
```

See Sybase documents for details on mirroring options.

Performance

The way you set up your database devices can affect performance. Spreading data across disks and disk controllers cuts down on I/O contention. Look at overall use of databases and make sure all action is not going to one disk (Figure 10.4 shows examples of good and bad disk use).

◆ Put heavily used databases and their logs on separate physical disks.
◆ Distribute active databases among the available disks.
◆ Don't use the master device, the sybsecurity device, log-only devices, or devices hosting high-performance databases as default devices.
◆ Balance system databases and user databases.

You can also use segments and table partitioning to place objects precisely. Segments are discussed (briefly) in Chapter 8 and partitions are discussed in Chapter 12.

Thresholds

SQL Server System 10 introduced thresholds as a way to monitor space use. When free space on a segment with a threshold falls below some level, the threshold manager executes a stored procedure you have created. Typically, the stored procedure does one or more of these things:

- Dumps the transaction log
- Prints a message to the errorlog
- Executes a remote procedure call to an Open Server to send mail or take some other action

There are two kinds of thresholds: last-chance thresholds and free-space thresholds.

Last-chance Thresholds

Last chance thresholds are created by SQL Server for transaction logs only and the logs must be on separate database devices than the data.

Putting a log on a separate database device makes it *thresholdable*. SQL Server automatically figures how many pages you need to back up the log. When free space falls below that number, SQL Server suspends user transactions and displays a message explaining that space is low and transactions are suspended.

```
Space available in the logs segment has fallen critically low in database
'pubs2'. All future modifications to this database will be suspended
until the log is successfully dumped and space becomes available.
```

At this point, you have enough space for a dump transaction.

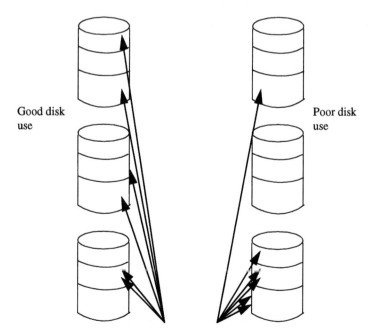

Good disk use

Poor disk use

FIGURE 10.4 Spreading data access among disks.

SQL Server also executes the stored procedure **sp_thresholdaction,** for which you define the action. Figure 10.5 shows a transaction log with a last-chance threshold.

If a transaction log is not on a separate device, it does not have a last-chance threshold. In the master database, for example, data and log are on the same database device (as shown in this fragment of **sp_helpdb** master output):

```
device                          segment
------------------------------- ---------------------
master                          default
master                          logsegment
master                          system
```

In the pubs2 database, user and system tables are on the **pubs_dev** device, but transaction logs are on the **pubs_log** device.

```
device                          segment
------------------------------- ---------------------
pubs_dev                        default
pubs_dev                        system
pubs_log                        logsegment
```

Getting Information on Thresholds with sp_helpthreshold

You can run **sp_helpthreshold** to get more information. In the target database, with no parameters, it reports on all thresholds in that database.

```
use pubs2
go
EXEC sp_helpthreshold
go
segment name          free pages  last chance? threshold procedure
--------------------  ----------- ------------ --------------------
logsegment                    40            1 sp_thresholdaction
```

♦ SQL Server allows 40 2K pages to dump this transaction log (the **pubs_log** device has 512 2K pages, or 1 megabyte in all). If you increase the size of **logsegment** with ALTER DATABASE, SQL Server automatically updates this number. You cannot modify the free pages value of a last chance threshold directly.

♦ This threshold is a last-chance threshold, created by SQL Server (1 means it is a last-chance threshold).

♦ SQL Server executes the threshold stored procedure **sp_thresholdaction** when the log size crosses the last-chance threshold.

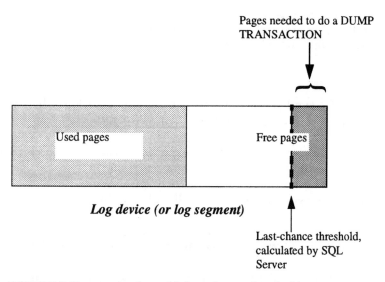

FIGURE 10.5 Transaction log with last-chance threshold.

The same **sp_helpthreshold** command for the master database returns no rows. Although the master database has a log, it is not on a separate device, so it cannot have a last-chance threshold.

```
use master
go
EXEC sp_helpthreshold
go
segment name            free pages last chance?    threshold procedure
----------------------  ---------- ---------------- --------------------

(0 rows affected, return status = 0)
```

Controlling Threshold Actions with sp_thresholdaction

Sybase supplies a description of the stored procedure **sp_thresholdaction,** but you have to create it and decide what action to take. SQL Server is able to handle the variables for:

- database name
- segment name (**logsegment** unless you have assigned a specific segment name to the log device)
- space left, in 2k pages
- status (1 for last-chance thresholds, 0 for all others)

```
CREATE PROCEDURE sp_thresholdaction
@dbname varchar(30), @segmentname varchar(30),
@space_left int, @status int
AS
....
```

To send a message to the Sybase errorlog when the threshold is crossed, add something like this after the AS:

```
PRINT "In database '%1! the segment '%2!' has '%3!' pages remaining.",
@dbname, @segmentname, @space_left
```

The message in the errorlog will look like this:

```
00:95/12/28 20:13:28.54 server background task message: In database
'pubs2' the segment 'logsegment' has '40' pages remaining.
```

A more useful version of the procedure might run a dump as well as printing a message.

```
CREATE PROCEDURE sp_thresholdaction
@dbname varchar(30), @segmentname varchar(30),
@space_left int, @status int
AS
DUMP TRANSACTION @dbname
TO tapedump1
PRINT "Dumped '%1!' '%2!' with '%3!' pages left."
@dbname, @segmentname, @space_left
```

Sybase documentation gives examples of **sp_thresholdaction** code. But remember—you have to create it. If you don't, nothing happens (except the message saying transactions are suspended and the suspension itself).

Aborting Transactions instead of Suspending Them

To abort transactions rather than suspending them when a threshold is crossed, use **sp_dbopton,** like this:

```
EXEC sp_dboption 'pubs2', 'abort tran on log full', 'true'
go
USE pubs2
go
CHECKPOINT
go
```

This means that users will have to re-enter any commands that got caught by the threshold.

Managing Last-Chance Thresholds with Ict_admin()

Another option to consider for last-chance threshold management is the function **lct_admin().** Its parameters are:

- lastchance—allows you to create a last-chance threshold in a database
- logfull—indicates whether a last-chance threshold has been crossed (returns "1" if it has)
- unsuspend—reactivates suspended tasks and puts the last-chance threshold out of commission (useful if tasks were suspended and you didn't create a last-chance threshold or created one that didn't help)
- reserve—tells you how many free log pages you need for a dump transaction

To use **lct_admin** to find out how many free pages you need to dump a 512-page log, try this command:

```
SELECT lct_admin ('reserve', 512)
go
-----------
        40
```

Free-space Thresholds

Free-space thresholds are thresholds you create yourself. Two typical examples are:

- Free-space thresholds for log devices, at a point before the last-chance threshold, so that you get some warning before the last-chance threshold is crossed (Figure 10.6)
- Thresholds for segments holding data, so that you can take action before they fill up (Figure 10.7)

Adding Free-space Thresholds with sp_addthreshold

In either case, you add a threshold with the **sp_addthreshold** command, giving

- The database name
- The segment name
- The amount of free space you want to allow
- The name of the stored procedure to execute when the threshold is crossed

You can have up to 256 thresholds per database. To add a threshold to the pubs2 database, at 80 pages of free space, use a command like this:

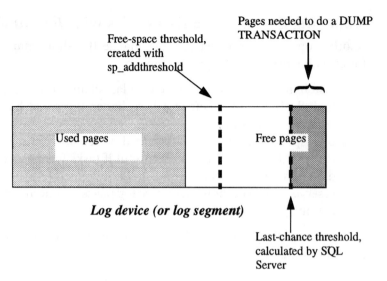

FIGURE 10.6 Last-chance and free-space thresholds on a log device.

```
EXEC sp_addthreshold 'pubs2', 'default', 80, 'sp_thresholdaction'
go
```

If you check thresholds in pubs2 with **sp_helpthreshold,** you'll see the new one. Notice that it is not a last-chance threshold (0 in the last chance column):

```
EXEC sp_helpthreshold
go
segment name          free pages  last chance? threshold procedure
--------------------  ----------- ------------ --------------------
logsegment                    40             1 sp_thresholdaction
default                       80             0 sp_thresholdaction
```

You add a free-space threshold to a log segment in the same way.

Thresholds must not be too close together or they cause constant action for minor changes. If you try to add a threshold that "crowds" an existing one, you'll get a message saying thresholds must be some distance (currently 128 pages) apart. Another way to get this information is to check the value of @@thresh_hysteresis. Thresholds must be separated by twice the value of this global variable.

```
SELECT @@thresh_hysteresis
go
-----------
       64
```

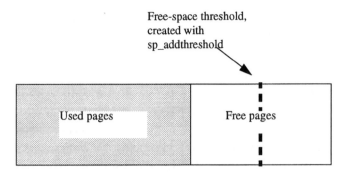

Data segment

FIGURE 10.7 Free-space threshold on a data segment.

An additional threshold for the pubs2 default segment would have to be at least 128 pages from the existing 80-page free-space threshold—have a minimum free space value of 208. If you try to add a threshold at 180 pages, as follows, you get a message:

```
EXEC sp_addthreshold 'pubs2', 'default', 180, 'sp_thresholdaction'
go
This threshold is too close to one or more existing thresholds.
Thresholds must be no closer than 128 pages to each other.
segment_name                     free_space
------------------------------   -----------
default                                   80
```

IN CASE YOU WONDERED WHAT "HYSTERESIS" MEANS:

Webster's New Universal Unabridged Dictionary, 2d ed. (New York: Simon and Schuster, 1993) defines it as a coming short, a deficiency, and notes that ". . . in physics, it is the lagging of an effect in a body when the force acting on it is changed, particularly a lag in the changes of magnetization behind the varying magnetizing force."

Coping with Thresholds

If you're experimenting with thresholds and set one that constantly suspends user activity, you can get some space with this command:

```
DUMP TRANSACTION pubs2
WITH TRUNCATE_ONLY
go
```

It removes the dumpable part of the transaction log, but makes no backup copy.

Other actions are change the threshold and drop the threshold.

You can also increase the size of the segment by adding space with ALTER DATABASE.

Changing a Threshold

You can change a threshold with **sp_modifythreshold,** changing the procedure to execute, the amount of free space, and the segment.

This procedure does not change the database affected. For that, you have to drop the threshold and add it again for the correct database.

This example changes the threshold for the pubs2 default segment to 120 (assuming you added it again after dropping it).

```
EXEC sp_modifythreshold 'pubs2', 'default', 80, null, 120
go
Dropping threshold for segment 'default' at 80 pages.
Adding threshold for segment 'default' at 120 pages.
```

Dropping a Threshold

You remove a threshold by specifying the database name, the segment name, and the free-space value. If you have several thresholds on a database segment, you can remove the one you want. To get rid of the pubs2 threshold just created, use this command:

```
EXEC sp_dropthreshold 'pubs2', 'default', 120
go
```

11

Operations

Overview

This chapter looks at some of the tasks a system administrator or database owner manages. They include:

+ Organizing user access
+ Transferring data
+ Setting database options
+ Monitoring a database with DBCC
+ Planning backups

User Access

This section doesn't cover user access exhaustively. It reviews logins, user accounts, groups, and permissions, noting some new features introduced in System 10 or System 11:

♦ Expanded login information
♦ Roles
♦ Encrypted passwords
♦ Password expiration
♦ Charge-back accounting
♦ GRANT with GRANT option
♦ REVOKE with CASCADE

LOGINS ARE NOT USERS (BUT USERS HAVE LOGINS)

An experienced consultant (let's call him LB) was setting up a friend (JB) to use his SQL Server to develop some databases for a class. LB created a SQL Server login with **sp_addlogin,** and then tried to GRANT CREATE DATABASE to JB. He kept getting the annoying message, "There is no such user JB." He made ugly comments (it was late). He checked syslogins—there was indeed such a person. He logged in as JB—it worked fine—but he still couldn't GRANT CREATE DATABASE!

JB (on the phone): "You need to create a user account for me in the master database."

LB (outraged):   "I did! It's right here!"

JB: "*User* account. Make me a *user* in the master database. Use **sp_adduser.**"

LB (unprintable):   "That's stupid! OK, OK. I'm making you a user. Here—I'm granting CREATE DATABASE again. Hmmmm. . . . Well, whatever it was, it's fixed now."

JB: "Thanks."

Every SQL Server user has to have a SQL Server login. That doesn't do anything but let you into the SQL Server. If there is a guest account in master, you can probably do some selects there, but in order to actually work, you need a user account for a specific database (you can have as many of these as make sense). If you're going to do anything in master (such as create databases), you need to have a user account in master.

Information about SQL Server logins is stored in master..syslogins. Information about user accounts is stored in the database's sysusers table.

Logins

You create a SQL Server login with **sp_addlogin.** The basic command requires the login name and a password with at least six characters. If users log into SQL Server directly, it's convenient to have the same SQL Server and operating system login name (but make sure the passwords are different!). If users log in through an application, this is not an issue.

```
EXEC sp_addlogin mike, secret
go
```

The password cannot be null and must be at least six characters long. It is encrypted. If you query syslogins (where login information is stored) for name and password, you get something like this:

```
SELECT name, password
FROM syslogins
WHERE name = 'mike'
go
name   password
-----  ----------------------------------------------------------------
mike   0x010491428479e9a960ea2d0b9ede504158a1639b53fa600dd9dd0446e15c
```

Should you forget your password, the system security officer (more about this later) has to replace your old password (unseen, since it's not human-readable) with a new one, so that you can log in. The parameters are the changer's password, your new password, and your login name.

```
EXEC sp_password 'bigBoss', 'UnknowN', 'mike'
go
```

You can also use **sp_password** to change your own password (and of course you have to be logged in to do this), but only if you remember it, since the two parameters you need are the old password and the new one. Login name is not necessary in this case.

If you want to get fancy with a SQL Server login, you can also specify:

♦ A default database (the one you "go to" when you log in)
♦ A default language
♦ A full name (useful for record keeping)

To give Mich a login with a login name, password, default database, and full name, use a command like this:

```
EXEC sp_addlogin 'mich', 'secret', 'pubs2', null, 'Michel T. LeFleur'
go
```

You can check for details on a login with the **sp_displaylogin** stored procedure.

```
EXEC sp_displaylogin mich
go
Suid: 8
Loginame: mich
Fullname: Michel T. Fleur
Configured Authorization:
Locked: NO
Date of Last Password Change: Dec 30 1995 6:06PM
```

Suid is the unique server login id number. Configured authorization, locked, and date of password change are discussed later in this chapter. A database owner uses **sp_adduser** to authorize a SQL Server login to use a particular database.

Roles

SQL Server supports three roles:

- ♦ sa_role (system administrator role) to allow a user to perform system administrator functions. These include all the commands that only the system administrator can run. (A user who has the sa_role can also be granted the semi-documented sybase_ts_role. Sybase tech support staff will walk you through this if you ever need it.)
- ♦ sso_role (system security officer role) to allow a user to act as a system security officer. This means the user can create login accounts, grant and revoke sso and operator roles, change passwords, and manage the auditing database sybsecurity (if auditing has been installed).
- ♦ oper_role (operator role) to allow a user to back up and load all databases.

At installation, the system administrator (sa) has all three roles by default. In a small system, you might want to leave it like that, perhaps giving the sa password to a user or two for backup.

For full accountability, set up the roles and grant them to users, then lock the installation "sa" account (see the section on locking logins for details). You can assign a role to more than one person. You might find it convenient to have a pool of system administrators, for example, so that essential functions can be performed as necessary. Because each user with a given role still has a personal login, you'll be able to track who ran a particular command—not possible if several users shared a login and password.

To make Mich an operator, use a command like this:

```
EXEC sp_role 'GRANT', oper_role, mich
go
```

If you run **sp_displaylogin** for Mich again, you'll see the role

```
Suid: 8
Loginame: mich
Fullname: Michel T. Fleur
Configured Authorization: oper_role
Locked: NO
Date of Last Password Change: Dec 30 1995 6:06PM
```

Roles go into effect the next time the user logs in *or* as soon as the user runs the SET ROLE command.

To activate his new operator role, Mich can do this:

```
SET ROLE "oper_role" ON
go
Authorization updated.
```

Groups and Users

Groups and users both belong to specific databases and are recorded in the database sysusers table. Because it's convenient to create groups before users, this section reviews groups first, then users.

Every user belongs to the *public* group by default. You can also assign a user to one other group per database. Groups are a useful way to manage access to objects. (In fact, that is the only purpose of groups.) If you establish permissions at the group level then, when you add new users, you need only add them to the appropriate group; they have their permissions established.

Keep the permission structure simple. GRANT and REVOKE to either users or to groups. Don't mix the two. If you GRANT and REVOKE permissions to users and groups, then the order in which you set up the permissions is critical. If you GRANT a permission to an individual and then REVOKE it from the group that user is in, the user does not have the permission.

It's a good idea to set up groups before you add users. Groups usually represent some natural role or responsibility, such as engineer or manager. To create a managers group in the pubs2 database, enter a command like this:

```
EXEC sp_addgroup 'managers'
go
```

Information about groups is stored in sysusers. You can get a report with **sp_helpgroup.** With no parameters, it shows all groups in the database. (Roles are listed as groups, but they don't have the same limitations: A user can have more than one role, and can have a role and be in a group.) Group ids (except for the public group) start at 16,384.

```
EXEC sp_helpgroup
go
Group_name                        Group_id
------------------------------    --------
managers                             16390
navigator_role                       16388
oper_role                            16386
public                                   0
replication_role                     16389
sa_role                              16384
sso_role                             16385
sybase_ts_role                       16387
test                                 16391
```

Add a user with **sp_adduser.** (You need to be the owner of the database and using that database when you execute **sp_adduser.**) The parameters are login name, name in database, and group name.

Name in database and group name are optional. Using different names for the SQL Server login and the database user name generally leads to problems. Don't do it unless you have a special reason or an application that controls user login and database use and needs different names.

To make Mich a user and a member of the managers group in the pubs2 database, type a command like this:

```
EXEC sp_adduser mich, mich, managers
go
```

You can get information about users with **sp_helpuser.** With no parameter, it reports on all users. If you give a user name, you see details for that user only. ("guest," by the way, is a kind of default user you can add to a database if you want to provide some access for people who don't have a user account in the database. Guest inherits whatever permissions the public group has.)

```
EXEC sp_helpuser
go
Users_name         ID_in_db Group_name       Login_name       Default_db
----------------   -------- ---------------- ---------------- -------
dbo                       1 public           bowman           master
guest                     2 public           NULL             NULL
mich                      3 managers         mich             pubs2
```

To move a user to a different group, use **sp_changegroup.** The parameters are the name of the new group and the user name. The group must already exist in the database. To move Mich to the "test" group, use this command:

```
EXEC sp_changegroup 'test', 'mich'
go
```

To take a user out of a group without putting him into a new one, use "public" as the group name. (Put quotes around it—it's a SQL Server keyword.)

```
EXEC sp_changegroup 'public', 'mich'
go
```

Aliases

SQL Server lets you create aliases for users. For example, if Ted does the same sort of work that Mich does, but isn't a pubs2 user, you can alias him to Mich, and he'll be able to act as Mich in pubs2. The command looks like this:

```
EXEC sp_addalias 'ted', 'mich'
go
```

Ted won't show up in a list of pubs2 users. However, if you run **sp_helpuser** with ted as a parameter, you'll find he is aliased to mich.

```
EXEC sp_helpuser 'ted'
go
```
The name supplied is aliased to another user.

Alias_name	ID_in_db	Group_name	Login_name	Default_db
mich	3	public	mich	pubs2

But what's the point? Why introduce this complicated scheme when all you have to do is give Ted a user account and put him in the same group as Mich? Unless you have a specific reason, don't use aliases. Keep your permission system simple and easy to understand.

SETUSER

SETUSER allows the database owner to "impersonate" a user, usually to give some help. If Mich is in over his head, trying to create a table, the database owner might lend a hand by doing the work for Mich ("as" Mich).

```
SETUSER 'mich'
go
```

The database owner is now, in effect, Mich, and has Mich's permissions. He can test accessing objects as Mich to verify that permissions are correct. Only the dbo can use the SETUSER command.

Managing Users

You can force users to change their passwords with the **sp_configure** "password expiration interval" option. To make passwords expire every week, set the value to seven:

```
EXEC sp_configure 'systemwide password expiration', 7
go
```

After a password expires, a user can still log in, but can execute no commands except **sp_password.**

You use **sp_password** to change a user's password. To change default database, default language, or full name for a login, use **sp_modifylogin.** You specify the login name, element you want to change, and the new value. If Mich changes his last name to LeFleur-Hollis and you want to update his login, you make an entry like this:

```
EXEC sp_modifylogin 'mich','fullname', 'Michel T. LeFleur-Hollis'
go
```

You can collect statistics on users with **sp_reportstats** and **sp_clearstats.** The first reports on use statistics for all users (no parameters) or for a specific user (give the login name as a parameter):

```
EXEC sp_reportstats 'mich'
go
 Name            Since       CPU   Percent CPU  I/O Percent I/O
 --------------- ----------- ----- ------------ --- -----------
 mich            Nov 11 1995    31  100.0000%    69  100.0000%


 Total CPU  Total I/O
 ---------- -----------
        31          69
```

SQL Server stores the statistics in **syslogins.**

You can set how often SQL Server writes CPU and I/O statistics to the **master..syslogins** table with **sp_configure** "cpu accounting flush interval" and "i/o accounting flush interval," respectively. The default for CPU is 200 machine clock ticks, while that for I/O statistics is 1,000 I/Os. To change the CPU flush interval, use a command like this:

```
EXEC sp_configure 'cpu accounting flush interval', 100
go
```

To start a new accounting period, use **sp_clearstats.** It prints out the current statistics (for all users if you give no login name, or for the named login) and then clears them, so that you start again. Here's how you remove the old values for Mich:

```
EXEC sp_clearstats 'mich'
go
```

Removing Users

SQL Server won't tolerate "orphan" objects, users, or groups. Before removing a group, you have to make sure it is empty. Before removing a user, you have to drop any objects the user owns. The process looks like this:

1. Remove objects the user owns and revoke rights the user has granted
2. Drop the user from the database (**sp_dropuser**)
3. Drop the corresponding login from SQL Server (**sp_droplogin**)

Better yet, set up production databases so that all objects belong to the database owner. This Eases table management, simplifies permission management, and prevents difficulties when you remove an object owner.

Whenever multiple users own objects, the permission structure gets complex, and owners are usually too lenient about giving access to their objects. If the database owner (dbo) owns everything (including stored procedures and the objects they reference), the dbo need only grant permission to execute the stored procedures. Other users don't have (or need) direct access to the underlying objects. With this scheme, it's easy to manage objects and users—you don't have to worry about objects they own or permissions they have granted.

If you don't have the database set up this way, and need to drop users who own lots of objects, you can leave the objects in place and lock the login. The user can no longer log in. The dbo can manage the objects and permissions.

```
EXEC sp_locklogin 'mich', 'lock'
go
```

Dropping a dbo is somewhat more complex. First use **sp_change-dbowner** to appoint a new dbo. If you want the new owner to inherit the current owner's aliases and permissions, specify "true" as your second parameter. To make Mike the new pubs2 dbo, use this command:

```
EXEC sp_changedbowner mike, true
go
```

The new dbo must not be a user in the database or have an alias there. You can drop the SQL Server login of the former dbo.

Permissions

You can enable users or groups to CREATE objects and allow them to use existing objects. The best way to handle this is to set up functional groups and make each user a member of an appropriate group. Then you can grant permissions to the group and all current and future members inherit them.

If the dbo owns all objects (as recommended), you don't need to grant any **CREATE** permissions except perhaps **CREATE PROCEDURE**. To grant **CREATE PROCEDURE** to everyone, use a command like this:

```
GRANT CREATE PROCEDURE
TO public
go
```

You can also grant permissions to roles.

To allow only members of the managers group to see the title and price columns in the titles table, first revoke all rights on the table to all users and then grant specific rights to the group:

```
REVOKE ALL on titles
FROM public
go
GRANT SELECT
ON titles (title, price)
TO managers
go
```

Rights you can grant include **SELECT, INSERT, UPDATE, DELETE, REFERENCE,** and **EXECUTE.** The first four apply to tables and views. **REFERENCE** applies to tables only. Users who create tables with constraints referencing other tables need **REFERENCE** rights to those tables. **EXECUTE** permission allows a user to run a specific stored procedure.

If you check the table permissions with **sp_helprotect,** the command and results look like this:

```
EXEC sp_helprotect titles
go
grantor     grantee      type      action  object        column   grantable
----------  -----------  --------  ------- ------------- -------  ---------
dbo         managers     Grant     Select  titles         price   FALSE
dbo         managers     Grant     Select  titles         title   FALSE
```

The last column is for **GRANT WITH GRANT OPTION.** It allows you to give a user rights to use an object and the ability to pass on those rights to other users.

According to Sybase documentation, you can use this option with individual users only, not with groups or public. There is a corresponding CASCADE option for REVOKE.

Use these options with caution. They tend to complicate the permission structure and weaken centralized control.

Another way to view permissions on a table is with **sp_column_privileges.** It gives a history of permissions for a specified column, taking table, owner, database, and column names as parameters. Here's an example command and a fragment of the output:

```
        EXEC sp_column_privileges titles, dbo, pubs2, price
        go
table_qualifier table_owner table_name column_name grantor grantee privilege is_
  grantable
----------------------------------- ------------------------------------------------
pubs2    dbo     titles  price   dbo    guest    REFERENCE      NO
pubs2            dbo       titles    price      dbo     ted    SELECT     NO
....
```

The related stored procedure **sp_table_privileges** provides similar information. The parameters are table name, table owner, and database.

Rules of Thumb for User Management

The dbo should own all tables and production stored procedures. The dbo should GRANT and REVOKE permissions to groups.

Loading Data

NON-LOGGING BCP

A developer can't figure out why the log keeps filling up. He is doing bcp, but he is using the non-logging bcp. Ah, some terms take a long time to die.

If you have no indexes on a table, and use bcp to copy data into the table, there is *minimal* logging. The allocation of space is still logged, but the details of each row are not. However, if you have a large number of rows, this logging of space allocation will require a large amount of space in the transaction log.

bcp is a utility for loading volume data into a table or for extracting table data out to a flat file. There are two speeds for bcp in a database: slow and fast.

♦ Slow bcp is similar to executing a number of INSERT statements to load the data—all of the rows are logged as they are inserted.
♦ Fast bcp is much speedier, with space allocation (but not individual inserts) logged.

Normally, SQL Server uses slow bcp. However, if you use the option:

```
EXEC sp_dboption 'select into/bulkcopy', TRUE
go
```

and if the table you are bcping into has no indexes or triggers (or you have removed them temporarily) SQL Server will use fast bcp. With fast bcp, you have to do some cleanup after you run the command.

- ◆ Dump the database
- ◆ Recreate any indexes or triggers you dropped temporarily
- ◆ Reset "select into/bulk copy" to false

For either type of operation, fast or slow, defaults defined for columns and datatypes in the target table are observed. SQL Server ignores rules and constraints to load data at maximum speed. You can make sure they are enforced by following this procedure:

1. Create a *dummy* table that has the same columns as the original table but no indexes or triggers.
2. Copy the new data to the dummy table with bcp.
3. Insert the data from the dummy table into the original table (with all indexes, triggers, and constraints in place) using a statement like:
   ```
   INSERT original_table
   SELECT * from dummy_table
   go
   ```

The last step will cause evaluation of the rules, triggers, and constraints, and report any errors.

Setting Database Options

While **sp_configure** options apply to the whole SQL Server (see Chapter 12), **sp_dboption** options are for individual databases. You can get a list of options by running **sp_dboption** with no parameters:

```
EXEC sp_dboption
go
Settable database options.
 database_options
 ---------------------------
 abort tran on log full
 allow nulls by default
 auto identity
```

```
dbo use only
ddl in tran
identity in nonunique index
no chkpt on recovery
no free space acctg
read only
select into/bulkcopy
single user
trunc log on chkpt
trunc. log on chkpt.
```

(The last two items are alternate spellings of the same option.)
You have to work in both the master and the user databases to execute
sp_dboptions commands.

    1. Run **sp_dboption** in the master database, giving the user database
name as part of the command

```
USE master
go
EXEC sp_dboption pubs2, 'dbo use only', true
go
```

    2. Return to the affected database and insert a checkpoint.

```
USE pubs2
go
CHECKPOINT
go
```

    To un-set any option, specify false instead of true. You cannot set
options on the master database. A few interesting options are discussed in
the following sections.

abort tran on log full

This option is part of your threshold strategy (discussed in Chapter 10).

    ♦ When the option is false (the default) the threshold manager suspends
transactions when the last-chance threshold is crossed. The suspended
transactions complete after log space becomes available.

    ♦ When the option is true, transactions are aborted rather than sus-
pended.

allow NULLS by default

If you don't specify a NULL/NOT NULL status for a column when you create a table, the default goes into effect:

- ♦ The SQL Server default is NOT NULL.
- ♦ The ANSI standard default is NULL.

If you need to be ANSI-compliant, use a command like this:

```
EXEC sp_dboption pubs2, 'allow nulls by default', true
go
```

The option has no effect on constraints.

To avoid confusion, explicitly spell out the NULL/NOT NULL status of each column in your CREATE TABLE statements. Defaults change, people do strange things, but clear NULL and NOT NULL statements speak for themselves.

auto identity

This option, when set to true, forces every row to have a unique identifier. If you create a table with no primary key, no unique constraint, and no IDENTITY columns, SQL Server adds a (secret) column with the IDENTITY property. It's not visible in an ordinary SELECT*, but you can see it by including SYB_IDENTITY_COL in the SELECT list.

no chkpt on recovery

The no chkpt on recovery setting has two uses. One is in a *warm standby* environment (see Chapter 7). The other is in certain instances when an 1105 error occurs ("Can't allocate space . . .").

Normally, when SQL Server completes recovery (every time you boot the server), the server issues a CHECKPOINT. This forces all dirty pages in cache to disk and writes a CHECKPOINT record in the log. In a warm standby environment or when an 1105 error occurs, you do not want the server to do this.

- ♦ In the warm standby case, this would not allow you to load any subsequent transaction dumps.
- ♦ In the 1105 error case, it may not be possible to issue a CHECKPOINT, because the database is full.

Issuing the CHECKPOINT in these cases causes the server to mark the database as not recovered.

The no chkpt on recovery setting instructs SQL Server *not* to do a CHECKPOINT at the completion of its recovery operation.

no free space acctg

This option is part of your threshold strategy. Use it to prevent threshold actions for all non-log segments. This can make recovery faster.

select into/bulkcopy

The **select into/bulkcopy** setting for the **sp_dboption** allows you to use WRITETEXT, SELECT INTO a permanent table, and fast bcp.

After you have set this option and executed one of the previous statements, you cannot use a DUMP TRAN command (unless it truncates the log)—you need to first do a DUMP DATABASE.

single user

When you set the **single user** option of the **sp_dboption** stored procedure, only one user at a time can access this database. Some SQL commands (DBCC CHECKDB) require you to be in single-user mode (or at least give more accurate results if you are in this mode).

trunc.log on chkpt

This option causes SQL Server to truncate the transaction log every time the automatic checkpoint process runs (about once a minute). This may be useful in development or test, or whenever logs are growing quickly and you do not need up-to-the-minute recovery. When you set this option:

- ♦ You cannot use DUMP TRAN (no incremental dumps) except one that truncates the log.
- ♦ You can use DUMP DATABASE, but if there is a media failure on one of the database devices, you can only recover back to the point of the last database dump.

If you do not set this option, the DUMP TRAN command is the only way to truncate the transaction log.

TRUNC.LOG ON CHKPT

This option is commonly pronounced "truncate log on checkpoint." Early in our SQL Server career, we were working on bulk copying in a huge amount of data. We turned this option on, and did our bulk copy with a batch size specified, so there would be a commit every 100,000 rows. After this commit, the log records for this batch could be truncated. We then set up a process to do a "CHECKPOINT" every few minutes, in order to truncate the log.

Sometime later, we learned that the option "trunc.log on chkpt" has nothing to do with someone executing the CHECKPOINT statement. The log is truncated approximately once a minute when the checkpoint process automatically wakes up and processes this database.

We sheepishly went back to the customer and suggested removing that CHECKPOINT code.

DBCC

DBCC is the database consistency checker. Run DBCC commands as part of your regular database maintenance program. It can identify and repair problems.

- ◆ Use DBCC CHECKALLOC, INDEXALLOC, and TABLEALLOC commands for checking space allocation
- ◆ Use DBCC CHECKDB and CHECKTABLE to check page use
- ◆ Use DBCC CHECKCATALOG to check system tables

Scheduling DBCC

DBCC CHECKALLOC and CHECKDB look at the whole database and can be time-consuming.

- ◆ If you have sufficient time, use CHECKDB and CHECKALLOC before every dump. With experience, you will discover that some databases never have any problems identified by DBCC commands.
- ◆ If there is not enough time to run CHECKDB and CHECKALLOC before every dump, you can run DBCC TABLEALLOC and DBCC CHECKTABLE for crucial tables before every dump, and run them for other tables on a nightly or weekly schedule.

Space Allocation

Figure 11.1 reviews space allocation

- ◆ DISK INIT creates space in allocation units (256 2K pages).
- ◆ The first page in an allocation unit is the allocation page. It records which pages in the allocation unit are in use and which pages are allocated to which tables.
- ◆ SQL Server allocates and deallocates table and index space in extents (8 2k pages) and records the changes on the allocation page.
- ◆ Each table and index has an object allocation map (OAM) which points to the allocation pages of allocation units reserved for that object.

CHECKALLOC

DBCC CHECKALLOC looks at all the allocation units and their pages in a database. It checks that all used pages are allocated and all allocated pages are used.

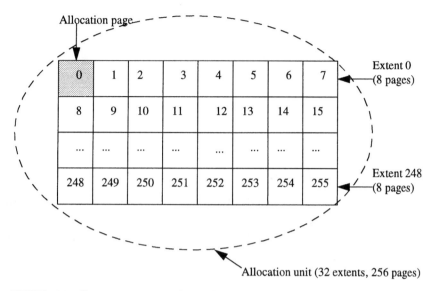

FIGURE 11.1 Allocation units and extents.

Run CHECKALLOC before you do any dumps so that you can identify and fix errors. In default mode (NOFIX) the command does not repair errors. Because CHECKALLOC reviews the whole database, you may decide to use it in NOFIX mode to identify errors and then run DBCC TABLE-ALLOC in FIX mode on specific tables.

The commands look like this (put the database in single-user mode to prevent spurious errors):

```
USE master
go
EXEC sp_dboption pubs2, 'single user', true
go
Database option 'single user' turned ON for database 'pubs2'.
Run the CHECKPOINT command in the database that was changed.
(return status = 0)
USE pubs2
go
CHECKPOINT
go
DBCC CHECKALLOC (pubs2)
go
```

Output gives you a display for each table in the database. A sample looks like this:

```
Checking pubs2
***************************************************************
TABLE: sysobjects        OBJID = 1
INDID=1   FIRST=1         ROOT=8          SORT=0
  Data level: 1. 3 Data Pages in 1 extents.
   Indid   :1. 1 Index Pages in 1 extents.
INDID=2   FIRST=16        ROOT=16         SORT=0
   Indid   :2. 1 Index Pages in 1 extents.
  TOTAL # of extents = 3
  ...
```

TABLEALLOC

DBCC TABLEALLOC makes the same checks as CHECKALLOC but on individual tables. The default mode is FIX. It is a good choice if you know what table is having problems. The command and output look like this:

```
DBCC TABLEALLOC(titles)
go
The default report option of OPTIMIZED is used for this run.
The default fix option of FIX is used for this run.
***************************************************************
TABLE: titles        OBJID = 208003772
INDID=1        FIRST=537      ROOT=529       SORT=1
       Data level: 1. 3 Data Pages in 1 extents.
         Indid    : 1. 1 Index Pages in 1 extents.
INDID=2        FIRST=449      ROOT=449       SORT=1
         Indid    : 2. 1 Index Pages in 1 extents.
TOTAL # of extents = 3
Alloc page 512 (# of extent=1 used pages=2 ref pages=2)
Alloc page 512 (# of extent=1 used pages=4 ref pages=4)
Alloc page 256 (# of extent=1 used pages=2 ref pages=2)
Total (# of extent=3 used pages=8 ref pages=8) in this database
DBCC execution completed. If DBCC printed error messages, contact a user
with
System Administrator (SA) role.
```

INDEXALLOC

DBCC INDEXALLOC is an index-level version of DBCC CHECKALLOC. The parameters are table name and index identification number. You can get the appropriate index number with this query:

```
SELECT o.name, o.id, i.name, i.indid
FROM sysobjects o, sysindexes i
WHERE o.id = i.id and o.name = 'titles'
go
name              id        name        indid
----------------- --------- ----------  ------
titles            208003772 titleidind      1
titles            208003772 titleind        2
```

Run DBCC INDEXALLOC for tileidind, like this:

```
DBCC INDEXALLOC('titles', 1)
go
The default report option of OPTIMIZED is used for this run.
The default fix option of FIX is used for this run.
*****************************************************************
TABLE: titles       OBJID = 208003772
INDID=1      FIRST=537      ROOT=529       SORT=1
      Data level: 1. 3 Data Pages in 1 extents.
      Indid    : 1. 1 Index Pages in 1 extents.
TOTAL # of extents = 2
Alloc page 512 (# of extent=1 used pages=2 ref pages=2)
Alloc page 512 (# of extent=1 used pages=4 ref pages=4)
Total (# of extent=2 used pages=6 ref pages=6) in this database
DBCC execution completed. If DBCC printed error messages, contact a user
with System Administrator (SA) role.
```

CHECKDB

The DBCC CHECKDB and CHECKTABLE commands check page links. (SQL Server is the cause of any problems the system detects—there is nothing you can do to damage a table.) Once a page is allocated, that page is linked with other pages for the same object. Each page has a header with pointers to preceding and following pages. When SQL Server adds pages for an object, the header pointers change.

Run DBCC CHECKDB before each DUMP DATABASE or DUMP TRANSACTION. Here's the command and some sample output.

```
USE pubs2
go
DBCC CHECKDB
go
Checking current database
Checking 1
The total number of data pages in this table is 3.
Table has 51 data rows.
Checking 2
....
Checking 8
The total number of data pages in this table is 256.
*** NOTICE: Space used on the log segment is 0.50 Mbytes, 50.00%.
*** NOTICE: Space free on the log segment is 0.50 Mbytes, 50.00%.
Table has 2079 data rows
....
Checking 336004228
The total number of data pages in this table is 1.
The total number of TEXT/IMAGE pages in this table is 6.
Table has 6 data rows.
```

```
Checking 672005425
The total number of data pages in this table is 110.
Table has 990 data rows.
DBCC execution completed. If DBCC printed error messages, contact a user
with System Administrator (SA) role.
```

CHECKCATALOG

DBCC CHECKCATALOG reads a number of system tables and ensures they are internally consistent. In particular, it reads the **sysobjects**, **syscolumns**, **sysprocedures**, **sysindexes**, **syssegments**, and **sysusages** tables. (The command is not time-consuming on most databases.)

One of the problems caught by DBCC CHECKCATALOG is a user type (datatype) identified for a column where that datatype does not exist in the **systypes** table. You should run DBCC CHECKCATALOG before running any DUMP command for a database. Here is the command and output.

```
USE pubs2
go
DBCC CHECKCATALOG
go
Checking current database
The following segments have been defined for database 6 (database name
pubs2).
virtual start addr    size    segments
--------------------  ------  ----------------
33554432              1024                   0
83886080              512                    2
```

CHECKTABLE

DBCC CHECKTABLE validates the internal consistency of a single table's data pages and index pointers. Fortunately, there are not often problems. DBCC CHECKDB does a CHECKTABLE for all the tables in the database.

```
USE pubs2
go
DBCC CHECKTABLE (titles)
go
Checking titles
The total number of data pages in this table is 3.
Table has 18 data rows.
DBCC execution completed. If DBCC printed error messages, contact a user
with System Administrator (SA) role.
```

Backup and Restore

Dumps and loads are performed by the Backup Server.

♦ The DUMP DATABASE and LOAD DATABASE statements are used to back up or restore an entire database.
♦ The DUMP TRANSACTION and LOAD TRANSACTION statements are used to perform an incremental dump and to restore from that incremental dump.

DUMP DATABASE Statement

The DUMP DATABASE statement makes a backup copy of a database. This copy captures the state of the database at the end of the dump. Other activities can continue in the database while it is being dumped.

The DUMP DATABASE statement copies the contents of all currently written pages in the database to the dump device. The size of a database dump may be significantly less than the size allocated for a database.

Beware of the INIT and NOINIT options on the DUMP DATABASE statement. The INIT option specifies that any existing dumps on the dump device will be overwritten with this dump. NOINIT specifies that this dump is appended to the dump device. NOINIT is the default! This means that if you do several DUMPs to the same device, and then try to LOAD from that dump file, you will load the first dump (the default on LOAD is the first file in the dump). This may not be what you had in mind.

LOAD DATABASE Statement

The LOAD DATABASE statement copies all the pages from the backup copy of the database into the database. To load a database dump, the database must already exist and cannot be in use. If you are replacing an existing database, there is no need to DROP the database first. The LOAD DATA-BASE statement overwrites the entire database and initializes any unallocated pages.

If the database does not yet exist, you must create it first. The most efficient way to do that is using CREATE DATABASE FOR LOAD which is much faster than issuing a CREATE DATABASE statement.

Even though the DUMP DATABASE statement creates a backup copy smaller than the original database, the database you are loading a dump into must be at least as big as space allocated for the original database. Using DUMP DATABASE and LOAD DATABASE together will not reduce the size of a database. Because the LOAD DATABASE statement initializes all unallocated pages, it may take a long time to issue a LOAD DATABASE statement, even if the dump is small.

DUMP TRANSACTION Statement

The DUMP TRANSACTION statement (see Table 11.1) copies the transaction log to a backup device and truncates the inactive portion of the log. There are also options that allow you to perform one or the other of these two tasks.

In order to issue a DUMP TRANSACTION statement that copies the transaction log to a dump device, the log must be on a separate SQL Server device. This is not necessary if you are using the WITH TRUNCATE_ONLY or WITH NO_LOG options (which do not copy the transaction log to a dump device).

The TRUNCATE_ONLY option removes the inactive part of the transaction log. It does not make a copy to a backup device. This is the statement to enter if SQL Server is unable to allocate space on the log segment.

The NO_LOG option only removes the inactive portion of the transaction log and

♦ It does not make a copy to a backup device
♦ It does not record its activity in the log
♦ There is some danger to the integrity of the database

Use this option only if DUMP TRANSACTION WITH TRUNCATE_ONLY fails because there is insufficient log space. Always do a DUMP DATABASE after issuing this command.

Use the NO_TRUNCATE option for two purposes:

♦ For making regular incremental (DUMP TRANSACTION) dumps when you do not want to load a whole series of incremental dumps in case of a failure. This option does not truncate the log with each DUMP TRANSACTION; therefore, by LOADing the original database dump and the latest transaction dump, you restore all transactions up to the point of the last DUMP TRANSACTION. Without this option, to

TABLE 11.1 DUMP TRANSACTION Statement

DUMP TRANSACTION	copies to log device	truncates the log
DUMP TRANSACTION . . . WITH TRUNCATE_ONLY		truncates the log
DUMP TRANSACTION . . . WITH NO_LOG		truncates the log
DUMP TRANSACTION . . . WITH NO_TRUNCATE	copies to log device	

recover, you would load each incremental dump taken since the last DUMP DATABASE.

◆ For up-to-the-minute recovery after losing a data device. If a data device is lost, you can still issue a DUMP TRANSACTION WITH NO_TRUNCATE statement and capture one last transaction dump that includes all transactions up to the point of data device failure.

The DUMP TRANSACTION statement also supports the INIT and NOINIT options described under DUMP DATABASE.

The LOAD TRANSACTION Statement

The LOAD TRANSACTION statement loads a backup copy of the transaction log and applies all the changes reflected to the database's transaction log.

DEVICE ERRORS

One of our customers called to tell us that she was trying to load a database dump, but was getting device errors. We suggested that she try an earlier dump, just to pinpoint where the problem was. Ultimately, she tried loading all of the dumps—and none were readable. After searching through operating system error logs, she discovered that she had been getting error messages on that particular tape drive for months. They had no good dumps—NONE!

1. Don't forget to look at your Sybase errorlog regularly!
2. Don't forget to look at your operating system error logs regularly!

DUMP/LOAD Schemes

You need to choose a backup strategy for your database based on:

◆ Ease of dumping
◆ Ease of loading
◆ How much data you are willing to lose in case of a device failure
◆ How long you are willing to have the database unavailable

Using Only DUMP DATABASE on a Database

DUMP DATABASE captures a copy of the database at the time of the dump. If you only use DUMP DATABASE on a database, you can only recover back to the time of the last dump and you lose all transactions since the last dump.

You can also use database dumps to copy a database. The commands to do a database DUMP are:

```
DUMP TRANSACTION WITH TRUNCATE_ONLY /* truncates the log */
DUMP DATABASE
```

The command to LOAD is:

```
LOAD DATABASE
```

This is the simplest approach. You would do a DUMP DATABASE regularly. If you do this once a day, then whenever there is a device failure, you would lose at most one day's worth of data. After the failure, you would find new disk space, drop and recreate the database, then LOAD the dump.

Using DUMP DATABASE and Incremental DUMP TRANSACTION

Using a DUMP DATABASE and Incremental DUMP TRANSACTION technique minimizes the amount of regular activity needed to maintain all transactions in a transaction dump. Using it, you minimize the size of each incremental dump, since, each time you do a DUMP TRANSACTION, SQL Server truncates the transaction log. It may take quite awhile to recover, however, since you must issue a series of LOAD TRANSACTION statements. If these dumps are on tape, each tape needs to be mounted in the correct order in order to recover.

The skeleton command to do a full dump is

```
DUMP DATABASE
```

The command to do an incremental DUMP is

```
DUMP TRANSACTION
```

The standard sequence to LOAD is

```
LOAD DATABASE
LOAD TRANSACTION /* load first incremental dump */
LOAD TRANSACTION /* load second incremental dump */
LOAD TRANSACTION /* load third incremental dump, and so;d3 */
```

With this scheme, there is more work to do for your regular dumps (you are executing DUMP TRANSACTION statements between your regular DUMP DATABASE statements). Your recovery is also more complicated, since you have to load many incremental dumps. When there is a failure, you only lose the changes since your last incremental dump. If you are doing DUMP DATABASE daily, and DUMP TRANSACTION hourly, then you will lose at most one hour's worth of transactions.

Using *DUMP DATABASE* and Accumulating *DUMP TRANSACTION*

Using a DUMP DATABASE and accumulating DUMP TRANSACTION technique requires a larger transaction log. Each incremental dump (DUMP TRANSACTION) takes longer because it contains the entire transaction log since the last DUMP DATABASE. Because you will only have to issue one LOAD DATABASE and one LOAD TRANSACTION statement, it reduces recovery time. If a failure happens, you will lose all transactions since the last incremental dump.

The command to do a full DUMP is

```
DUMP DATABASE
```

The command to do an incremental DUMP is

```
DUMP TRANSACTION WITH NO_TRUNCATE
```

The standard sequence to LOAD is

```
LOAD DATABASE
LOAD TRANSACTION /* load last incremental dump */
```

The DUMP complexity of this scheme is the same as the previous one. However, loading is simplified, since you need only do two loads (a database dump and one transaction log dump). The potential for lost transactions is also the same.

Up-to-the-Minute Recovery

With an Up-to-the-Minute Recovery you can recover *all* transactions that happened up to the point of a device failure. It minimizes the size of each incremental dump because, each time you do a DUMP TRANSACTION, the server truncates the transaction log. To recover from a failure you must issue a series of LOAD TRANSACTION statements, so recovery may take quite awhile. Also for recovery, if these dumps are on tape, you must mount each tape in the correct order.

When a data device fails, you must capture one last transaction log dump using the DUMP TRANSACTION WITH NO_TRUNCATE option. You will not lose transactions, but the database is unavailable while completing the loads.

The command to do a full DUMP is

```
DUMP DATABASE
```

The command to do an incremental DUMP is

```
DUMP TRANSACTION
```

After a device failure occurs on a data device

```
DUMP TRANSACTION WITH NO_TRUNCATE
```

The standard sequence to LOAD is

```
LOAD DATABASE
LOAD TRANSACTION /* load first incremental dump */
LOAD TRANSACTION /* load second incremental dump */
LOAD TRANSACTION /* load third incremental dump, and so on;d3 */
LOAD TRANSACTION /* the WITH NO_TRUNCATE dump */
```

The DUMP TRANSACTION WITH NO_TRUNCATE is a "dying gasp" dump. This dump preserves all of the transactions in the transaction log at the point of failure. Note that this applies to a failed "data" device. If the log devices fail, you cannot recover the transactions since the last transaction log dump. This is why it is important to consider using mirroring to protect the transaction log. A log device failure is catastrophic. A data device failure is recoverable.

Backing Up the Master Database

It is important to back up the master database along with other databases. You need to back up the master database any time there are changes to it.

Some examples of commands that make changes to the master database are:

- ♦ ALTER DATABASE
- ♦ CREATE DATABASE
- ♦ DISK INIT
- ♦ DISK MIRROR
- ♦ DISK UNMIRROR
- ♦ DISK REMIRROR

Many stored procedures make changes, too. Consider:

- ♦ **sp_addlogin,**
- ♦ **sp_addremotelogin**
- ♦ **sp_addsegment**
- ♦ **sp_addserver**
- ♦ **sp_addumpdevice**

- ◆ **sp_configure**
- ◆ **sp_dropdevice**
- ◆ **sp_droplogin**
- ◆ **sp_dropsegment**
- ◆ **sp_dropremotelogin**
- ◆ **sp_extendsegment**
- ◆ **sp_logdevice**

12

System 11 Tuning Features

Overview

System 11 (known internally at Sybase as "Cougar") is a performance release. Many of the new features are responses to specific customer needs or make previously untuneable options configurable.

The features that relate most directly to query tuning are covered in Chapter 2. They include:

- Dictating the order of joins with SET FORCEPLAN ON
- Changing the number of tables the optimizer considers at one time when evaluating joins with SET TABLE COUNT
- Using DBCC TRACEON (302) to get information on optimizer choices
- Using new features in SET SHOWPLAN to learn more about query plans

This chapter is more concerned with system internal tuning options introduced in System 11. They fall into these general categories:

- Administrative changes

♦ Buffer manager changes
♦ Data storage changes
♦ Transaction log changes
♦ Lock manager changes
♦ Housekeeper task changes

Of course, these features also have a strong effect on how queries work, and some show up as new options in SQL commands (PREFETCH, MRU), so the division is rather artificial.

As always with tuning, focus on a specific problem and test your solution thoroughly. Make sure to use a data set and user base close to your real-life situation.

Administrative Changes

Since System 11 adds many new configurable options (the total is now over 80) Sybase has modified the **sp_configure** system stored procedure to

♦ Add new options and change some old ones.
♦ Change the **sp_configure** output to display options in groups, and show the memory used by each option. A new system procedure, **sp_displaylevel,** lets you indicate how many of the **sp_configure** options you want to see. You can choose the basic, intermediate, or comprehensive level.
♦ Allow you to make and save configuration option changes through a configuration file and to start SQL Server from the file.

Configuration Options

In System 11, Sybase has added a number of configuration options and changed the names and parameters of others. Table 12.1 lists options as they were available during beta test. Check your document set for final values.

♦ Units are listed only if they are interesting (bytes, machine clock ticks). If there is no entry, the value is just an integer (number of locks, number of default languages).
♦ Static/dynamic indicates when options go into effect. Dynamic options go into effect as soon as you change them. Static changes take effect after you restart SQL Server. Previously, you had to run the RECONFIGURE command to put dynamic changes into effect. This is allowed but no longer necessary. (The RECONFIGURE command will probably be dropped in future releases.) A few options are neither dynamic

TABLE 12.1 Configuration Options

Option	Default	Units	Static/ Dynamic	Old Name
additional network memory	0	multiples of 2048 bytes	static	additional network memory
address lock spinlock ratio	100	ratio	static	
allow nested triggers	1 (on)	on/off	static	nested trigger
allow remote access	1 (on)	on/off	static	remote access
allow sql server asynch i/o	1 (on)	on/off	static	trace flag 1603
allow updates to system tables	1 (on)	on/off	dynamic	allow updates
audit queue size	100	records	static	audit queue size
configuration file	0	path	dynamic	
cpu accounting flush interval	1000	machine clock ticks	dynamic	cpu flush
cpu grace time	200	milliseconds	static	ctimemax
deadlock checking period	500	milliseconds	dynamic	
deadlock retries	5000			
default character set id	1		static	default character set id
default database size	2	Mb	static	database size
default fillfactor percent	0	% (1-100)	static	fillfactor
default language id	0		dynamic	default language
default network packet size	512	bytes- multiples of 512	static	default network packet size
default sortorder id	50	#	static	default sortorder id
disk i/o structures	256	#	static	cnblkio
event buffers per engine	100	#		
executable code size		not configurable	calculated	sql server code size
freelock transfer block size	30	#	dynamic	
housekeeper free write percent	20	% (1-100)	dynamic	
i/o accounting flush interval	1000	machine clock ticks	dynamic	i/o flush
i/o polling process count	10	#	dynamic	cmaxscheds
identity burning set factor	5000	$\% *10^7$	static	identity burning set factor
identity grab size	1		dynamic	
lock promotion HWM	200	#	dynamic	
lock promotion LWM	200	#	dynamic	
lock promotion pct	100	%	dynamic	
lock shared memory	0 (off)	on/off	static	trace flag 1611
max asynch i/os per engine	2147483647		static	cnmaxaio_engine
max asynch i/os per server	200		static	cnmaxaio_server
max engine freelocks	10	%	dynamic	
max network packet size	512	bytes	static	maximum network packet size
max number network listeners	15		static	cmaxnetworks

TABLE 12.1 *(Continued)*

Option	Default	Units	Static/ Dynamic	Old Name
max online engines	1		static	max online engines
memory alignment boundary	2048	bytes (in 2k increments)	static	calignment
min online engines	1		static	min online engines
number of alarms	40		static	cnalarm
number of devices	10		static	devices
number of extent i/o buffers	0	# 8-page extents	static	extent i/o buffers
number of index trips	0		dynamic	cindextrips
number of languages in cache	3		static	cnlanginfo
number of locks	5000		static	locks
number of mailboxes	30		static	cnmbox
number of messages	64		static	cnmsg
number of oam trips	0		dynamic	coamtrips
number of open databases	12		static	open databases
number of open objects	500		static	open objects
number of pre-allocated extents	2		static	cpreallocext
number of remote connections	20		static	remote connections
number of remote logins	20		static	remote logins
number of remote sites	10		static	remote sites
number of sort buffers	0		dynamic	csortbufsize
number of user connections	25		static	user connections
o/s asynch i/o enabled	0			
o/s file descriptors	0			
page lock spinlock ratio	100	rows/spinlock	static	
page utilization percent	95	% (1-100)	dynamic	
partition groups	64		static	
partition spinlock ratio	32		static	
permission cache entries	15		dynamic	cfgcprot
print deadlock information	0 (off)	on/off	dynamic	trace flag 1204
print recovery information	0	on/off	static	recovery flags
procedure cache percent	0	%		procedure cache
recovery interval in minutes	5	minutes	dynamic	recovery interval
remote server pre-read packets	0 (off)	on/off	static	pre-read packets
runnable process search count	2000			
shared memory starting address	0	not configurable	calculated	mrstart
size of auto identity	10	precision $10^{precision}$	dynamic	
sort page count	0	pages	dynamic	csortpgcount
sql server clock tick length	100000	microseconds	static	cclkrate
stack guard size	4096	bytes (2K increments)	static	cguardsz
stack size	platform specific	bytes (2K increments)	static	stack size

TABLE 12.1 *(Continued)*

Option	Default	Units	Static/Dynamic	Old Name
systemwide password expiration	0	days	dynamic	password expiration interval
table lock spinlock ratio	20	ratio	static	
tape retention in days	0	days	static	tape retention
tcp no delay	0 (off)	on/off	static	trace flag 1610
time slice	100	milliseconds	static	time slice
total data cache size	n/a	n/a	calculated	
total memory	platform specific	2k units	static	memory
upgrade version	1100	not configurable	calculated	upgrade version
user log cache size	2048	bytes	static	
user log cache spinlock ratio	20	ratio	static	

nor static but *calculated*. This means SQL Server figures the value—you cannot configure it directly.

♦ Old name shows the option name in previous releases. If there is no old name, the option is new.

sp_configure Output

The **sp_configure** output has changed. Options are now grouped under these headings:

♦ Backup/Recovery
♦ Cache Manager
♦ Configuration Options
♦ Disk I/O
♦ General Information
♦ Languages
♦ Lock Manager
♦ Memory Use
♦ Network Communication
♦ O/S Resources
♦ Physical Memory
♦ Physical Resources
♦ Processors
♦ SQL Server Administration
♦ User Environment

You can examine options and their values for a particular group by giving the group name as an option in the **sp_configure** command. To see backup/recovery options only, use a command like this:

```
EXEC sp_configure "Backup/Recovery"
go
```

The output looks like this:

```
Group: Backup/Recovery
Parameter Name                    Default   Memory Used Config Value Run Value
------------------------------   --------- ----------- ------------ ---------
allow remote access                  1           0          1           1
print recovery information           0           0          0           0
recovery interval in minutes         5           0          5           5
tape retention in days               0           0          0           0
```

A few options appear in more than one group. The "allow remote access" option, for example, is in both the Backup/Recovery group and the Network Communication group: The option setting has implications for each group.

The **sp_configure** output now has five columns:

♦ The parameter name column reflects **sp_configure** option name changes. They are somewhat more descriptive than in earlier versions.
♦ The default value is the starting value for SQL Server. It stays in effect until you change it.
♦ The new Memory Used column shows how many kilobytes of memory the option uses.
♦ The Config Value column shows the value you set with **sp_configure.**
♦ The Run Value shows the value currently in effect.

If the option is dynamic, the value you supply goes into effect immediately and appears in both the Config Value and Run Value columns. For static options, the value shows up in the Config Value column, but is not activated (and is not reflected in the Run Value column) until the next time you restart SQL Server.

SERVER WON'T START

I (Jim) got caught by this . . . let's just say several times.

I take the server down, and try to restart it. It won't start—something about a bad configuration value, or not enough memory.

The problem was—someone (might even have been me) had changed one of the configuration settings (maybe several months ago), and the server hadn't been restarted since. When SQL Server tried to boot, the configuration settings were unacceptable.

Advice: After changing any of the configuration settings that aren't "dynamic", that is, that don't take effect immediately, take the server down and back up as soon as possible. At least this way, if the server won't start, you will remember what you just changed, and have some idea of what went wrong.

Configuration on System 11 is much smarter, and will often warn you if the SQL Server thinks you are using settings that will be a problem. But you may still get caught by this (especially if you try to edit the configuration files directly).

To recover from this, you can use buildmaster with the -r option to reinitialize the configuration settings for the server to their default values. On System 11, you can modify the configuration file. Because of this problem, it is important to save a copy of your sp_configure output, and your configuration file, in order to restore the values to a "useful" set.

Configuration Files

A configuration file is an operating system ASCII file holding current configuration run values. You can read and edit it. Configuration files come in handy for using the same basic setup with more than one SQL Server, keeping track of exactly what your current configuration is, and testing.

SQL Server creates a configuration file in $SYBASE each time you modify a configuration option. The default file name is the SQL Server name with an appended sequential number (GLORY.001, GLORY.002, etc.) When you're working on configuration options, the number of configuration files can grow rapidly: You need to check the location periodically and prune old files.

SPACE WARS

A consultant was working on some labs for a performance and tuning class. Not surprisingly, this involved a lot of playing around with configuration options. It wasn't until she started having space problems that she checked out the rapidly growing $SYBASE directory and found a suspicious collection of files with her server name and a three-digit number suffix. Each file was small, but the total space eaten was . . . not small.

She looked more closely and discovered they were configuration files. Installation alone had generated 13 configuration files! Each one in that group came from SQL Server turning the "allow updates" option on or off as it set itself up.

A fragment of the configuration file looks like this:

```
[Backup/Recovery]
      recovery interval in minutes = DEFAULT
      print recovery information = DEFAULT
      tape retention in days = DEFAULT
[Cache Manager]
      number of oam trips = DEFAULT
      number of index trips = DEFAULT
      procedure cache percent = DEFAULT
      memory alignment boundary = DEFAULT
```

```
[Named Cache:default data cache]
     cache size = DEFAULT
     cache status = default data cache
[Named Cache:pubs_cache]
     cache size = 1M
     cache status = mixed cache
```

In the **sp_configure** output, as noted earlier, some options appear in more than one group. This is not true of the configuration file. You'll find only one line for the "allow remote access" option; it is under the Network Communication group, not the Backup/Recovery group. Options show DEFAULT if you haven't changed the value.

If you don't want to rely on the configure files SQL Server creates (perhaps you want more control over the name, location, and timing) you can make your own. To set up a configuration file in $SYBASE/config. file with the current SQL Server configuration run values, use a command like this:

```
EXEC sp_configure 'configuration file', 0, 'write',
'$SYBASE/config_file'

go
```

Other options for the third parameter are:

◆ Read—checks configuration file values and reads valid ones into SQL Server.
◆ Verify—validates values in the configuration file to make sure they are valid.
◆ Restore—creates a new file with current SQL Server configuration values.

You can hand-edit a configuration file to change values and then use the READ option to pass the values to SQL Server. Dynamic values go into effect immediately, static ones after you restart SQL Server.

Finally, you can hand-start SQL Server using a configuration file with the **dataserver** command like this:

```
dataserver -c configuration_file_name
```

Options previously set with **buildmaster -y** and the (undocumented) DBCC TUNE command are now incorporated into **sp_configure.** Ordinarily, you start SQL Server with a GUI tool or the **startserver -f** RUN_SERVER command (using the RUN_SERVER file SQL Server generates during installation). The dataserver command is included in the RUN_SERVER file.

Buffer Manager Changes

The buffer manager in SQL Server maintains a working set of data pages in a buffer (data) cache, so that many of the pages needed by applications are in memory, cutting down on physical reads. When a page is required by an application, the buffer manager first looks to see if it is in cache. If not, the buffer manager identifies available space in cache and reads the page from disk.

The buffer manager in SQL Server 11 has three major enhancements that will result in performance improvements for your applications.

- ♦ A logical memory manager allows you to partition memory into multiple distinct data caches, each of which you can name and bind objects to (tables, indexes, or databases).
- ♦ Variable block-size disk I/O permits reads and writes of 1, 2, 4, or 8 pages at a time, at the discretion of the optimizer.
- ♦ A new cache placement strategy changes how some pages are aged out of cache, at the discretion of the optimizer.

Logical Memory Manager

Prior to System 11, SQL Server had a single buffer (data) cache (see Figure 12.1).

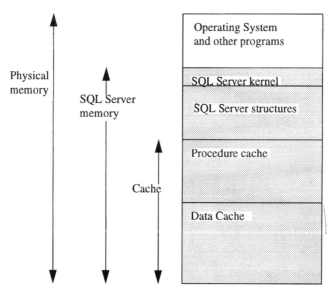

FIGURE 12.1 Physical memory, SQL Server memory, and data cache.

Now the new logical memory manager allows you to configure multiple named data caches. You may assign individual tables, indexes, text columns, image columns, or databases to a named buffer cache (see Figure 12.2).

Choosing Named Data Caches

What does this mean for your applications?

- First, you can assign a heavily used table to its own named data cache. If this cache is sufficiently large, then once all of the pages of the table have been read into cache, the entire table stays in cache. Access to other objects will not force these pages out of cache. This means that you won't use physical I/O to access this table.
- Second, it is now possible to integrate online transaction processing (OLTP) and decision support systems (DSS) on the same SQL Server. On previous releases, a single DSS query might read many pages into cache, forcing the important pages for an OLTP application out of cache. Now you can establish one cache for the important OLTP application tables and a separate cache for the DSS application tables (or databases). The two applications no longer have cache conflicts.
- Third, the new logical memory manager reduces contention for logical memory manager resources. There are certain very short logical memory manager activities that are single-threaded per cache. On previous

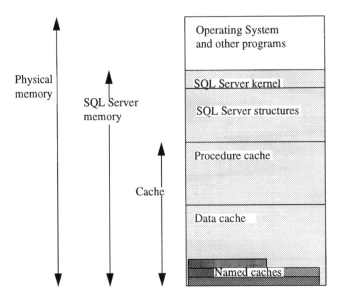

FIGURE 12.2 Named data caches.

releases this could be a bottleneck when the SQL Server was executing on many CPUs in an SMP environment. Multiple named data caches distribute access and consequently reduce contention across the multiple named caches.

Following are some suggestions for using private caches.

- Create a named data cache for **tempdb.** All commands involving work-tables or temporary tables use **tempdb,** so giving it its own cache cuts down on contention with other activities.
- The sysindexestable for a database with heavy OLTP usage is accessed a lot. If you put this table in its own cache, you may improve performance.
- In a DSS environment with many ad hoc queries, put **sysobjects, syscolumns,** and **sysprotects** (all used in query parsing and compiling) in a separate cache.
- If you place the index for a randomly accessed table in its own cache (one that is big enough to hold the entire index), the logical memory manager will keep all of the index pages in cache. (Note that you can place a clustered index in a different named buffer cache from its data pages.)
- Logs for active databases can also benefit from separate caches.

The downside is that you must establish the named caches effectively. If you partition your data cache into named caches, you are limiting how much cache various objects can occupy. This may not be optimal. If your DSS queries are run at night, and your OLTP queries during the day, you may want to let the logical memory manager manage cache in a single data cache. You may also want to consider multiple configurations depending on usage.

To avoid problems plan your strategy.

- Give SQL Server as much memory as you can.
- Identify problem areas by looking at I/O use, query plans, and changes in object size.
- Test any changes you make to be sure they don't slow down other critical areas while boosting performance in one.
- Don't starve the default data cache or you may have trouble restarting.

Using Named Data Cache Commands

The system stored procedure **sp_helpcache** gives you information on how caches are used. The following display is from a small system with no named caches set up. It has a total SQL Server memory of 7.5 Mb.

Cache Name	Config Size	Run Size	Overhead	Mem Avail for Named Cache	Mem Config to Named Caches
default data cache	0.00 Mb	5.60 Mb	0.29 Mb	5.60 Mb	0.00 Mb

```
There is 5.60 Mb of memory left over that will be allocated to the default
cache
```

--------------------------- Cache Binding Information: ------------------			
Cache Name	Entity Name	Type	Index Name
---------	----------	----	---------

You set up named caches with **sp_cacheconfig** and then bind them to objects with **sp_bindcache.** To assign two megabytes of memory to **tempdb,** use a command like this:

```
EXEC sp_cacheconfig "temp_cache", "2M"
go
```

You need to reboot SQL Server to put the change into effect. You can bind **tempdb** to the named cache (before or after the reboot) with this command:

```
EXEC sp_bindcache "temp_cache", tempdb
go
```

The **sp_helpcache** display changes to show the new cache (new values are bolded in this example).

```
EXEC sp_helpcache
        go
```

Cache Name	Config Size	Run Size	Overhead	Mem Avail for Named Cache	Mem Config to Named Caches
default data cache	0.00 Mb	5.60 Mb	0.20 Mb	**5.57 Mb**	**2.00 Mb**
temp_cache	**2.00 Mb**	**2.00 Mb**	**0.13 Mb**		

```
There is 3.57 Mb of memory left over that will be allocated to the default
cache
```

--------------------- Cache Binding Information: ------------------			
Cache Name	Entity Name	Type	Index Name
-----------	----------	----	---------
temp_cache	**tempdb**	**database**	

You can also use **sp_cacheconfig** with no parameter to see the new values.

```
EXEC sp_cacheconfig
        go
```

Cache Name	Status	Type	IO Sz	Wash Sz	Config Value	Run Value
default data cache	Active	Default			0.00 Mb	3.56 Mb
default data cache	Active	Default	2 Kb	512 Kb	0.00 Mb	3.56 Mb
temp_cache	**Active**	**Mixed**			**2.00 Mb**	**2.00 Mb**
temp_cache	**Active**	**Mixed**	**2 Kb**	**512 Kb**	**0.00 Mb**	**2.00 Mb**
					------------	--------
				Total	**2.00 Mb**	**5.56 Mb**

♦ Status is Active, Pend/Act, or Pend/Del. Active means the cache is currently available. Pend/Act shows you have configured the cache and it will go into effect after the next restart. Pend/Del indicates you have deleted the cache and it will be removed after the next restart.

♦ Type is Default, Mixed, or Log Only. Default is for the default data cache, while mixed and log only are for user-defined caches.

♦ I/O Sz is the black size for the cache (see the next section for an explanation).

♦ Wash Sz shows how large the wash buffer is (see the New Cache Strategy section for a definition of wash buffer).

Two commands allow you to modify caches:

♦ To change cache size, rerun **sp_cacheconfig** with a different value. This command reduces **temp_cache** to 1 Mb.

```
EXEX sp_cacheconfig "temp_cache", "1M"
go
```

♦ To keep the cache but change the objects you bind to it, use **sp_unbindcache**. (This command takes effect immediately—you don't need to reboot SQL Server.)

```
EXEC sp_unbindcache "temp_cache"
go
```

♦ To remove a named data cache, change its size to 0. SQL Server deletes it at the next restart.

```
EXEC sp_cacheconfig "temp_cache", "0"
go
```

You can assign a number of objects to a named cache. If you create a **pubs_cache** named cache for the pubs2 database, for example, you can bind both the titles and authors table to it with separate **sp_bindcache** commands.

```
EXEC sp_bindcache 'pubs_cache', pubs2, titles
go
EXEC sp_bindcache 'pubs_cache', pubs2, authors
go
```

The binding section of **sp_helpcache** output then looks like this:

```
------------------ Cache Binding Information: ------------------
Cache Name              Entity Name             Type            Index Name
----------              -----------             ----            ----------
pubs_cache              pubs2.dbo.titles        table
pubs_cache              pubs2.dbo.authors       table
```

The two tables share the named cache. To bind system tables, first put the database in single-user mode.

Variable Block-Size I/O

SQL Server 11 provides support for 1-, 2-, 4-, and 8-page I/O in the data cache. The default is 1 page (2K on most systems, 4K on Stratus). For queries where SQL Server accesses pages in sequence, reading 8 pages on one physical I/O is much more efficient than using 8 I/Os for the same amount of data (see Figure 12.3).

You take advantage of these large I/Os by creating multiple buffer pools in a given named data cache. SQL Server chooses to use a larger I/O if it has a pool available for that size I/O, and if the optimizer believes that the operation would benefit.

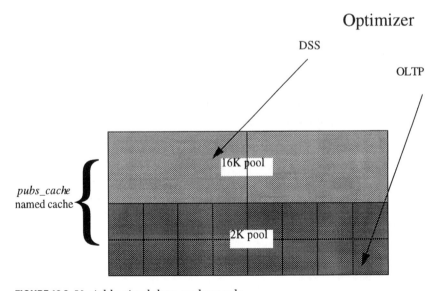

FIGURE 12.3 Variable-sized data cache pools.

Choosing Pools

As a starting point you may want to create a 2-page (4K) buffer pool that can be used by the **syslogs** table in the key databases on your server. Early experience in beta sites indicates that this will provide a performance improvement for many applications—the default I/O for logs is 4K.

Other areas that may benefit from large I/O include operations that

- ◆ Use table scans or nonclustered index leaf level scans
- ◆ Use blob (text or image) data
- ◆ Perform UPDATE STATISTICS
- ◆ Use SELECTINTO and BCP (on heaps)
- ◆ Search for ranges on tables with clustered indexes

Again, there is a downside. When you establish a large I/O buffer pool, you are taking space away from your default 2K buffer pool. If you create a 4K buffer pool and SQL Server is never able to take advantage of 4K I/Os, then space is wasted.

Make sure you don't "starve" your default cache: It's the only one that is active during startup recovery.

Using Pools

A number of new SQL commands allow you to work with block size.

- ◆ You create one buffer pool for each IO size that you want to allow for this cache (1, 2, 4, or 8 pages) with the **sp_prdconfig** stored procedure.
- ◆ You recommend a larger I/O size *for a specific table, index, text, or image object* with the **sp_cachestrategy** stored procedure.
- ◆ You recommend a larger I/O size *for this session* with the SET PREFETCH command.
- ◆ You recommend a larger I/O *on individual SELECT, UPDATE, and DELETE statements* with the PREFETCH keyword.

The system procedure **sp_cachestrategy** has the highest precedence, followed by the SET PREFETCH command. The individual SELECT, UPDATE, and DELETE with PREFETCH come last.

Assuming you have a 1Mb named data cache bound to the pubs2 database, you can make half of it a 4K pool with this command:

```
EXEC sp_poolconfig "pubs_cache", "512k", "4k"
go
```

Output from **sp_cacheconfig** shows two pools for **pubs_cache:** One is 2K and the other is 4K.

Cache Name	Status	Type	IO Sz	Wash Sz	Config Value	Run Value
default data cache	Active	Default			0.00 Mb	3.52 Mb
default data cache	Active	Default	2 Kb	512 Kb	0.00 Mb	3.52 Mb
pubs_cache	Active	Mixed			1.00 Mb	1.00 Mb
pubs_cache	Active	Mixed	2 Kb	204 Kb	0.00 Mb	0.50 Mb
pubs_cache	Active	Mixed	**4 Kb**	100 Kb	0.50 Mb	0.50 Mb
temp_cache	Active	Mixed			1.00 Mb	1.00 Mb
temp_cache	Active	Mixed	2 Kb	204 Kb	0.00 Mb	1.00 Mb
				Total	2.00 Mb	5.52Mb

To suggest particular pool sizes for tables, you have several options. For any of the options, you first bind the table to a cache. (In this case, the table's database is bound to the cache, so binding the table to the same cache doesn't change anything.)

```
EXEC sp_cacheconfig, "pubs_cache", pubs2, titles
go
```

The SET PREFETCH command determines whether large I/O (prefetching) is available for this session. By default it is on.

```
SET PREFETCH ON
go
```

You can specifically enable prefetching for a table, index, text, or image object.

```
EXEC sp_cachestrategy titles, PREFETCH, "on"
go
```

Finally, you can recommend prefetching in a query, update, or delete by specifying PREFETCH and the pool size (in kilobytes) in the index clause:

```
SELECT *
FROM titles (index titleidind PREFETCH 4)
go
```

None of these commands involving PREFETCH will have any effect if you don't have large I/O buffer pools set up so that they are available to the object or if prefetching has been turned off on a higher level.

New Cache Strategy

Prior to SQL Server 11, pages read from disk were placed in memory at the *most recently used* (MRU) side of the buffer (data) cache chain and moved sequentially down the chain toward the *least recently used* (LRU) side. Changed (dirty) buffers were written to disk when they passed a location called the wash marker. Unchanged (clean) buffers moved from the LRU end of the chain back up to the MRU end to be used again. If SQL Server needed a page already in cache the page returned to the MRU end before it reached the wash marker (see Figure 12.4).

This *LRU* strategy is good for OLTP workloads: Commonly used pages stay in cache and other pages age out of cache SQL Server tends to use this approach for:

◆ Pages used several times in a query
◆ Some index pages and OAM (object allocation map) pages
◆ Pages modified by a command

However, it does not work as well for DSS. If a SELECT statement causes a table scan on a very large table the buffer manager brings the table pages into cache at the MRU end, eventually forcing out of cache most pages from other objects.

SQL Server 11 introduced a second buffer cache strategy called *fetch and discard* or *MRU* (see Figure 12.5). This strategy places pages near the LRU end (just in front of the wash marker) if the buffer manager believes that the page will not be needed again soon (or if you advise it). Pages already in the cache and needed again move to the MRU end of the cache. The buffer manager chooses the strategy when:

◆ The table is a work table or the outer table in a join
◆ A table scan is expected to use more than about half of the buffers in the buffer pool

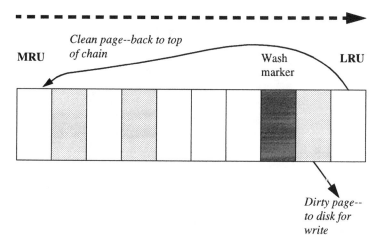

FIGURE 12.4 LRU strategy.

♦ Range queries the clustered indexes
♦ Queries covered by an index scan a nonclustered index leaf level

(Some pages stay in cache for more than one "trip" from the MRU end to the LRU end. See Sybase documentation on **sp_configure** "number of oam trips" for more information.)

This fetch and discard cache strategy improves the interaction of **DSS** and **OLTP** applications. The DSS queries will not tend to drive the commonly needed page for the OLTP application out of cache.

For example, if a query uses two tables, the inner table (which may be accessed many times) is read into cache with the LRU strategy, while the outer table (which may be accessed only once) uses the fetch-and-discard strategy.

You can configure wash buffer size (the area between the wash marker and the end of the LRU side of the chain) with the **sp_poolconfig** stored procedure (see Figure 12.6).

```
EXEC sp_poolconfig pubs_cache, "1M", "wash=256"
go
```

♦ Setting the value too high means that too much of the buffer holds clean pages—in effect, the buffer becomes smaller.
♦ On the other hand, a low value means few clean pages may be available and performance may slow.

The default value for the wash size is 256 or 20 percent of the total if the pool has less than 512 buffers.

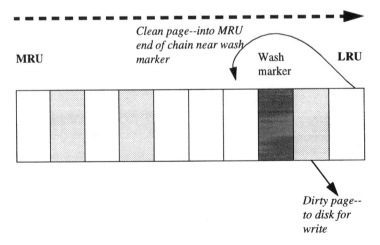

FIGURE 12.5 Fetch and discard strategy.

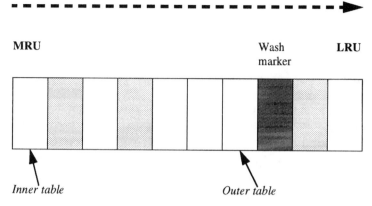

FIGURE 12.6 Combination strategy.

You can set the strategy in two ways:

♦ By specifying it in the **sp_cachestrategy** stored procedure. MRU is the option SQL Server considers by default. Turn it off if you want to recommend LRU strategy.

```
EXEC sp_cachestrategy titles, MRU, "off"
go
```

♦ Recommend MRU or LRU strategy in a query, update, or delete in the index clause:

```
SELECT *
FROM titles (index titleidind MRU)
go
```

The stored procedure MRU/LRU setting has higher priority than the query setting.

Data Storage Changes

System 11 introduces a number of data storage changes you can use to tune your applications.

♦ The new MAX_ROWS_PER_PAGE option lets you specify how full data and index pages are. It is covered in Chapter 8.
♦ Changes to page allocation let you specify whether SQL Server searches the OAM page chain before allocating new extents.

♦ Changes to data storage let you partition table data if the table does not have a clustered index. This can decrease page contention where there is heavy insert activity.

Searching the OAM Page Chain

When allocating new pages to tables or indexes, SQL Server checks the object's OAM (object allocation map) to find unused pages. If inserts add large numbers of rows, the OAM scan can slow performance. You can force SQL Server to add new extents (instead if re-using pages) by setting the **sp_configure** "page utilization percent" below 100. Since a low page utilization percent leads to more empty pages, you may want to set this value during heavy inserts and then return to the original value.

♦ A value of 100 causes the OAM scan.
♦ A lower value means the method of allocating pages is dependent on the relationship between used and unused pages (used pages/(used pages + unused pages)). If the ratio is lower than the page utilization percent, SQL Server allocates a new extent rather than searching the OAM pages.

Bulk copy always adds new extents during inserts: The page utilization percent has no effect.

Partitioning Heap Tables

Heap tables are tables that have no clustered indexes. This means the data is stored in no particular order and inserts always go to the last page in the double-linked page list. During the insert, the page is locked and unavailable to other users as shown in Figure 12.7.

The situation with some updates (those treated as delete-inserts) is similar.

♦ Updates that do not change the size of the row cause no data moves.
♦ Updates that increase the size of the row but force no other rows off the page cause no writes to new pages.
♦ Updates that don't fit on the current page become deletes followed by inserts, and the row is inserted on the last page.

You can decrease page contention with table *partitions:* Each partition has its own page chain and last page. A table with 10 partitions, for example, has 10 last pages. Inserts (and updates treated as delete-insert combinations) are randomly distributed among the partitions as shown in Figure 12.8.

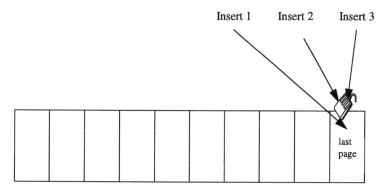

FIGURE 12.7 Inserts to heap tables.

Choosing What to Partition

Heap tables with lots of concurrent insert activity are partitioning candidates. For best results, partition a table before populating it with data. Otherwise, existing data will stay in its current location and only new data will go to partitions. To improve I/O as well as reduce lock contention, put partitions on segments spanning separate physical disks. You cannot partition tables that have a clustered index (and most tables have a clustered index) or system tables.

Creating Partitions

Partitioning table data is a many-step process:

1. Initialize a database device with DISK INIT.
2. Put the database the table belongs to on the device with CREATE or ALTER DATABASE.
3. Add a segment for the device with **sp_addsegment.**
4. Create the table on the segment with CREATE TABLE.
5. Specify the partitions with ALTER TABLE.

For example, you might decide to make the pubs2 database larger by 2 Mb, and set up a new segment you can use for the titles3 table partitions. You begin by initializing the disk.

```
DISK INIT
NAME = 'pubs_dev',
VDEVNO=2,
PHYSNAME = 'D:\sybase\data\pubs.dat',
SIZE = 1024
go
```

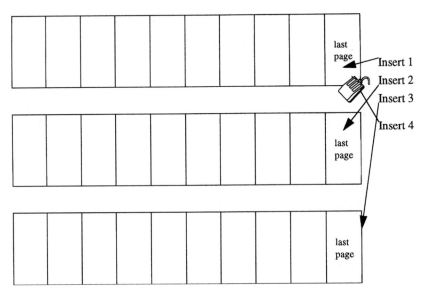

FIGURE 12.8 Partitioned heap table and inserts.

Next, you use the ALTER DATABASE command to make the new space available to the database.

```
ALTER DATABASE pubs2
ON pubs_dev=2
go
```

Then you create a segment on the new device.

```
EXEC sp_addsegment pubsseg, pubs2, pubs_dev
go
```

When the segment is available, create the table on the segment.

```
CREATE TABLE titles3
      (title_id tid not null,
      title varchar (80) not null,
      type char (12) not null,
      pub_id char (4) null,
      price money null,
      advance money null,
      total_sales int null,
      notes varchar (200) null,
      pubdate datetime not null,
      contract bit not null )
ON pubsseg
go
```

Finally, use the ALTER TABLE command to partition the table.

```
ALTER TABLE titles3
PARTITION 5
go
```

You can get information on partitions with the **sp_helpartition** system procedure.

```
EXEC sp_helpartition titles3
go
partitionid firstpage   controlpage
----------- ----------- -----------
          1        1026        1027
          2        1281        1282
          3        1288        1289
          4        1296        1297
          5        1304        1305
```

The control page records the last page in the page chain.

To remove partitions, use the ALTER TABLE command with the UNPARTITION keyword. You must remove partitions before you drop or truncate the table, create a clustered index on the table, or use **sp_placeobject**.

Transaction Log Changes

The transaction log also provides you with some opportunities for tuning. You can

- ♦ Set the size of user log caches, which are buffers for transaction log writes
- ♦ Set the ratio of user log cache spinlocks
- ♦ Examine the new syslogshold table to find the oldest transaction in each database

Tuning User Log Caches

Each user connection has a user log cache. The default size is 2,048 bytes. The transaction log is a heap table, so all inserts are contending for the same last page. The user log caches cut down on contention by buffering the writes. SQL Server flushes a user log cache to the transaction log when the user log cache is full or the transaction completes. If the value is too low, the user log fills up and flushes before the end of a transaction; if it is too high, you waste memory.

The size should be no larger than the largest transaction log insert generated by your application. To configure the cache to 3,000 bytes, use a command like this:

```
EXEC sp_configure "user log cache size", 3000
go
```

The user log caches are governed by spinlocks. While one process is accessing a user log cache, others wait. The default is 20 caches per spinlock. To change the value to 10, try a command like this:

```
EXEC sp_configure "user log cache spinlock ratio", 10
go
```

Since each spinlock uses as much as 256 bytes of memory, setting the value unnecessarily low (and increasing the total number of spinlocks) can cut down on the amount of memory available for procedure and data caches. For a SQL Server with only one engine, this command has no effect: SQL Server uses only one user log cache spinlock.

Using syslogshold

Syslogshold is a new system table in the master database. It holds a maximum of two rows for each database:

- ♦ Information on the oldest active transaction in the database that has been written to the transaction log (if a transaction is only in the user log cache, it won't appear in syslogshold)
- ♦ Information on the Replication Server truncation point for the transaction log

The DUMP TRANSACTION command removes all pages from the transaction log between the first page of the log and the page before the oldest uncommitted transaction. If an uncommitted transaction stays in place undetected, available log space decreases, despite the best intentions and plenty of DUMP TRANSACTION commands. Now you can find these trouble spots and take action (urge the guilty user to commit or kill the process yourself).

A query on syslogshold (while a query in the pubs2 database is incomplete) looks like this:

```
SELECT dbid, spid, name
FROM master..syslogshold
go
dbid    spid    name
------  ------  ----------------------
6       8         $user_transaction
```

The results show that the oldest active transaction has an spid of 8. If you run **sp_lock,** you'll see that spid 8 is holding many locks in the pubs2 database.

```
        EXEC sp_lock
        go
```

The class column will display the cursor name for locks associated with a cursor for the current user and the cursor id for other users.

```
spid    locktype              table_id    page         dbname      class
------  --------------------  ----------  -----------  ----------  ----------------
    8 Sh_intent               432004570            0 master      Non Cursor Lock
    8 Ex_intent               976006508            0 pubs2       Non Cursor Lock
    8 Ex_page                 976006508         1304 pubs2       Non Cursor Lock
    8 Ex_page                 976006508         1305 pubs2       Non Cursor Lock
    8 Ex_page                 976006508         1306 pubs2       Non Cursor Lock
    8 Ex_table                976006508            0 pubs2       Non Cursor Lock
```

You can join **syslogshold** with other system tables (**sysprocesses,** for example) to get precise information on problem transactions.

DUMP TRAN WITH_NOTHING_HAPPENS

I was on-site at a customer site doing training. The system administrator came to me to talk about a serious problem he was having. The log had filled up unexpectedly. The log was set to truncate automatically in this development database (truncate log on checkpoint). He had run the DUMP TRAN process and it worked successfully, that is, there were no complaints from the server. But the log did not decrease in size. He had tried this several times to no avail. (This had happened before, but had somehow resolved itself mysteriously.)

I called *my* technical support (JTP) and we reviewed what could actually cause the server to successfully process the DUMP TRAN, but not decrease the size of the log. After much review and discussion (we hadn't seen this before) we could only come up with the fact that a transaction *must* be open somewhere. The log cannot be truncated past the point of the earliest still open transaction. Nothing that happened after that moment can be truncated.

We discussed this with the system administrator. He felt that it was unlikely because the development team had a strong method for transaction management in their software and didn't keep open transactions. We puzzled around for awhile. We then started a search through the development teams. Who was logged in? We got them to log out. The problem was still there. We finally discovered one of the senior managers was still in with a connection. What was it? We walked to his desk.

(Fortunately, everyone was in a single building.) "What are you doing?" Well, he had logged out of his development environment and major applications as requested. We studied his desktop. What was this process minimized over here in the corner? Oh, that? He monitored other folks and their working connections. He had thrown together a small application that ran **sp_who** so he could see what was going on. "It's been there for days." He forgot it was there. How did he build it, we asked? "It's just a trivial default application model that only executes **sp_who.**" How did you set up the connection? "With the simple defaults."

Aha! In his development environment, the default for a connection was to open a transaction. This application did no data modifications, but by default it did open a connection and start a transaction. This was the long running transaction that was blocking the DUMP TRAN process. No one thought to look for something so innocuous.

Since that day, we have come upon this many times. It is critical to understand the default behavior of your applications and application development environments. (It is also necessary to be aware of where you use chained transactions.) We have since built procedures to report on open transactions that get to the problem much more quickly. (With System 11, the user log cache feature removes this contention when there is a small transaction or just a BEGIN TRANSACTION, and you can use **syslogshold** to find the oldest transaction.) When you execute DUMP TRAN with_nothing_happens, think about open transactions.

Lock Manager Changes

System 11 introduces some configurable lock manager features.

◆ The **sp_configure** deadlock checking interval and lock promotion options are covered in Chapter 2.

◆ The **sp_configure** number of locks option lets you change the default number of locks for SQL Server.

◆ The address spinlock ratio, freelock transfer block size, max engines freelocks, page lock spinlock ratio, and table lock spinlock ratio are specifically for tuning locks on multiple engine systems.

Configuring the Number of Locks

The default configuration for SQL Server is 5,000 locks. Use **sp_lock** to monitor lock use at different times and with different applications and numbers of users to see if this number is adequate. Sybase recommends increasing the number of locks by increments of 1,000 and estimates that each concurrent user needs 20 locks.

Too many locks can cut down on the amount of memory available for other uses: Each lock takes 72 bytes of memory. You may need to increase total memory to get the locks you need.

To increase locks to 6,000, use this command:

```
EXEC sp_configure "number of locks", 6000
go
```

Configuring Locks for Multiple Server Engines

A *spinlock* is a lock that protects SQL Server internal structures. When one process has access, other processes wait (spin patiently). In System 11, multiple engine SQL Servers can configure the number of spinlocks in some critical areas. Single engine SQL Servers do not have this ability. See Sybase documentation for a complete explanation of this complex topic.

Housekeeper Task Changes

The housekeeper task, a low priority background activity, is in charge of writing dirty buffers to disk when SQL Server is idle. Increasing SQL Server activity stops the housekeeper task.

This housekeeping activity makes the checkpoint task examine whether it can checkpoint the database. These increased checkpoints can lead to faster recovery. The downside is that if an application keeps changing the same page, the housekeeper may be more diligent than is required and write too many times.

The housekeeper task is configured in terms of the percentage of increased database writes. The default, 20 percent, means that the housekeeper starts working when SQL Server is idle and keeps at it until total writes increase by 20 percent. At this point, the housekeeper task shuts down. You can change the percentage with **sp_configure.** To set it at 25 percent

```
EXEC sp_configure "housekeeper free write percent", 25
go
```

A value of 100 makes the housekeeper work constantly. A value of 0 disables the task.

I N D E X